Work-Based Mobile Learning

Concepts and Cases

edited by
Norbert Pachler, Christoph Pimmer
and Judith Seipold

PETER LANG
Oxford · Bern · Berlin · Bruxelles · Frankfurt am Main · New York · Wien

Bibliographic information published by Die Deutsche Nationalbibliothek
Die Deutsche Nationalbibliothek lists this publication in the Deutsche National-
bibliografie; detailed bibliographic data is available on the Internet at
http://dnb.d-nb.de.

A catalogue record for this book is available from the British Library.

Library of Congress Cataloging-in-Publication Data:

Work-based mobile learning : concepts and cases / Norbert Pachler, Christoph
Pimmer and Judith Seipold (eds.).
    p. cm.
Includes bibliographical references and index.
ISBN 978-3-03911-982-0 (alk. paper)
    1. Employees--Training of--Computer-assisted instruction. 2. Mobile
communication systems in education. 3. Organizational
learning--Technological innovations. I. Pachler, Norbert. II. Pimmer,
Christoph, 1979- III. Seipold, Judith, 1976-
    HF5549.5.T7W652 2010
    658.3'12402854678--dc22

                        2010043273

ISBN 978-3-03911-982-0

© Peter Lang AG, International Academic Publishers, Bern 2011
Hochfeldstrasse 32, CH-3012 Bern, Switzerland
info@peterlang.com, www.peterlang.com, www.peterlang.net

Printed in Germany

Work-Based Mobile Learning

Contents

vi

List of Figures

List of Tables

INTRODUCTION

NORBERT PACHLER, CHRISTOPH PIMMER
AND JUDITH SEIPOLD

1 Work-based mobile learning: an overview

The central question of this book is how mobile devices can be used to support learning and competence development in work contexts. With this volume, *Work-based mobile learning: concepts and cases*, we offer a multi-faceted collection of different concepts and cases of mobile learning in work environments from international contexts. The book is targeted at both practitioners – trainers or managers in charge of in company training – and researchers, who are interested in designing, implementing or evaluating work-based mobile learning. As the handbook is – to our knowledge – the first title that is explicitly dedicated to the new and emerging field of work-based mobile learning, the contributions represent a starting point to build on, and to further develop and refine the empirical, conceptual and theoretical repertoire for this field.

This chapter provides a brief introduction to work-based mobile learning as well as an overview of the various chapters of this book. Beyond the key messages of the individual contributions, we also briefly discuss themes that emerge across the different chapters on work-based mobile learning, issues according to which we have structured the book. The specially commissioned chapter on work-based learning (WBL) following this introductory chapter is intended as a starting point for the analysis and interpretation of subsequent chapters, which explicitly problematise mobile learning in work contexts. As mobile devices allow the generation of multimedia material, in the first section of the book we feature a number of cases involving the collection and sharing of, as well as the reflection on multimedia evidence of, situated learning experiences. The second section centres on scenarios in which mobile devices support learning 'on demand' directly in the processes of work, particularly in contexts of highly mobile learners. Simulations and laboratories as alternative learning contexts for real-world situations which prepare learners for work are the topic of investigation of the third section. While the use of mobile technologies can be beneficial from an individual or organisational perspective, it also raises a number of ethical questions which need to be addressed; the fourth section deals with this topic. Finally, in consideration of the rapid technological and conceptual developments in this field, we take a look at the near future: in the section five, we present two studies exploring possible mobile learning scenarios in the near future.

Importance and motivation

Mobile devices such as mobile phones boast a range of different functionalities from communication, multimedia capture to personal information management (Livingston, 2004). The cost of telecommunication has steadily decreased (compare e.g., Eurostat, 2008), making mobile technologies affordable to the vast majority of people in and beyond the Western world. No wonder, therefore, that mobile devices were identified in recent Horizon Reports (New Media Consortium, 2009, 2010) as the technologies with the highest likelihood of entry into the mainstream of learning-focused institutions within the coming years. The use of mobile devices is not limited to private spheres but takes an important role also in work contexts. Indeed, the penetration of mobile devices in the work environments of business professionals is reported to have been tremendous over the last decade (Dzartevska, 2009). In this context, mobile devices have the power to transform the way we work and learn: they arguably alter the nature of knowledge work as well as the balance between training and performance support (Traxler, 2007a). In this way, transformations brought about by mobile phones can result in greater efficiency and supervision but also in the weakening of home and work boundaries (Traxler, 2010).

Despite the increasing use of mobile devices in work contexts a lack of known concepts and practices of how mobile learning can be used for learning in and across work contexts exists at the time of writing this book: we are not aware of any guide or systematic approach to work-based mobile learning. Also, research in this field can be said to be at a very early stages (see e.g., Pimmer, Pachler and Attwell, 2010).

Goals and scope

In order to address this shortcoming, we offer in this book a number of different concepts and cases of mobile learning in work environments. The central question across the different contributions is how mobile devices can be used to support learning in work contexts. The handbook is targeted at practitioners – trainers and managers in charge of in-company training – as well as researchers in this field, who are interested in practical and conceptual advice on designing, implementing and evaluating mobile learning in work environments. Accordingly, the contributions to this book are very much centred on conceptual and pedagogical issues.

Work-based learning and mobile learning

The exploration of mobile devices for learning and competence development in work contexts must be seen as an emerging, and still rather immature area of professional development. For this book, we construct and conceptualise the notion of work-based mobile learning with reference to current approaches to work-based learning *and* mobile learning: for *work-based learning* we use a broad and inclusive definition drawing on Evans, Guile and Harris (2010). They understand work-based learning as learning *at work, for work and through work*, an approach that bridges embedded workplace learning perspectives and those that frame WBL as (a series of) programmes. This breadth in scope we deem appropriate for the contributions featured in this book: it contains chapters in which mobile learning is embedded in placements as part of (higher) education programmes (*learning for/through work*), learning that is offered in the form of compliance training at the workplace (learning *at* work) and contributions which focus more on social, cultural and political dynamics of workplace learning (learning *through work*). Our understanding of *mobile learning* is based on the processes of coming to know, and of being able to operate successfully in, and across, new and ever changing contexts with and through the use of mobile devices. Therefore, instead of a technical orientation, our focus is on an educational perspective given the affordances that mobile devices provide for meaning-making (Pachler, 2009; Pachler, Bachmair and Cook, 2010).

We put forward a multi-faceted and rich collection of concepts and cases of mobile learning in work environments from an international perspective ranging, for example, from students in placement settings in the UK and service technicians in machine industries in Germany, to bakery apprentices in New Zealand and indigenous park rangers in Australia. Throughout the book, a mixture of mobile and blended learning scenarios are reported:

- with heterogeneous groups of learners (professional workers, employees, apprentices, students ...),
- in manifold industries and work contexts (machine building, health sector, craft, education, transport ...),
- based on different forms of learning and teaching (creating and consuming content, reflecting, solving problems, discussing, simulating, assessing ...),
- on diverse content/topics (health and safety, electrical engineering, biosecurity, dental hygiene, therapy, geomorphology ...),
- aimed at the development of multifaceted skills and competences (interpersonal, inter-professional, tacit ...).

The book demonstrates that mobile devices can be used in manifold ways in professional learning and development. Upon closer examination it is possible, however, to discern some patterns and issues emerging across individual chapters according to which we have structured the book:[1]

- Introduction
- Section 1: Assessment and identity formation: Collecting, sharing and reflecting
- Section 2: Learning and work processes: Providing information on demand
- Section 3: Mobile simulations and laboratories: Preparing learners for work
- Section 4: Ethical issues relevant for (researching) mobile learning
- Section 5: Near-future scenarios for work-based mobile learning

Introduction

Chapter 2   Work-based learning: Setting the scene

When implementing and researching mobile learning in work environments, practitioners and researchers can draw on a wide knowledge base in the academic discipline of work-based learning. The chapter 'Setting the scene' by Karen Evans, a leading figure in work-based learning, provides an introduction to the 'state of the art'. This is built on by the remainder of the book, which illustrates how the concepts outlined by Evans can be valuable for the analysis and interpretation of mobile learning in work contexts.

---

1   We are aware that the reported cases and concepts cannot be matched disjunctively, but we feel that the following categorisation reflects the main focus of the respective contributions.

Beyond exemplifying the broad notion of work-based learning discussed above, Evans characterises work-based learning as learning 'that expands human capacities through purposeful activities where the (following) purposes derive from the context of employment':

- enculturation;
- competence, license to practise;
- improving practice, innovation and renewal;
- wider capabilities;
- equity, ethics and social justice;
- vocational/professional identity development.

These purposes can be widely identified in and across various chapters: *enculturation* is, for example, evident in Ruth Wallace's contribution (Chapter 6), who reports on how mobile learning enables marginalised learners in presenting their work practices and showing 'how we do things here'. *Competence, license to practise* refers to learning that is necessary for performance to occupational standards. This, for example, is reflected in Geoff Stead and Martin Good's cases (Chapter 8) as well as in Claudia de Witt et al.'s project (Chapter 7). Both contributions refer, inter alia, to the use of compliance training in the transport sector. Improving practice, innovation and renewal is also a focus in some of the chapters: Lucy Stone (Chapter 4), for example, explains that teaching assistants have found 'innovative and creative ways of using the mobile devices'. The project by Ceridwen Coulby et al. (Chapter 3) was centred on the assessment of wider capabilities such as interpersonal and inter-professional skills that can enable learners to 'do the next job as well as the current one'. The importance of equity, ethics and social justice for mobile learning in work contexts is mentioned in several chapters and the topic is the focus of the fourth section of this book. In the analysis of work-based mobile learning vocational/professional identity is also taken into account: Selena Chan (Chapter 5), for example, discusses how mobile devices have enabled apprentice bakers to construct showcases of their vocational identity trajectory.

Evans introduces key theoretical and conceptual perspectives in a field that is much more mature than mobile learning. However, she identifies a number of divergent, competing and even contradictory lines of inquiry. In identifying three significant theoretical domains of WBL (expertise and competence, power relations, practice and micro-interaction) she offers a framework suitable also for the exploration of mobilities of work-based learning. This book features a wide range of theoretical approaches that can be positioned within these categories (and their intersections) such as Schön's reflective practitioner, Kolb's learning cycle, communities of practice or concepts taken from the field of knowledge management. Particularly popular is Activity Theory and activity systems which are widely used as conceptual frameworks in work-based learning and mobile learning (see Pimmer, Pachler and Attwell, 2010).

With the concept of *recontextualisation* Evans offers a fresh approach to WBL: she considers the processes of knowledge recontextualisation – knowledge put to work in different environments – to be at the heart of WBL. This includes ways in which different forms of knowledge are recontextualised as people move between sites of learning and practice in and across universities, colleges and workplaces. This approach might be of interest to work-based mobile learning, as many of the chapters discuss how mobile phones bridge learning across different contexts. For example, Stone (Chapter 4) shows how mobile devices allow teaching assistants who learn in many different spaces to 'map their learning in one space onto their learning in the other spaces'.

Finally, Evans argues for a social ecological approach that provides a way into understanding the complexity of factors that impact on education and lifelong learning without losing sight of the whole. She posits that an ecology can be used to understand the motivations of adult learners in using technologies in work and in related learning. Notably, the metaphor of an ecology has also been used in recent theoretical work in the field of mobile learning (see Pachler, Bachmair and Cook, 2010).

Having shown examples of how WBL concepts discussed in the chapter by Evans can help to analyse the use of mobile devices for learning in work contexts, in the remainder of this introductory chapter we briefly summarise the other contributions to the book which introduce cases and concepts of work-based mobile learning. A key question we try to address in this context is *why* and *how* mobile devices have been used and how they can enhance learning and competence development. Instead of considering mobile learning as an extension of e-learning on mobile devices, we attempt to identify in our overview its particular characteristics reported across the different chapters.

Section 1   Assessment and identity formation:
Collecting, sharing and reflecting

A key functionality of mobile devices such as mobile phones is that they allow users the generation of multimedia materials in the form of audio, images and even video. Although these functions have been supported by a number of other devices for a long time, it is the integration in one lightweight, ubiquitous device that provides new and simple opportunities for learning, a characteristic referred to as convergence in the literature (Pachler, Bachmair and Cook, 2010).

In all the cases reported in this section of the book, learners collected and reflected on situated learning experiences: for example, they recorded their thoughts for self-assessment purposes, they collected evidence of their experiences and achievements with the help of mobile devices and they reflected on their work practices. However, in all cases the generation of materials through mobile devices is only described as one step in an overall learning scenario. Mobile devices helped to trigger learning activities which can be considered from different, conceptual, technical and social perspectives. In all chapters, the collection phase was part of an integrated, blended learning *concept*. In these mobile-learning contexts 'blended' can imply the use of the materials generated with the mobile device online sessions or face-to-face classroom activities. In all the cases, examples are reported where learning in more informal contexts – such as learning in the workplace – is linked with learning in more formal contexts – such as learning in classroom settings or tutorial support. From a technical point of view the mobile devices are never used as stand-alone tools but they are integrated with wider 'systems' such as e-portfolios, social networking sites or virtual institutional learning environments. Taking a social perspective into account, the collection phase mostly involved further actors in the learning process such as tutors and teachers who provided feedback or who recognised learners' achievements; this can be seen as a new opportunity for assessing and recognising competence development. In addition to educational professionals, learners shared their experiences with peers. In some cases also the wider social communities including workmates, employers, friends and even family are reported to have been involved.

Demonstrating personal capabilities and sharing situated learning experience with a (wider) social community results in the construction and transformation of the learners' vocational identity; this is an aspect highlighted in two of the chapters in this section. Across the contributions the affinity of the learners to and their ownership of mobile devices are also underlined as crucial elements: it is deemed useful to deploy technology which is readily available to the learners and to draw on existing competences in the handling of familiar devices.

Chapter 3   *Mobile technology and assessment: A case study from the ALPS programme*

In their contribution, Ceridwen Coulby, Nancy Davies, Julie Laxton and Stuart Boomer explore how Dental Hygiene and Therapy students can use mobile devices to assess interpersonal and inter-professional competences such as team work, communication and ethical practice within work-based placements. In addition to having to deal with a poor IT infrastructure, students on placements can feel unprepared, experience a lack of feedback on their performance and receive limited support when reflecting on their work. These issues are addressed by way of a blended learning concept: after carrying out a particular task, students answer a set of questions designed to help them reflect on and learn from their experiences. Mobile devices also provided students with the opportunity to audio-record their thoughts aloud. The learners found the assessments helpful for their reflective practice. Students requested peer feedback before developing an action plan to improve their future performance. The assessments were collected in e-portfolios which allowed students and tutors to engage in discussions about the assessment and wider placement issues. The e-portfolio was appreciated by the learners for their reflection on action and enabled dialogues between students and tutors which increased the level of remote support for students.

Chapter 4   The WoLF Project: Work-based Learners in Further Education

Lucy Stone describes very similar learning activities in the context of teacher education in busy, early years settings including kindergarten, primary school classrooms and special educational needs settings. While usually working environments of teaching assistants provide little support for the recording and subsequent reflection of learning experiences, the Teaching Assistants (TA) in this project were enabled to collect evidence of their placement work with mobile devices (PDAs). In addition to conducting self-assessments of their study skills, they also used the PDAs to capture spontaneous moments or examples of theory they were putting into practice with still images, video files and voice recordings. The devices opened up new opportunities for TAs to develop their portfolios and, thereby, promoted reflection in practice. While the learners used the mobile devices to capture moments to reflect on them at a later stage, the biggest impact appears to have been the sharing and discussing of the TAs' experiences with their peers and tutors in face-to-face classes or through online activities through the learning platform.

Chapter 5   Becoming a baker: Using mobile phones to compile e-portfolios

Selena Chan shows how learners used mobile phones to collect situated learning experiences in the workplace and how they shared their experiences with teachers and with their wider social community. Chan explores the learning activities of apprentice bakers with a particular focus on the learners' conceptualisation of their vocational identity as a process of belonging to a workplace, becoming and then being a baker. Apprentices documented authentic multimedia evidence of their situated learning experiences as their skill acquisition developed. They shared this evidence on social networking sites not only with other apprentices and teachers but also with friends, workmates, employers and family. Apprentices were able to develop narratives to showcase their occupational identity trajectory from novice to recognised, competent trades practitioner. Mobile phones are considered key in the project as they provide opportunities to document relevant aspects of apprentices' skill development. Chan also notes that the opportunity to share concrete evidence of skill acquisition, which in the past could not be easily disseminated, has enhanced apprentices' initial self-recognition and eventual self-acceptance of occupational/vocational identity transformation.

Chapter 6   *The affordances of mobile learning that can engage disenfranchised learner identities in formal education*

Ruth Wallace also centres her chapter on learner identities, although in a completely different context: she explores the affordances of mobile technologies in recognising and engaging disenfranchised adult learners in indigenous workplace learning. In this example, indigenous rangers use mobile devices to document work practices and to share the materials generated with colleagues. More precisely, they produced multilingual digital stories of regular tasks such as mixing chemicals or explaining financial management. They also recorded formal training lessons and stored them in their office. These materials were then reused in further sessions before undertaking specific tasks, to induct new staff or to refresh learning outcomes from previous training. The deployment of mobile devices is reported as crucial because the learners are already experts in using the technology. Mobile devices supported indigenous rangers' learning and the demonstration of their strengths in their own context, language and time. In this way, mobile learning led to an active construction of knowledge and learner identities. Mobiles enabled indigenous rangers to manage the knowledge in ways that are described as empowering rather than embarrassing to senior cultural leaders, people with low-level English skills or learners who prefer to review material often. The technology allowed them to demonstrate their competence and value as workers in their community.

Section 2   Learning and work processes: Providing information on demand

Providing ad-hoc access to information, collaborative knowledge building and context-aware information management are central issues of the chapters that are included under the heading 'learning and work processes'. Referring to field studies, the authors critically evaluate and discuss specific needs of workers and learners in situations that are typical for their professional fields. Their need to react in complex situations that are often constituted in situ is not only a demanding day-to-day routine for workers and learners but also challenging for those providing mobile learning environments and technologies. In addition to the provision of contextualised content, mobile devices can allow learners to document problems in specific situations in order to better illustrate and discuss their uncertainties with others. Multimedia materials generated in this way can then be used for further learning and training purposes. A concept similar to this is currently also being developed in the clinical context (see Pimmer, Pachler, Gröhbiel and Genewein, 2009; Pimmer, 2009). This section of the book is based on three contributions by authors from Germany and the United Kingdom who give insights into the professional areas of truck drivers, apprentice electronics engineers, workers in the passenger transport and logistics (PTL) industries, service technicians and machine building and plant construction companies and are providing solutions for work-based mobile learning in complex and fast evolving professional fields.

Chapter 7 *Mobile learning in the process of work: Participation, knowledge and experience for professional development*

The provision of learning content, the compilation of glossaries and assessments in the form of tests is the focus of Claudia de Witt, Sonja Ganguin, Maciej Kuszpa and Sandro Mengel's chapter. Looking at the learning needs and habits of two professional groups – electronics engineers and truck drivers – the authors describe the assessment of the framework in which learning takes place within these two groups. Their specific needs, which are based on the structure of their professions, are evaluated as well as their use of ICT and mobile devices for information retrieval and knowledge production. Learning is covered under the structural framework of participation and information retrieval which are both strongly connected to interpersonal interaction and activity. The target group analysis allows first insights into the role of mobile devices within specific work processes and situations and considers them as the basis for future didactic/teaching and learning concepts in order to support individualised learning as well as collaborative knowledge building using mobile devices.

Chapter 8 *Mobile learning in vocational settings: Lessons from the E-Ten BLOOM project*

Geoff Stead and Martin Good describe an EU-supported project that was realised in Austria, Germany and the UK and which focuses on the passenger transport and logistics industries. Besides the infrastructural importance of the use of mobile devices within an industrial sector that is inherently mobile, the use of mobile devices to support basic skills such as driving regulations, customer service, literacy, numeracy, IT skills and health and safety, etc., is highlighted. The study refers to a broad basis of qualitative and quantitative methods such as background contextual research, workplace questionnaires, focus groups and real workplace trials. The study evaluates the status quo of the use of mobile devices, ICT and face-to-face teaching and chooses an approach of content provision for learning that considers different factors resulting in the following key needs for providing mobile learning contexts: easy and context-related customisation of the devices and contents, the supportive and changing status of mobile learning in relation to other forms of knowledge building, as well as personalisation, flexibility and ease of access.

Chapter 9   *From know-how to knowledge: Exploring Web 2.0*
              concepts for sharing hands-on service expertise

With a shift from production to service, companies rely more and more on highly qualified technicians who are confronted with installations and repair tasks at the customers' sites, as Liza Wohlfart, Simone Martinetz and Alexander Schletz describe in their chapter. A central aspect in the day-to-day routine of technicians is changing contexts to which they have to respond in adequate ways. A number of factors – such as time pressure, informal communication or high mobility within and across different physical sites – frames and constrains the work and learning processes of these technicians. Against this background, the authors describe a concept that is aimed at providing fast, on-demand support during practical work processes and at enabling some sort of pre-qualification in potential problems. In this context, mobile learning can support technicians' problem-solving processes. Mobile phones can, for example, enable technicians to document and discuss current problems. Within such communicative and collaborative interactions with colleagues by using mobile devices, tacit knowledge of products and processes is collected, distributed and shared. This leads to a shift from tacit to explicit knowledge which can be harnessed for the task of situative problem solving.

Section 3   Mobile simulations and laboratories:
            Preparing learners for work

Simulations and laboratories as alternative learning contexts for real-world situations are the topic of investigation of authors from the United Kingdom, Austria and Mexico whose chapters are covered in this section.

The use of text messages by undergraduates studying Applied Geomorphology and in the context of a Teaching Qualification in Adult Literacies (TQAL) as well as an example of the use of online laboratories of electrical engineering students offer insights into the simulation of situations by using mobile devices and the construction of an online learning environment to provide remote or mobile work-based experimental practice. By using mobile-learning concepts such as mobile simulation and laboratory-situated learning, contexts can be augmented. Also, learners are able to engage in activities that are considered basic in terms of their professional skills and knowledge, but that are – for different reasons – not available for learners in their real-world environments.

Chapter 10   Online laboratories in interactive mobile learning environments

Michael E. Auer, Arthur Edwards and Danilo Garbi Zutin frame their chapter with an approach based on e-learning with a particular focus on technology. They highlight the shift from training partners providing information for learning to self-initiated information retrieval by learners in order to train themselves. This shift originates from the flexibility gained through the features of mobile devices and wireless networks and includes the result that the traditional place for work-based learning, i.e. on-the-job learning, is replaced by site unspecific locations and times. Learners can engage in knowledge building also in places other than the workplace and mobile systems can replace the training partner. This is the central starting point for the authors to discuss the implementation of mobile learning in work-based learning contexts.

With their chapter, the authors cover an area of work-based mobile learning that tends to move away from on-site experiences and the learners' professional and private everyday life – one of the central reference points of many of the other authors contributing to this book. Whilst other authors try to adopt learner agency and cultural practices that originate in the everyday use of mobile and web-based technologies, Auer et al. argue for 'personnel who can function optimally in the workplace' and, at the same time, for the creation of circumstances where learners are able to refer to their previous experiences and to learn in continuous, stimulating and enjoyable environments. Thus, the optimisation of the work-based learning process includes not only the minimisation of such factors applying to appropriation of knowledge-building, but also the acceptance of learners' perceived interests, preferences and goals.

After giving an example of learning with online laboratories, the authors conclude their chapter with the description of technical details of an online learning environment that they developed to provide remote or mobile work-based experimental practice in the area of engineering.

Chapter 11   Work-based simulations: Using text messaging and the role of the virtual context

Mobile learning in the form of simulations using SMS text messages is the topic of investigation in the project described by Sarah Cornelius and Phil Marston. Undergraduate students of Applied Geomorphology receive text messages referring to flood disaster scenarios in order to get involved in work-related tasks and real-world experiences and to foster their decision-making abilities. The use of theoretical knowledge to real situations was one of the aims of this project. The authors refer to an activity theory approach to evaluate learners' experiences with text message simulations and a text message-based mentoring scheme that is developed for work-based adult literacies practitioners. Real-time learning in varying and real-life contexts by using mobile devices is seen as an alternative to prepare learners and workers for situations where real-world experiences would be too costly, sensitive, dangerous or logistically impossible. In such a framework, different aspects have to be considered, such as a complex set of issues associated with the virtual context of the simulation scenario and the work context of the learners themselves.

Section 4 Ethical issues relevant for (researching) mobile learning

For a long time ethics has been one of the dominant public issues in relation to the everyday use of mobile devices: the infringement of personal rights, the responsibility of companies in selling ring tone subscriptions to minors or 'happy slapping' and bullying are some of the most prominent issues that have impacted on the attitudes of schools towards the use of mobile devices for teaching and learning. The issue of ethics is, of course, also highly relevant in relation to workplace mobile learning and research. By referring to teaching and nursing professions, authors from the United Kingdom and Australia investigate responsibilities that workers and researchers have with regard to the physical and mental integrity of others. On the basis of a literature review and field studies, categories are elaborated that can be used as guidelines for the responsible use of mobile technologies in work and learning contexts and to ensure accountability towards others in their learning process and work routines.

Chapter 12   Ethical professional mobile learning for teaching and nursing workplaces

The complexities and confusion faced by teachers and nurses in their use of work-based mobile learning is the starting point for Kevin Burden, Sandy Schuck and Peter Aubusson in discussing ethical issues that arise in contexts of mobile learning. Data collection by means of picture taking, data exchange and distribution are not just central functions of mobile devices and mobile learning, but they are also issues that have to be considered from the perspective of vulnerability of the people depicted and/or recorded.

With reference to basic ethical principles, rules, norms and values of professionals engaged in mobile learning as well as to power, accountability and vulnerability that are established in and through social interaction, the authors provide guidelines for ethically responsible use of mobile devices in professional contexts that can be generalised and used in contexts of teaching and nursing and beyond: trust and confidentiality, genuine collaboration, transparency, the analysis of consequences and risks and accountability of activities.

Chapter 13   *Ethical concerns relevant to researching work-based mobile learning*

Starting with a short history of ethics in different professional fields and in research with a focus on privacy, ownership and copyright, Jocelyn Wishart critically discusses the notion of ethics with a view to the needs and rights of vulnerable people such as patients in hospital and young children.

Informed consent, personal information and images, ownership, data protection and user-generated content are considered to be key issues of ethics in mobile learning and research. They are viewed as a contemporary addendum to already established ethical principles and can be used as a scheme that can be discussed with professionals before they start using mobile devices in the field. One of the central issues of considering ethics in mobile learning is the awareness of personal needs and the needs and rights of others as well as a process in which values, norms and rules are negotiated in advance in order to respects the rights of those involved in mobile-learning processes.

Section 5   Near-future scenarios for work-based mobile learning

This section of the book features two studies focusing on future aspects of mobile learning. Both chapters discuss learning that is 'just in time' and 'when necessary'. While an initial approach to the use of mobile devices for learning in work contexts might be in the provision of learning modules, the supportive function of mobiles in immediate work contexts appears to be a more promising but also challenging aspect in the near future. This is a finding that was already reflected in other studies: a multinational IT company, for example, shifted its focus for mobile learning from the delivery of formal learning modules to just-in-time performance support systems (Ahmad & Orion, 2010). Other commonalities across the two chapters include approaches that are more collaborative than didactic, focusing on social interactions between learners and experts or between peers facilitated by mobile devices. A particular potential for the near future appears to exist in the field of life sciences and health care, where both chapters report and analyse a number of different scenarios. Unsurprisingly, some of the issues raised in this section have already been mentioned in other contributions to the book: examples include the use of mobiles for the compilation of e-portfolios or their use to record learning experiences. Some possible scenarios, however, have not been covered in other book chapters: these include the use of a 'handheld projection device' for tutorial support. However, new developments in the field of Tablet PCs such as the iPad may enable this kind of learning scenario in the foreseeable future. Despite great advances in the field of mobile technologies, some issues such as interoperability, connectivity or power remain to be resolved. Across the two contributions in this section it is also interesting to note how the methods applied – the *Futures Technology* Workshop, the *Cognitive Forseight* toolkit, the *Building Visions for Learning Spaces* cards and the scenario-based Delphi approach – framed the scenarios in terms of richness and creativity.

Chapter 14   Mobile learning in corporate settings:
Results from an expert survey

The question of whether and how mobile devices can be used to support employees' learning processes in the near future is also addressed in a study conducted by Christoph Pimmer and Urs Gröhbiel. A group of international experts, researchers and practitioners was asked to evaluate four scenarios: sales representatives learning with personalised learning objects;

engineers accessing learning materials on display goggles; nurses documenting the handling of work tasks and apprentices who answer daily questions from their classroom teacher to reflect on their learning progress at work. Experts were also invited to describe additional scenarios they expect to come on stream in the near future. These scenarios were classified according to their immediacy and relevance to the work process (just-in-time and just-in-case) and whether learning involves social interaction or solely human-computer interactivity. Participants in the study anticipated mobile learning in companies in the near future mostly in the form of learning 'just-in-case', based on human-computer interactivity, as the implementation of this kind of scenario seems to be relatively easy. Other findings of the survey show that social interaction in learning processes received the most positive evaluation, as did content-based scenarios with examples focusing on contextualised learning. The integration of learning at work was described as the most important area of inherent tension to be addressed: challenging but very promising at the same time. While reflection that occurs in scenarios based on the production and sharing of learning material was positively highlighted, experts expressed reservations in terms of the mastery of technical and didactic skills in order to produce learning materials of sufficiently high quality.

Chapter 15   Future scenarios for workplace-based mobile learning

Jocelyn Wishart and David Green explore future scenarios for mobile learning developed by a number of experts in a series of workshops in Great Britain. Out of twelve scenarios, six are centred on workplace mobile learning – a fact that underlines the growing importance of this field. The scenarios include college and tourism students on placements communicating with peers and tutors or creating e-portfolios; trainees using a futuristic handheld projection device that enables multimedia communication with tutors; student doctors accessing external services and expertise at the point of care; a holistic portfolio containing life and work experiences to encourage life-long learning across different contexts; and inter-professional networks where mobile phones bridge local and remote expertise. Across the scenarios developed and analysed Wishart and Green note an increasing use of just-in-time and 'when necessary' training, an increasing amount of peer-to-peer networking and collaboration and an approach to teaching and learning that is more collaborative than didactic. Mobile learning is reported as being particularly useful in specific subjects, especially those where both theory and practice are studied or those which involve field-work and data collection such as in the sciences, geography and vocational subjects. Other emerging issues for workplace mobile learning include both ethical and practical implications such as cultural barriers, resistance to change as well as ethical and privacy concerns.

Conclusion and outlook

Considering the 'enormous amount of interest and momentum and invest-ment going into mobile technologies' (Traxler, 2007b) we focus in the book on how learners and organisations in work contexts can make use of this development in order to enhance or enable learning. While mobile devices have not primarily been developed for learning and education, the chapters provide a number of examples of how learners and organisations use and harness the pervasive technology for learning purposes in work contexts. We contend, however, that the deployment of technology for (mobile) learning is neither apolitical nor beneficial per se for the people and parties involved. A number of ethical and political issues have to be considered when using work-based mobile learning.

Whilst we have tried to provide a first appraisal of the field of work-based mobile learning, we are fully aware that this volume can represent all but a starting point in the exploration of the complex issues in hand. However, we very much hope, and believe, the book offers a rich collec-tion for both practitioners and researchers to build on and to develop and refine the knowledge base for this field. Practitioners can, for example, apply and evaluate the concepts presented in further professional environments.

Researchers are invited to contribute with further empirical findings to a better understanding of critical factors and causalities in this emerging field. There is also a need to consolidate the still very fragmented theoretical base which is currently being used. Mirroring Sawchuck (2010), who notes that no single theory or area of research can 'lay claim to any sort of definitive account of the multi-dimensional phenomena of workplace learning research as a whole' we believe that this is also true for the exploration of mobile learning in work contexts. While we fully acknowledge the value of the applied theoretical concepts, we also encourage fertilisation across different lines of research in order to more holistically explore the complexities of mobile learning in work contexts.

Given the wide range of different concepts and cases presented in this book, we do not see the use of mobile devices as a one-size-fits-all approach to learning in and across work contexts; instead, we consider them as tools that are suited for learning in particular settings; some of which are presented in this book. We also hope the cases show that mobile learning goes far beyond the delivery of e-learning modules on small devices. In this sense, we believe that mobile learning has some unique characteristics and transformative potentials impacting on work environments and beyond.

Obviously, we have not been able to offer an exhaustive perspective on such a wide-ranging topic in this book. We have, for example, not provided cases of how mobile devices and augmented reality can be combined to enhance human visual perception and, possibly, contribute to learning. While some chapters have shown that the use of mobile devices can impact on learners' identities, we only marginally discuss how new practices triggered by mobile devices are transforming society as a whole, for example, in shifting our work-life balance. These are all aspects that might well be discussed in a future edition.

References

Ahmad, N., & Orion, P. (2010) *Smartphones make IBM smarter, but not as expected.* Available online at <http://www.allbusiness.com/media-telecommunications/telecommunications/13738659-1.html> (accessed 01/05/10)

Dzartevska, A. (2009) 'Developing a mobile learning platform for a professional environment.' In Ryu, H., & Parsons, D. (eds) *Innovative mobile learning: techniques and technologies* (pp. 273–301). Hershey, NY: Information Science Reference

Eurostat (2008) 'Science and technology.' *Europe in figures – Eurostat yearbook 2008.* Available online at <http://epp.eurostat.ec.europa.eu/portal/page/portal/eurostat/home/> (accessed 01/05/10)

Evans, K., Guile, D., & Harris, J. (2010) 'Rethinking work-based learning – For education professionals and professionals who educate.' In Malloch, M., Cairns, L., Evans, K., and O'Connor, B. (eds), *The SAGE Handbook of Workplace Learning.* London: Sage

Livingston, A. (2004) 'Smartphones and other mobile devices: the Swiss army knives of the 21st century.' In *Educause Quarterly 27*(2), pp. 46–57

New Media Consortium / EDUCAUSE (2009, 2010) *The Horizon Report.* Available online at <http://www.nmc.org/horizon> (accessed 10/08/10)

Pachler, N., Bachmair, B., & Cook, J. (2010). *Mobile learning: structures, agency, practices.* Springer

Pimmer, C. (2009) 'Work-based mobile learning in the health sector: Concept of a mobile learning system exemplified by educational scenarios of junior doctors.' Paper presented at the *3rd WLE Mobile Learning Symposium: Mobile Learning Cultures across Education, Work and Leisure.* WLE Centre, IOE London, UK

Pimmer, C., Pachler, N., & Attwell, G. (2010) 'Towards work-based mobile learning. What we can learn from the fields of work-based learning and mobile learning.' In *International Journal of Mobile and Blended Learning (IJMBL) 2*(4). *Special Issue: Mobile learning in the context of transformation*

Pimmer, C., Pachler, N., Gröhbiel, U., & Genewein, U. (2009) 'Arbeitsintegriertes Lernen im Gesundheitswesen. Konzept für ein mobiles Kollaborations – und Lernsystem am Beispiel der ärztlichen Weiterbildung.' In *bwp@ Berufs und Wirtschaftspädagogik – online 15*

Sawchuck, P. (2010) 'Researching workplace learning: an overview and critique.' In Malloch, M., Cairns, L., Evans, K., and O'Connor, B. (eds), *The SAGE Handbook of Workplace Learning.* London: Sage

Traxler, J. (2007a) 'Defining, discussing and evaluating mobile learning: The moving finger writes and having writ.' In *The International Review of Research in Open and Distance Learning 8*(2)

Traxler, J. (2007b). JISC Podcast. Available online at <http://www.jisc.ac.uk/media/avfiles/news/interviews/podcast25johntraxler.mp3> (accessed 13/05/10)

Traxler, J. (2010) 'Sustaining mobile learning and its institutions.' In *International Journal of Mobile and Blended Learning (IJMBL) 2*(4). *Special Issue: Mobile learning in the context of transformation*

KAREN EVANS

2 Work-based learning: Setting the scene

Abstract

Work-based learning (WBL) is, at root, about relationships between the fundamental human, social processes of working and learning. The process of defining and scoping the field of work-based learning brings oppositions, tensions and exclusions to the fore. In offering expanded definitions of work-based learning, bridging embedded workplace learning perspectives and those that frame work-based learning as a class of programmes, this scene-setting chapter argues for an inclusive approach that expands and rethinks the field. Theories and perspectives cluster in ways that are of particular significance to an inclusive understanding of mobilities of work-based learning. Clusters focus respectively on cognition/expertise and on practice-based, organisational learning with critical theories bringing insights that problematise and challenge some of the dominant assumptions in both. This points to the need for a more dialogic approach in which robust lines of inquiry in different domains are opened up more fully to an exploration of overlaps, gaps and points of connection. A social ecological approach allows the relationships between work and learning to be explored through the dynamics of different scales of activity: societal, organisational and personal. While the agency of the learning individual is foregrounded as highly significant for mobile work-based learning, a social ecological approach avoids the pitfalls of individualistic interpretations by capturing the interdependent and embedded processes involved.

Introduction

Work-based learning (WBL) is coming of age. Setting the scene for a book of this kind means introducing the main players and perspectives in a field that is both burgeoning and maturing. As noted above, WBL is, at root, about relationships between the fundamental human, social processes of working and learning. I have shown, in Evans et al., 2010, how the process of defining and scoping the field of work-based learning brings oppositions, tensions and exclusions to the fore. In offering expanded definitions of WBL, bridging embedded workplace learning perspectives and those that frame WBL as a class of programmes, I argue for an inclusive approach that expands and rethinks the field rather than inventing yet further terminology. In this approach, WBL is defined as:

- learning at work, for work and through work;
- ...that expands human capacities through purposeful activity;
- ...where the purposes derive from the context of employment.

Theories and perspectives cluster in ways that are of particular significance to an inclusive understanding of mobilities of work-based learning. Clusters focus respectively on cognition/expertise and on practice-based, organisational learning with critical theories bringing insights that problematise and challenge some of the dominant assumptions in the field. Sawchuk (2010) in an authoritative review of the field asks what counts as 'robust' research and inquiry in the field concluding that each of these domains contains robust lines of inquiry each of which encompasses a sufficient, if not complete, set of factors and considerations. This points to the need for a more dialogic approach in which robust lines of inquiry in different domains are opened up more fully to an exploration of overlaps, gaps and points of connection. This process, I argue, leads to an elaboration of the diversity of purposes that derive from the context of employment, and thus to an expanded understanding of the scope and nature of work-based learning and how knowledge is 're-contextualised' as people and practices move and change in work, education and community settings. Finally, I argue for a social ecological approach that allows the relationships between work and learning to be explored through the dynamics of different scales of activity: societal, organisational and personal. While the agency of the learning individual is fore-grounded as highly significant for mobile work-based learning, a social ecological approach avoids the pitfalls of individualistic interpretations by capturing the interdependent and embedded processes involved.

Exploring tensions

The history of work-based learning is strewn with oppositions and exclusions that have to be resolved if WBL is to become more strongly positioned as well as better defined. These are encapsulated in tensions between participatory and acquisition-based views of learning; insufficient attention to power relations and inequalities of access to learning; failure to combine organisational, individual and wider socio-economic perspectives in much current theorising and practice. Crucially for this volume, and for inquiry into the potential of mobile learning, there has been a failure in the past to recognise the combined significance of on-the-job, off-the-job, near-the-job learning as well as learning beyond the workplace.

For example, there is a marked divergence between the university-appropriated conceptions of WBL and the concepts associated with 'workplace learning'. For 'workplace' perspectives that emphasise the social, cultural and political dynamics of workplaces, the lenses used bring into focus the work practices that other lenses sometimes miss but can also produce 'tunnel visions' of a different kind. They distance themselves from versions of WBL conceived of as a class of higher education programmes since such conceptions often disconnect the use of work as a resource for learning from the political realities and social relations of the workplace as experienced by employees. For those whose priorities are rooted in workplace learning, the 'work experience' or the 'placement' is seen as a source of learning which involves only a partial workplace presence which excludes many of the features of the employer–employee relationships that are so crucial in influencing workplace learning experiences.

The use of socio-cultural lenses does reveal how learning at work is embedded in production processes and social relations. But situated analyses of work and learning also often fail to make connections between the organised and planned (often termed 'formal') types of programs that incorporate elements of work-based learning and the workplace learning that is embedded in 'everyday work' within the social dynamics of organisations; between the workplace and wider life–work relationships and the careers of workers as they move into and out of communities of social practice (and indeed participate in several simultaneously). When the analytic lenses of the social organisation of learning in the here-and-now of the enterprise are used exclusively, the learning individual is either out of focus or beyond the range of view.

Can approaches which use theoretical concepts for analyzing the constitution of practice connect with those that focus on the challenges, problems and opportunities that arise for people in their places of work? To what extent can practice be used as a resource to rethink theory and how can better understandings of power relations make visible the assumptions that underpin public policy in this field?

Mapping the theoretical domains: Connection and overlap

Theoretical domains of significance can be mapped to highlight their areas of potential and actual overlap. A first step towards a more dialogic approach is to explore new thinking at the intersections (see Figure 2.1).

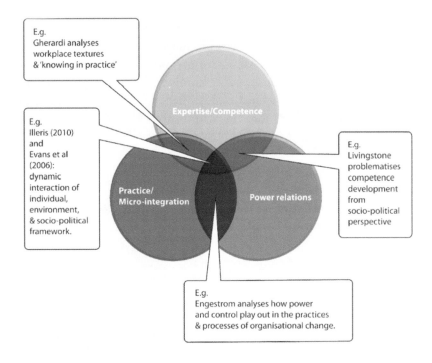

Figure 2.1 Theoretical domains of work-based learning

Sawchuk (2010) argues that 'ignoring, criticizing and dismissing contribu-tions based on topic/method choice narrows the potential for the devel-opment of truly robust lines of research inquiry'. With the proviso that the contributions to the debate have to qualify for consideration by taking sufficient aspects into account, differing positions and perspectives 'have something important to contribute and to receive from to the others'. Mapping the ways in which three significant theoretical domains intersect potentially offers a framework for exploring the mobilities of work-based learning.

Domain 1, focusing on the development of expertise and individual competence, is rooted in theoretical perspectives on behaviour and cog-nition. These range from those that have behaviourist roots that equate behaviour with performance, to the generative versions (Norris, 1991) that emphasise capabilities. Many of these pay attention to the processes and contexts in ways that move well beyond some narrower 'HRD' preoccupations with individual, organisational and economic outcomes.

Eraut's approach recognises that 'learning' in the workplace is often not recognised or named as such. It is embedded in other key purposes, notably those of enculturation, innovation and licenses to practise. Eraut (2004, 2007) explains that different types of cognition are linked to the social situation and it is the particular work context and its social relations that trigger information processing and problem-solving. A limitation of Eraut's models is that they derive mainly from studies of professionals and graduate employees in fields such as accountancy, engineering and nursing. However, Eraut's analyses of the interplay between confidence, challenge and support – 'if there is neither a challenge nor sufficient support to encourage a person to seek out or respond to a challenge, then confidence declines and with it the motivation to learn' (Eraut, 2004 p. 269) – have salience for workers of all skills levels, as Taylor and Evans (2009) and Belfiore et al. (2004) have shown.

Domain 2, focusing on power relations, raises more fundamental concerns over the politics of learning and work that shape policy discourses and pervade the contemporary workplace. Here, significant lines of research inquiry are rooted in various versions of critical theory. They show how the realities of the employment relationship are manifested in the intensification of work; differential access to informal learning opportunities and career progression; 'learning poor' as opposed to 'learning rich' environments; power relations between managers and workers and the extent to which employee 'voice' is heard or unheard (see Evans and Rainbird, 2002). The conflict inherent in the wage relationship is a central plank of analyses that reveal the contradictions that occur because 'managements have to pursue the objectives of control and releasing creativity, both of which are inherent in the relationship with workers and which call for different approaches' (Edwards, 2003, p. 16). Sawchuk, reviewing research in this tradition, shows how this has systematically revealed the historical processes by which collective bargaining processes have included and impacted upon quality of work-life/learning, paid education leave and the systematic linkages between continuing education and the workplace. In particular, Forrester (2001, 2005) and Rainbird et al. (2004) have shown how British Trade Unions have constructed a workplace learning agenda.

Domain 3, focusing on practice and micro-interaction in workplace activities, provides detailed insights into naturally occurring processes – what actually happens in everyday workplace interactions. A focus on structural factors can lose sight of the complexities of practice and how social practices both reflect and shape culture and the social structures including work organisations. In the domain of practice-focused studies, leading theoretical perspectives linked to strong lines of research inquiry are offered by Lave (1991, 2009) and by Luff, Hindmarch and Heath (2000). Luff et al.'s sociological work-based studies focus on what occurs in practice and how it occurs. These micro-interaction studies are rooted in the theoretical traditions of socio-linguistics and semiotics and use forms of discourse and conversation analysis that have been able to shed light on the ways in which practice is reproduced, renewed and innovated (see also Stubbe, 2003). While these studies do not focus on learning per se they connect with the kinds if questions about the 'situated' nature of learning that Lave, from a social anthropological perspective has influentially tackled elsewhere. Situated learning (see Lave and Wenger, 1991) takes account of social interaction and physical activity. Learning is embedded in a cultural-social context of everyday activities. Learning always takes place in relation to people and their contexts. A key construct is the 'community of practice' – the idea that learning is constituted through the sharing of a purposeful activity. Lave, whose concepts have been appropriated, critiqued and misrepresented in various ways, has in 2009 revisited her accounts to explain their theoretical roots in historical-materialism.

The three domains overlap in ways that have already produced some key points of connection. At the *intersections between practice/mediation and expertise*, Gherardi's studies are influential in showing how the 'texture' of work organisations is continuously created and recreated through the complex interplay of historical, cultural, material, structural and normative factors. Gherardi (2000) and Gherardi and Nicolini (2006) recognise organisational learning as relational and dynamic. Gherardi's work, while analysing texture, also focuses strongly on 'ways of knowing', 'knowing in practice' and the range of knowledge forms (procedural, declarative, implicit, reactive) that are central to Eraut's research. At the *intersection of power relations and expertise/competence*, numerous researchers have shown how the labour market has progressively been redefined in a rationale of competences, which aims to 'measure the individual against the ideal worker that the skills matrix represents' (Moore, 1987, p. 230) and becomes an instrument for 'cultural control' of workplace learning (see Evans, 1998; Solomon, 2001). Strong lines of research rooted in this perspective are exemplified by Livingstone's research programme in which large-scale data sets collected in North America and beyond have been utilised to explore social regularities in patterns of participation, outcomes, learning and skills. Livingstone (2006a,b; 2007) has argued that inadequate skills utilisation in workplaces, rather than skills deficits, is the problem for workers and the issue to which public policy should be attending, a stance also confirmed by Evans and Waite (2009) and Felstead et al. (2009) in the UK context. Livingstone's surveys, and those of Felstead et al. (2009) have provided strong evidence of large scale and widespread involvement in learning activity among adults in the workforce coupled with evidence that little of this is effectively captured and utilised in the work processes of their paid employment. At the *intersection of 'situated' theories of practice and critical theories of power relations* in workplace learning, Engeström's work (2001, 2007, 2008) has played a leading role in drawing attention to the workplace dynamics of power and control through detailed, practice-focused analyses of organisational change processes. These differ from interaction studies and analyses of situated cognition in their focus on boundary crossings and multiple meditations between 'subject' and 'object' within divisions of labour, community and workplace rules, as well as their distinctive 'change laboratory' approach.

Through these intersections, further connections can be forged that facilitate a holistic, integrative approach. At the intersection of all three domains, Illeris et al.'s models (2003, 2004, 2010) and the perspectives developed by Evans et al. (2006) show how learning at work is enmeshed in the dynamics of technical-organisational, social-cultural and individual factors. Illeris's model starts with the learning individual, revealing organisational and societies tensions and also spaces for action. By contrast, Evans et al. (2006) start with the workplace as a site in which production of goods and services is the driving purpose, not learning per se. They show how research struggles to pay due heed to all of these scales of activity. Thus much of the work on the socio-cultural factors involved in communities of practice focuses on the immediate work setting or group and is not well situated in an understanding of the dynamics of wider institutional and regulatory context. Although there are strengths in understanding learning as participation, this approach often fails to recognise that, in paid work, the employment relationship is often contradictory and sometimes antagonistic in ways that fundamentally influence participation and learning. Similarly, research on reflective practice has tended to focus mainly on the individual worker/learner. Activity theory, especially of the type developed by Engeström (2001) attempts to link local working practices with wider organisational frameworks. However, it takes the wider regulatory frameworks that underpin the relationship between managers and workers, for granted and pays relatively little attention to individuals. Evans et al. 2006 have attempted to bring these considerations together in a holistic and relational approach to the facilitation of workplace learning, focusing on the interdependencies of activities and actors at three overlapping levels of activity, showing how:

- regulation of the employment relationship and Government initiatives have significant impact on opportunities for, and nature of, workplace learning;
- workplaces can be characterised as more expansive or restrictive as learning environments; and
- dispositions and tacit skills of workers/employees influence the nature of the working environment and the ways in which workers react to and interact with that environment.

While learning has to be understood as integral to practice, attention also has to be paid to the environment as a whole, including the regulatory framework that governs the employer-employee relationship. The work environment affects how far formal learning can be a positive trigger for the more informal. A short-term timeframe and a narrow view of learning, dominated by measurable changes in performance, will not enhance the learning environment and can stifle innovation.

Facilitating work-based learning:
Towards a theoretically informed and inclusive approach

For the purposes of this volume, keeping all three scales of activity in view
is a means to the end of facilitating and improving work-based learning
through the use of mobile technologies. This requires, as a first priority, the
development of theoretically informed and evidence-based understandings
of the scope of work-based learning. Work-based learning usually starts
in the work setting, through activities that derive their purposes from the
context of employment. These activities generate the work-based knowledge that we all develop through everyday practice: intellectual resources
from outside the workplace can be drawn on to deepen and expand understanding and practice. These are the processes that have to be modeled into
work-based learning, together with the recognition that paid employment
is not the only form of work that matters in work-based learning. A key
hypothesis is that work-based learning can be enhanced through the use
of creative technologies. Drawing in new intellectual resources to deepen
and expand our understanding and practice is made more possible, more
feasible with digital technologies now available. 'Mobility' in learning has
new meanings as the locations and social spaces in which work is carried
out diversify and work itself becomes mobile and distributed.

Can a rethought concept of WBL that goes back to the nature of
these interlocking relationships break out of the narrow preoccupations
of education and training professionals with 'programmes' and 'standards'
to accommodate the complexities of the social relations of production and
the potential offered by mobile learning in the workplaces of real life? In
so doing, can it offer an integrative way forward in a fragmenting field?

With the starting point that the workplace (whether in a hospital, business, voluntary organisation, school or college etc.) is a crucially important
site for learning and for access to learning, I have shown that analytical
perspectives on work-based learning have to take the social and organisational context of work and learning more fully into account. They also
have to explore work-based pedagogies that originate from research into
how people learn in, for and through work.

These are aspects that have to be addressed in our search for ways to improve the relationship between learning and work. The relationships between work and learning have to be explored at different levels, 'zooming' in and out (to use a metaphor derived from use of an internet map or viewing tool) to gain an integrated view of the 'whole' and how the integral parts come together in ways that are best understood interdependently, holistically and in terms of location and cultural context.

An inclusive approach that expands and rethinks WBL, rather than inventing yet another terminology, leads towards an elaboration of the purposes that derive form the context of employment – the question begged by the opening definition – in ways that extend far beyond the dominant assumptions that these purposes equate to employers' needs or the dictates of policy.

Work-based learning is 'for' people in work at all levels of the workforce at different ages and life stages. The purposes of WBL go far beyond those of assisting people into work by having some experience of the workplace to offer employers. According to whether the worker is a 'learner' preparing for work, a new entrant to work or an experienced worker developing, supervisory or managerial responsibilities, learning takes place very differently depending on the specific context, on the status and role of the worker and his or her prior work and learning experience. Different types of worker-learner require different arrangements in the workplace and, where applicable, in the educational support provided beyond the workplace, to maximise learning. Work-based learning may start with shop floor activities that focus on 'health and safety' perhaps; or overcoming a technical problem – in which subject-based, procedural, and personal forms of knowledge are utilised. The impetus may come from Trades Union membership or membership of a professional body. There are also aspects of WBL that are sectorally rooted. Each employment sector has its own history of policy and qualification development, its own culture of skills and practice recognition and improvement. Specific work-based learning *activities* such as projects, cases or problems can take their impetus from the job, the wider environment of work or the knowledge base. They might start with a work challenge or problem that has to be solved or they might be triggered by the need to share knowledge and experience with others as part of participatory management strategies. Finding ways of responding to unforeseen occurrences or new circumstances often engages groups and teams in in-company or intra-organisational WBL while professional networks often respond to challenges by forms of co-operation that operate far beyond organisational boundaries.

Therefore, WBL takes place individually and collectively in the workplace and beyond and the purposes of an expanded WBL derive from the highly differentiated contexts of employment that people experience. These contexts themselves extend beyond the paid employment that is the focus for so much theorising and research, to the contexts of self-employment, contract-based employment and indeed unpaid employment in contexts such as those of voluntary or community organisation.

The purposes that derive from the contexts of employment are the following:

Purpose	Relates to ...
enculturation	The purpose of 'learning how we do things here'
competence, licence to practise	The learning necessary for performance to occupational standards, demands of increasing regulation, health and safety standards, keeping abreast of new systems and technologies
improving practice, innovation and renewal	Learning to do what has not been done before: this involves significant WBL and occurs every time a new set of demands is introduced, particularly in the public sector
wider capabilities	It encompasses the development of professional and occupational capabilities; learning to 'do the next job' as well as the current one; learning to work in different cultures and environments
equity, ethics and social justice	Refers to the process of systematically reflecting on practice within a set of professional concerns about ethics, values, priorities and procedures
vocational/ professional identity development	New entrants 'thinking and feeling' their way into a vocation/profession and coming to identify with it and with others who participate in it; experienced workers developing and reconstructing identities in and through work as positions, roles and contexts change

Each of these purposes can be understood from the perspectives of employee and professional body interests as well as those of the employer and from the perspective of employment and the wider society. For example, the pursuit of 'brands' and mission statements has made corporate encultura-tion processes more visible; shop floor enculturation may be compliant or resistant. Practice improvement is a purpose that is often driven from the 'bottom up' in organisations; innovation is more often 'top down'. Increas-ingly employee-driven innovation (see Evans & Waite, 2010) is a focus of attention, with implications for knowledge flows and power relations between levels of the workforce. In the development of wider capabilities, the impetus may come from the organisation or the profession as well as the workers' interests in positioning themselves for career development.

In ethics, equity and social, justice, theorising practice as a way of resolving professional concerns (see Guile and Young, 1995) leads to the development and improvement of models and procedures. The organi-sation of learning through Trades Union structures and representatives foregrounds social justice, recognising that workplace cultures can foster the learning of racism (see Allan et al., 2004) as readily as the learning of tolerance and co-operation. As Quarter (2000) has shown in '*Beyond the Bottom Line*', companies that embrace the aims of corporate social respon-sibility may support learning opportunities in and through the workplace that reflect wider ethical, equity or social justice purposes.

Knowledge recontextualisation and mobilities in work-based learning

The dynamics of knowledge and pedagogy have always to be kept in view in this expanded view of WBL. The pursuit of all these purposes brings different types of knowledge (personal, procedural, ethical, propositional) with fundamentally different logics into play. At the heart of WBL lie processes of knowledge recontextualisation, as knowledge is put to work in different environments. A fresh approach developed by Evans, Guile and Harris (2009) and Evans et al. (2010) concentrates on the ways in which different forms of knowledge are re-contextualised as people move between sites of learning and practice in universities, colleges and workplaces. All knowledge has a context in which it was originally generated. Contexts are often thought of as settings or places but contexts in our use extend to the 'schools of thought', the traditions and norms of practice, the life experiences in which knowledge of different kinds is generated. For knowledge generated and practised in one context to be put to work in new and different contexts, it has to be recontextualised in various ways that simultaneously engage with and change those practices, traditions and experiences. The starting point (Evans, Guile and Harris, 2010) is the idea that concepts and practice change as we use them in different settings. This approach to recontextualisation has drawn on (a) developments of Bernstein's idea that concepts change as they move from their disciplinary origins and become a part of a curriculum (Bernstein, 2000; Barnett, 2006) and (b) van Oers' (1998) idea that concepts are an integral part of practice and that practice varies from one sector or workplace to another. Both of these notions have been substantially expanded in order to embrace the ways in which learners/employees change as they recontextualise concepts and practices and the extent to which this process may spur innovation in workplaces as much as in educational contexts.

At the level of the learning individual, the following principles, adapted from Evans and Niemeyer (2004), have particular salience for mobile work-based learning:

1. Engagement is essential for learning to take place.
2. Learning may be situated in three ways:
   - in *work practices*,
   - in the *culture* of the workplace and
   - in the *social world* of the participants.
3. When learning is well-situated in each of these three ways, engagement, learning outcomes and potential for recontextualisation are all enhanced.

4. When learning is poorly situated in any of these three respects, engagement, outcomes and recontextualisation potential may be diminished.

Mobile work-based learning has more potential to situate learning in these ways than has been realised to date. Mobilities in work-based learning focus on the learning individual and the creation of new learning spaces but are also enmeshed in the multiple purposes have derive from, and are embedded in, the contexts of work. The ways in which adults learn in and through the workplace are rooted in educational trajectories and their complex intertwining with social institutions (of labour market, workplace, community) and social roles (of employee, citizen, family member) at different stages of the life-course.

The spatial dimensions of workplace learning can facilitate learners' motivations and outcomes towards skills development. Kersh (2010), for example, shows how the workplace, as a type of learning space, can be associated with positive attitudes and outcomes for adult learners. Drawing on both the theoretical (e.g. Solomon et al., 2006; Fuller & Unwin, 2004, Evans et al., 2006) and her own empirical research, Kersh argues that the workplace often symbolises an environment that is perceived as different from a classroom-like setting where the learner might have had negative prior experiences.

Similarly, understandings of on-the-job learning are connected to the place of that kind of learning and, in particular, that this place is not off-the-job (Solomon et al., 2006: 3). In addition, the workplace may offer rewards such as improved career prospects (for example promotion) which provide an additional incentive for learning. Developing confidence in the workplace is another crucial stimulus. Research into UK Workplace Skills for Life (SfL) provision (Wolf and Evans 2011) yields important examples. While the aim is to boost skills relating to economic productivity, SfL is focused quite narrowly on one spatial environment – the workplace – but learners' motivations are much more broad and relate to a wider range of differing environments and resources. Apart from using their newly developed skills in the workplace, employees are shown to recontextualise their skills in other contexts, for example their family environments and community activities. (Evans & Waite, 2009, 2010) Explorations of mobilities in learning in adult life are most often focused on highly mobile professional workers, who take the lion's share of any companies' resources for training and staff development. Yet mobilities are at least as significant for employees on the 'shop floor' and those involved in providing a range of public services. Many of the 'Skills for Life' workplace literacy learners referred to above valued the relative convenience and accessibility of workplace learning in so far as it fitted in more smoothly with their lives at work and at home. The benefit of learning with colleagues in a familiar setting was important for the bus driver 'because at least it's in familiar settings as opposed to I've got to find a room, J49 and Fred Bloggs will be in there waiting for you'. Similarly, an employee of an engineering company told us that he preferred 'learning at work because you're working with the people you're learning with …they can have the chats, and …conversations and …discuss it amongst yourselves if they're struggling with anything'. The important point here is that the access to learning through the workplace space is supported and enriched by the social interactions of the workplace. It is not, in that sense, 'individualised' (see also Evans 2009). The expansion of new technologies, such as the internet, email, mobile phones etc., also makes an impact on virtual *working* space, further loosening the boundaries between different types of environments. However, in order to engage in various types of virtual learning and virtual working space, employees need IT skills. There is a growing tendency for 'online paperwork'. In many organisations it is expected that employees are able to complete or work with various forms (e.g. reports, orders, invoices etc.) online. All those factors may create some stress and pressure for the staff in a range of workplaces. Employees who lack confidence in their IT skills may feel threatened and de-motivated if they are 'forced into' doing or engaging in IT-based activities without prior training. On the other hand, once trained, the use of electronic resources for mobile learning can opens up new possibilities for them.

A social ecological approach

Building on Bronfrenbrenner (1979), the usefulness of the social ecology metaphor is that it provides a way into understanding the complexity of factors that impact directly or indirectly on education and lifelong learning without losing sight of the whole. Every contextual factor and every person contributing or influenced is part of a complex ecology or system of social relations and relationships that sustains the system through a set of interdependencies. According to Weaver-Hightower's (2008) overview, the four categories of

- actors,
- relationships,
- environments and structures,
- processes

lie at the heart of social ecological analyses. These differ in the degree of significance that is accorded to personal agency, through which actors 'depending on their resources and power, are able to change ecological systems for their own benefit' (p. 156) Because ecologies are self-sustaining through interdependencies that operate without centralised controls, individuals and groups have spaces in which to exercise agency in ways that can influence the whole dynamic, through the interdependencies involved. Furthermore, Biesta et al. (2007) argue that people do not act *in* structures and environments – they act through them. This resonates with conceptualisations of agency as bounded rather than structured (Evans, 2002). These perspectives are significant for the ways in which workers can use the workplace as a learning space for end that extend far beyond it.

In research that starts with the workplace, individual agency is argued to be best understood when individual worker/learner perspectives are built into the dominant social–organisational view of learning at work. This perspective has been integral the central thesis of *Improving Workplace Learning* (Evans, Hodkinson, Rainbird and Unwin, 2006) which has elaborated, through an integrated programme of research, the three scales of activity

introduced earlier in the chapter. At the 'macro' level, wider social structures and social institutions can be fundamental in enabling or preventing
effective learning from taking place. This includes the legal frameworks
that govern employees' entitlements, industrial relations and the role of
Trades Unions as well as the social structuring of business systems. At the
intermediate scale of activity, the nature of the learning environment in
the organisation or network can expand or restrict learning (see Fuller &
Unwin, 2003, 2004). Establishing cultures that support expansive learning
environments is problematic. For most employers, workers' learning is not
a priority and a lower-order decision. As Hodkinson & Rainbird (2006)
have noted, first-order decisions concern markets and competitive strategy.
These in turn affect second-order strategies concerning work organisation
and job design. In this context, workplace learning is likely to be a third-order
strategy (see also Keep & Mayhew, 1999). This means that improvements
to workers' learning always have to be balanced against other priorities. The
interdependencies of interests play out as senior managers exert influence
over the culture of an organisation and its approach to supporting workplace
learning. For the individual worker, their past experiences, dispositions and
present situation will affect the extent to which they take advantage of the
opportunities afforded by their immediate work environment. Moreover,
the challenge is to create the conditions in which all workers can take advantage of learning opportunities in and through the workplace, redressing the
imbalance between workers in lower level jobs and those in professional
and management roles. One mechanism may be through entitlements to
learning, established in law, through collective bargaining or through the
interventions of enlightened managers, trade unionists, trainers and cow-
orkers. Another mechanism is to build worker confidence through the
recognition of tacit skills, discussed in more detail by Eraut (2000, 2004)
and Evans, Kersh and Kontiainen (2004). One of the pitfalls of identifying these three scales of activity is that they become fixed levels of analysis.
Instead, as already argued, it is more appropriate to keep the three scales
in view in the same way that one might in 'zooming in and out' in internet
maps in ways that keep the interdependencies are kept in view. The ways in
which employees can themselves, individually or collectively, influence their
employment and life chances in and through the workplace environment
have been documented through previous and current research.

Conclusion

Mobilities in learning have to be understood as part of a wider dynamic, keeping in view the macro organisational and policy environments and the interdependencies set up within and beyond the workplace. This has to include the recognition that workers are both part of the work system and have lives outside it; they are engaged in multiple overlapping structures and 'communities of social practice' that can themselves be analysed in terms of social-ecological interdependencies. Thus, a social ecology of learning can be used as a key to understanding motivations of adult learners in using technologies in work and in related learning; in research into adults' experiences of the spatial aspects of mobile learning; and in first attempts to model interrelationships in ways that enable practitioners and learners to design interventions and plan for change. Improving work-based learning means paying attention to what people want and need; and to the different expressions of interests that come from work groups differently located in the social landscapes of organisations and labour markets.

References

Allan, H., Larsen, J., Bryan, K. & Smith, P. (2004) 'The social reproduction of institutional racism: internationally recruited nurses' experiences of the British Health Services.' *Diversity in Health and Social Care 1*(2), pp. 117–126

Barnett, M. (2006) 'Vocational knowledge and vocational pedagogy.' In Young, M. & Gamble, J. (eds), *Knowledge, Curriculum and Qualifications for South African Further Education*, Cape Town: HSRC Press

Belfiore, M., Defoe, T., Folinsbee, S., Hunter, J., & Jackson, N. (2004) *Reading work: Literacies in the new workplace.* Mahwah, NJ: Erlbaum

Bernstein, B. (2000) *Pedagogy, symbolic control and identity: Theory, research, critique.* Rev. edn. Lanham, MD: Rowman and Littlefield

Biesta, G., & Tedder, M. (2007) 'Agency and learning in the lifecourse: towards an ecological perspective.' *Studies in the Education of Adults 39*(2), pp. 132–149

Bronfenbrenner, U. (1979) *The ecology of human development.* Cambridge, MA: Harvard University Press

Edwards, P. (ed.) (2003) *Industrial relations: theory and practice*. 2nd edn. Oxford: Blackwell

Engeström, Y. (2001) 'Expansive learning at work: toward an activity theoretical reconceptualization.' *Journal of Education and Work 14*(1), pp. 133–156

Engeström, Y. (2008) 'Enriching activity theory without shortcuts.' *Interacting with Computers 20*, pp. 256–259

Engeström, Y. & Kerosuo, H. (2007) 'From workplace learning to inter-organizational learning and back: the contribution of activity theory.' *Journal of Workplace Learning 19*(6), pp. 336–342

Eraut, M. (2007) 'Learning from other people in the workplace.' *Oxford Review of Education 33*(4), pp. 403–422

Eraut, M. (2004) 'Informal learning in the workplace', *Studies in Continuing Education 26*(2): 247–274

Eraut, M. (2000) 'Non-formal learning and tacit knowledge in professional work'. *British Journal of Educational Psychology 70*, pp. 113–136

Evans, K. (1998) *Shaping futures: Learning for competence and citizenship*. Aldershot: Ashgate

Evans, K. (2002) 'Taking control of their lives?' *Journal of Youth Studies 5*(3), pp. 245–269

Evans, K. (2009) *Learning work and social responsibility: Challenges for lifelong learning in a global age*. Dordrecht: Springer

Evans, K., Kersh, N., & Kontiainen, S. (2004) 'Recognition of tacit skills: sustaining learning outcomes in adult learning and work – re-entry.' *International Journal of Training and Development 8*, pp. 54–72

Evans, K., Hodkinson, P., Rainbird, H., & Unwin, L. (2006) *Improving workplace learning*. Abingdon: Routledge

Evans, K., Guile, D., & Harris, J. (2009) *Putting knowledge to work*. London: Institute of Education, University of London (WLE Centre)

Evans, K., Guile, D., & Harris, J. (2010) 'Rethinking work-based learning for education professionals and professionals who educate.' In Malloch, M., Cairns, L., Evans, K. & O'Connor, B. (eds), *The Sage Handbook of Workplace Learning*. London: Sage

Evans, K., Guile, D., Harris, J., Allan, H. (2010) 'Putting knowledge to work: a new approach.' *Nurse Education Today 30*(3), pp. 245–251.

Evans, K. & Niemeyer, B. (eds) (2004) *Reconnection: Countering social exclusion through situated learning*. Dordrecht: Springer

Evans, K., & Rainbird, H. (2002) 'The significance of workplace learning for a learning society.' In Evans, K., Hodkinson, P., & Unwin, L. (eds), *Working to learn: Transforming learning in the workplace*. London: Routledge

Evans, K. & Waite, E. (2009) 'Adult learning in and through the workplace.' In Ecclestone, K., Biesta, G., & Hughes, M. (eds) *Lost in transition? Change and becoming through the lifecourse.* London: Routledge

Evans, K. & Waite, E. (2010) 'Stimulating the innovation potential of routine workers through workplace learning.' *TRANSFER – European Review of Labour and Research 16*, pp. 243–258

Evans, K., Hodkinson, P., Rainbird, H., & Unwin, L. (2006) *Improving workplace learning.* Abingdon: Routledge

Forrester, K. (2001) 'Modernised learning: an emerging lifelong agenda by British Trade Unions?' *Journal of Workplace Learning 13*(7), pp. 318–325

Forrester, K. (2005) 'Learning for revival: British Trade Unions and workplace learning.' *Studies in Continuing Education 27*(3), pp. 257–270

Fuller, A., & Unwin, L. (2003) 'Learning as apprentices in the contemporary UK workplace: creating and managing expansive and restrictive participation.' *Journal of Education and Work* 16 (4), pp. 407–426

Fuller, A., & Unwin, L. (2004) 'Expansive learning environments: integrating personal and organizational development.' In Rainbird, H., Fuller, A., and Munro, A. (eds) *Workplace learning in context.* London: Routledge

Felstead, A., Fuller, A., Jewson, N., & Unwin, L. (2009) *Improving work as learning.* Abingdon: Routledge

Gherardi, D. (2000) 'Practice-based theorizing on learning and knowing in organizations: an introduction.' *Organization 7*(2), pp. 211–223

Gherardi, D. and Nicolini, D. (2006) *Organizational knowledge: The texture of workplace learning.* London: Blackwell

Guile, D. & Young, M. (1995) *Further professional development and FE teachers: Setting a new agenda for work-based learning.* In Woodward, I. (ed) *Continuing professional development. Issues in design and delivery* (pp. 235–268). London: Cassell

Hodkinson, P., & Rainbird, H. (2006) 'Towards and intergrated cultural approach.' In Evans, K., Hodkinson, P., Rainbird, L., & Unwin, L. (eds), *Improving workplace learning.* Abingdon: Routledge

Illeris, K. and Associates (2004). *Learning in Working Life.* Fredricksberg, DN: Roskilde University Press

Illeris, K. (ed) (2009) *International perspectives on competence development.* New York: Routledge

Illeris, K. (2010) 'Workplaces and learning.' In Malloch, M., Cairns, L., Evans, K., & O'Connor, B. (eds), *The Sage Handbook of Workplace Learning.* London: Sage

Keep, E. & Mayhew, K. (1999) 'The assessment? Knowledge, skills and competitiveness.' *Oxford Review of Economic Policy 15*(1), pp. 1–15

Kersh, N. (2010) 'The spatial dimensions of Skills for Life workplace provision.' Paper prepared for the Seminar 3 in ESRC seminar series 'New Spaces of Education: The Changing Nature of Learning in the 21st Century'. University of Nottingham School of Education. 11 February

Lave, J., & Wenger, E. (1991) *Situated learning.* Cambridge: Cambridge University Press

Lave, J. (2009) *Apprenticeship in critical ethnographic practice.* Chicago: University of Chicago Press

Livingstone, D. (2006a) 'Contradictory class relations in work and learning: Some resources for hope.' In Sawchuk, P., Duarte, N., & Elhammoumi, M. (eds) *Critical perspectives on activity: Explorations across education, work, and everyday life* (pp. 145–159). New York: Cambridge University Press

Livingstone, D. (2006b) *Informal learning: conceptual distinctions and preliminary findings.* New York: Peter Lang

Luff, P., Hindmarch, J., & Heath, C. (eds) (2000) *Workplace studies: Recovering work practice and informing system design.* New York: Cambridge University Press

Moore, R. (1987) 'Education and the ideology of production.' *British Journal of the Sociology of Education 18*(2) pp. 227–242

Norris, N. (1991) 'The trouble with competence.' *Cambridge Journal of Education 21*(3), pp. 331–334

Quarter, J. (2000) *Beyond the bottom line.* Westport, Connecticut: Quroum Books

Rainbird, H., Fuller, A., & Munro, A. (2004) *Workplace learning in context.* Abingdon: Routledge

Sawchuk, P. (2010) 'Researching workplace learning: an overview and critique.' In Malloch, M., Cairns, L., Evans, K., & O'Connor, B. (eds), *The Sage Handbook of Workplace Learning.* London: Sage

Solomon, N., Boud, D., & Rooney, D. (2006) 'The in-between: exposing everyday learning at work.' *International Journal of Lifelong Education 25*(1), pp. 3–13

Solomon, N. (2001) 'Workplace learning as a cultural technology.' *New Directions for Adult and Continuing Education 92*(1), pp. 41–51

Stubbe, M. (2003) 'Multiple discourse analyses of a workplace.' *Interaction Discourse Studies 5*(3), pp. 351–388

Taylor, M., Evans, K., and Mohamed, E. (2009) 'Formal and informal training for workers with low literacy: Building an international dialogue between Canada and the United Kingdom.' *Journal of Adult and Continuing Education 15* (1), pp. 37–54

van Oers, B. (1998) 'The fallacy of decontextualisation.' *Mind, Culture and Activity 5*(2), pp. 143–152

Weaver-Hightower, M. (2008) 'An ecology metaphor for educational policy analysis: A call to complexity.' *Educational Researcher 37*(3), pp. 153–167

Wolf, A., & Evans, K. (2011) *Improving literacy at work.* Abingdon: Routledge

Assessment and identity formation:
Collecting, sharing and reflecting

CERIDWEN COULBY, JULIE LAXTON, STUART BOOMER
AND NANCY DAVIES

3   Mobile technology and assessment:
    A case study from the ALPS programme

Abstract

This chapter explores the use of mobile devices for assessment purposes within work-based placements. Dental Hygiene and Therapy students at the University of Leeds used mobile devices to access learning material and complete self and peer assessments of their interpersonal skills whilst on work placement. These assessments were then reviewed by university tutors using an e-portfolio system which allowed students and tutors to open a dialogue regarding the assessment and wider placement issues. This case study is part of the Assessment and Learning in Practice Settings (ALPS) programme of teaching and learning research.[1] The students found the assessments helpful to their reflective practice and the use of the mobile device for reflection *in* action; and the e-portfolio for reflection *on* action (Schön, 1983) completed the learning cycle, encouraging greater depth of reflection (Patton, 2002). The combination of the mobile device and the e-portfolio also provided students with pastoral support, as it provided the students with a link to the university and access to their friends, as well as an opportunity for the tutor to support and guide the students' learning from a distance. Mobile devices provide new and exciting opportunities

---

1   Assessment and Learning in Practice Settings (ALPS) is one of 74 Higher Education Funding Council for England (HEFCE) funded Centres for Excellence in Teaching and Learning (CETL) created in 2004. For more details see <http://www.alps-cetl.ac.uk> (accessed 10/08/10).

for learning and assessment. However, we must be mindful that without a pedagogically-based rationale for their use, technical and infrastructure issues can rapidly reduce student engagement.

Introduction

Importance of work-based learning

In higher education the majority of health and social care curricula comprise a blend of classroom instruction, simulation and work-based placement. Placements are a vital part of health and social care education as the workplace provides opportunities for learning and assessment of competences and professional attributes that cannot be replicated in simulations or classroom settings (Billett, 2001). The authenticity of these experiences prepares the student holistically for professional practice, enabling them to become accustomed to the culture, tools and signs (Vygotsky, 1978) of their profession, beginning the journey from mere observers to full participants within a community of practice (Lave and Wenger, 1991).

Within Dental Hygiene and Therapy, by the time of graduation the student needs to have acquired the skills to allow them to function in the postgraduate arena (D'Andrea, 2004). Within the dental professions this is regulated by the General Dental Council (GDC). In order to ensure that students have acquired the necessary skills to practise, there has been a greater emphasis on the use of primary care outreach schemes (i.e. placements within community clinics) in the teaching of the dental professions. This is explicitly stated in the curriculum documentation for dental undergraduate training (GDC, 2002).

Whilst it is recognised that work-based placement is an essential component in preparing health and social care students for practice, this teaching and learning environment is not without practical and more complex issues.

Access to IT

From a practical perspective, access to computers can be unreliable or restricted due to lack of integration between National Health Service organisations IT infrastructures. In addition, students can experience significant delays in obtaining user accounts whilst on placement; while others may not be provided with one at all (Roberts, 2009). The implication of this is a lack of access to current information, learning materials and social networks. Mobile technology can offer a solution to these issues; though historical fears of interference with medical machinery (DoH, 2009), and of risk to patient confidentiality within health and social care settings provide challenges to the implementation of such projects.

Lack of feedback and pastoral support

On a deeper level, all health and social care graduates are expected to perform procedures and interact with service users professionally as soon as they start work. However, studies show that some students feel unprepared for practice (Goldacre, Davidson and Lambert, 2003a, Goldacre et al., 2003b, Evans and Roberts, 2006). Two issues that students experience are lack of feedback on their performance during the placement (Norcini, 2007) and insufficient secondary support when reflecting on their placement learning (Competence in practice assessment tool ALPS 2009 – ongoing research). Also, while the student may be visited by their tutor or another representative from the University during their placement, these visits are limited by availability of the tutor and the number of students to be visited (Waterhouse et al., 2008). This can be unsatisfactory from both the student and tutor perspective, as the student can feel isolated and experience a lack of support (Tang, 2003), while the tutor is unaware of the quality and breadth of the learning taking place.

A possible solution?

The aim of the ALPS programme is to ensure that students graduating from health and social care programmes feel confident and competent to practice when starting their professional careers. Work-based placements provide the most appropriate learning environment in which to foster these attributes, however as we have identified placement learning is not without issue. ALPS has sought to address these issues and improve the student experience by supplying timely access to learning resources, reference information and social networks in addition to formalised feedback processes and a link with their university-based tutor.

Why mobile technology?

In response to the difficulties experienced by students regarding access to IT in practice, ALPS chose to examine mobile technology as a possible remedy. The use of mobile technology for learning is a rapidly growing trend in education, with practitioners from primary, secondary, further and higher education sectors piloting the use of mobile technology both in and out of the classroom (Kukulska-Hulme & Traxler, 2005; Ally, 2009; Vavoula, Pachler and Kukulska-Hulme, 2009). A significant proportion of research into the use of technology for learning has been in the field of healthcare (Garrett & Jackson, 2006; Kneebone et al., 2008; Dearnley et al., 2007; Coulby et al., 2009), due to working practices and curriculum design (Dearnley, 2007).

Assessment tool solution for feedback

ALPS has also sought to improve the 'readiness' of students to practise through the use of interprofessional assessment tools. All 16 ALPS professions identified common competences that are core to their professions; team working, communication and ethical practice. These competences were developed into assessment tools for use by all of the professions in health and social care situations; such as 'Gaining consent' and 'Knowing when to consult or refer'. The tools encourage and enable the student to seek more assessment opportunities from a wider variety of sources, including self, peers, health and social care professionals of the same or other professions and service users (patients). The flexible nature of the tools allow different professions to use the tools in a way and at a level that is appropriate for them.

e-Portfolio solution for pastoral support

ALPS further investigated the methods of delivery and completion of assessments, examining the immediacy of access to learning and the timeliness of responses inherent in the ALPS mobile assessment cycle. ALPS assessments completed on a mobile device are automatically delivered back to an online e-portfolio. In this e-portfolio both tutor and student are able to review the assessment and comment on it. The tutor then feeds forward to the student, shaping the students' future practice. By providing students with mobilised generic assessments, tutors back at the university are able to view the students' holistic progress through the placement, and how they are progressing with their colleagues, peers or patients. This link between tutor and student allows the tutor to provide the student with a high level of scaffolding (Vygotsky, 1978) when required (typically at the beginning of the placement), fading as the student moves towards full participation (Lave and Wenger, 1991).

ALPS is a large scale, multi-faceted programme with over 500 students using student-led ALPS assessments delivered via mobile devices. The University of Leeds alone has 6 cohorts of students using the devices; 49 medical, 40 diagnostic radiography, 12 audiology, 42 adult nursing, 11 mental health nursing and 19 dental hygiene and therapy students. Due to the large amount of data that a programme of this size generates, this chapter will use a case study to illustrate some of the main learning points from the ALPS programme.

Dental Hygiene and Therapy case study

Conceptual and professional background

The University of Leeds offers a graduate Diploma in Dental Hygiene and Therapy (Dental H & T). The 15 module course is spread over 27 months, with students undertaking placements in clinical practice outside the University during their final year of study. The aim of the course is to train registered Dental Care Professionals (DCPs) who can work within a team framework taking on the role of both a dental hygienist and a dental therapist. The three areas of common competency identified by all 16 ALPS professions are essential for the Dental H & T students at Leeds, who are required to demonstrate their communication, team working and ethical practice skills as well as procedural skills by collating evidence whilst on placement.

The underpinning learning theory upon which the Dental H & T programme is based is that of Experiential Learning (Kolb, 1984). This is a four-stage cycle of learning whereby 'concrete experience' should lead to 'reflective observation' resulting in 'abstract conceptualization', i.e. analysing what you have observed and formulating hypothesise for future action which is then applied during 'active experimentation'. This, in turn, begins the cycle again.

However, criticisms of Kolb suggest that this cycle is an over-simplification of experiential learning, highlighting the constructivist nature of this theory, with its implication that learning takes place within the learner's own mind (Piaget, 1950), rather than being socially constructed (Wertsch, 1997). There is also no recognition of the effect of context, i.e. the learning environment itself (Billet, 2001), or of interpretation. Interpretation of the learning that takes place within a given situation is shaped by the community of practice to which they belong (Lave and Wenger, 1991), the individuals' own background and experiences, and any external requirements that may be in place (Fuller and Unwin, 2004).

Despite these shortcomings, the simplicity of Kolb's theory is a useful tool when used with undergraduate students as it provides an accessible introduction to reflection. When applied to clinical training, Kolb's theory emphasises the importance of reflection, indicating that merely being told how to carry out a procedure and given the opportunity to practise it is not sufficient to promote total understanding. Rather, learners must subsequently reflect on the task before drawing conclusions and eventually complete the cycle by applying the knowledge in a future task. This is a continuous process (or cycle) with further reflection and conceptualisation being completed prior to subsequent related tasks. This reflective practice is fundamental to learning both as a student and within the postgraduate arena through continual professional development (Pitts, 2007).

The timing of reflection is also important, whether 'in action' (during the event, or straight after) or 'on action' (later, with the benefit of time to consider and appraise action taken) (Schön, 1983). Most health and social care programmes, including Dental H & T, utilise reflection on action due to practical constraints, such as student workload when out in practice and access to IT.

Fleming (2009) identifies that retrospective reflection (reflection on action, Schön 1983) may result in weaknesses not being identified until a later time, when they may be more difficult to alter. Therefore, frequent in action reflection, either exclusively by the learner or by the learner utilising feedback from others, can inform student practice at an earlier juncture.

ALPS assessments are designed to capitalise on both reflection in action and on action by utilising mobile devices to encourage instant reflection and the e-portfolio for retrospective reflective practice. The assessments encourage students to gather feedback from a variety of sources to aid their reflection and provide them with alternative interpretations of their performance, thus recognising the collaborative nature of learning and meaning-making (Wertsch, 1997).

The main outcome of this assessment process is to create reflective practitioners (Schön 1983) who can utilise reflective practice as a form of sustainable assessment (Boud, 2000) throughout their careers. Dental H & T staff were quick to see the potential benefit of involving others in reflection and one of the aims of utilising the devices and tools within this area was to enhance the students' experience within placement by supporting students' self reflection with the use of peer-assessment and remote tutor contact.

The Dental H & T students are sent on placement in pairs, providing excellent opportunities for peer-assessment that can be used to enhance the student experience (Falchikov, 1995; Topping, 1998). The process enables them to see the way other students have approached tasks and, in so doing, develop their ability to exercise judgement over their own work.

Work-based learning is intended to provide students with a realistic picture of what they will experience post-qualification. Within the Dental H & T programme this means that the students see and treat a greater number of patients during the working day. The net result of this may be that, while the students gain more practical experience, there is a reduction in the time that is available to gather feedback and reflect on learning experiences. The risk here is that the students perform more *tasks* while reflecting and ultimately learning *less* than intended. It is hoped that utilising the ALPS mobile assessments will encourage the type of essential reflective learning which will ultimately create more confident and competent professionals.

Methodology

An interpretative phenomenological approach (Smith, 1999) to qualitative data analysis was taken in this study, as we were interested in analysing the whole student experience. Focus groups were held to gather feedback from the students which were audio-recorded and then transcribed prior to thematic analysis.

Training for staff and students was seen to be key to the project as identified in earlier work (Kneebone and Brenton, 2005; Laxton and Coulby, 2009), therefore several training sessions were planned.

Initially, the dental tutors were provided with mobile devices and trained in their usage. A smaller cohort of tutors also received face-to-face training on the ALPS e-Portfolio. The students were provided with their devices later in the year, allowing staff to get used to the devices and provide additional support for students during their training session.

Mobile devices were handed out to 19 second year Dental H&T students to use whilst on their paediatric clinical placement. They were asked to complete mobile assessments on 'Gaining consent' (i.e. asking for and being granted permission to perform a procedure on a patient) and to submit both peer-assessment and self-reflection on this subject.

The Dental H & T students were advised to complete an assessment after performing a tooth extraction on a child for the first time, as this was an ideal situation to demonstrate their ability to 'gain consent'. The students worked through a set of questions designed to help them reflect on and learn from their experience. They could either use the slide-out or on-screen keyboard to type or the audio record feature to capture their thoughts aloud. Students then requested peer feedback before reflecting again on the experience and developing an action plan to improve their future performance.

Once the completed assessment arrived in the e-portfolio, the university tutor could then send feedback and advice via the built-in blog feature. This enabled a dialogue between student and tutor which increased the level of remote support for students undertaking clinical placements (see Figure 3.1).

As well as mobile assessment, the devices improved the access to learning material for the Dental H&T students. Their tutor was able to send supporting material directly to the students, in a variety of formats, i.e. video demonstrations of a tooth extraction and links to helpful websites.

Students were invited to attend focus groups post placement in order to discuss their experience.

On 15/02/2010 09:04:47 ALPS Tutor said:

Thank-you for completing this assessment, could you now add some comments of your own now that you have a little more time to reflect on this episode. I would be interested to hear your views on 1. The gaining consent process 2. The actual procedure of the extractions 3. Completing the assessment tool/using the PDA 4. How you might improve the consent process and the extraction procedure in the future. Is this the same extraction case as you partially completed in June or is it a different one?

On 15/02/2010 09:10:47 Student Demo11 said:

This extraction case was a new one. I never got round to completing the first one as it was difficult to arrange time when myself/peer were on clinic together, it is also a bit of a time issue on a busy clinic. I think the more you do the assessments, the quicker/easier they seem. Gaining consent from the patient was relatively straight forward, the child was very young so consent discussed with parent. Child informed fully of procedure and understood treatment plan to extract tooth. I felt quite confident carrying out the extraction as I had done the procedure once before, child was very co-operative and I felt I still maintained a good rapport with patient after procedure.

edit delete

On 15/02/2010 09:18:17 ALPS Tutor said:

Thanks, do you feel having completed the task earlier (i.e. having extracted a tooth before) made it easier to complete the consent and explain the procedure to the parent/child? Can you maybe also think of the terminology you used for this child who you say was quite young and the terminology you would use with an older child. I note that your comments in the assessment are quite short, is this due to time constraints? As it is quite slow to type in lots of text on the PDA, you could think of using the audio recording option which will allow you and your peer to put your comments on in a shorter period of time.

On 15/02/2010 09:22:23 Student Demo11 said:

I did feel that the task was easier because I had completed an extraction before. I explained to the child that we would have to send the tooth off to sleep and give the poorly tooth a wiggle out so that it wouldn't hurt him any more. He was quite excited that we would then put the naughty tooth in an envelope to take home for the fairies. We found out about the audio recording option at the recent ALPS meeting and I think this will make things a lot easier and quicker on the clinical sessions. Thank-you for your feedback.

edit delete

Figure 3.1 A dialogue between student and tutor within the e-portfolio

Results

In ALPS a commitment was made to issue devices to whole cohorts of students in order to portray an inclusive view of attitudes towards mobile learning. Many other studies (see examples in Kukulska-Hulme and Traxler, 2005; Ally, 2009) have taken a voluntary approach to the use of devices, thus producing a bias in results. Here we hope to portray the true range of opinion towards the mobile devices as an aid to learning.

Additionally, this cohort of students, while expressing an interest in interprofessional feedback, did not approach other professions for assessment feedback. This could be due to the confidence of the students used to having feedback 'given to them' rather than taking advantage of a student-led process, but equally this demonstrates the lack of ease students can feel when engaging with health professionals outside of their own discipline (Hall, 2005).

19 students attended two separate focus groups. They were prompted to discuss their experiences and the following themes were identified:

Theme 1: Use of mobile technology for feedback and reflective learning

Theme 2: Use of e-portfolio for pastoral support

Each theme will be illustrated using direct quotes from students attending the focus groups.

Theme 1: Use of mobile technology for feedback and reflective learning

The device

All of the students found the assessment tool software easy to use, although many (at least 10) experienced issues with the mobile device itself, such as technical failures, short battery life and the loss of content from storage cards. This did result in a lack of motivation for some (5) students:

'Mine wasn't working properly.' Student 5

'Yes I had to take mine to the Helpdesk a couple of times because it kept deleting things ...' Student 2

Despite these technical problems, 6 of the 19 students went on to complete regular assessments while 8 completed at least one. Some students did not complete assessments and the reasons given for this were lack of opportunity (i.e. no child tooth extractions) or malfunction of their device.

Although students did experience difficulties with the devices, they were able to see positive aspects within the project. For example, students commented that having a device to access email on placement was an advantage as this helped to combat feelings of isolation. Several of the students used the device to access Facebook so much they exceeded the device storage capacity and had to seek technical support.

We believe that the negative attitude towards the devices themselves among some students had several reasons. Primarily, experiencing technical difficulties was off-putting to students as it required action from them to access help, taking up their time. However, there are some more complex explanations. The device itself may be perceived by the student as the delivery mechanism for 'extra work'; therefore, the device becomes an object of dislike, not for what it is but for what it represents.

Alternatively, some students exhibit a lack of enthusiasm for using a new form of technology, as not all students are 'digital natives' or used to using technology in terms of learning (Ramanau, Sharpe and Benfield, 2008). Others may have been initially interested but then experienced technical difficulties resulting in them 'giving up' on the device.

Paradoxically, 2 students reported that they thought the devices slow or as something else to carry around but then used the device so much for social use that files were automatically removed from the device due to file size. The students' actions, i.e. use of the device, are inconsistent with what they said. This could be reflective of the little-tapped market for mobile learning; perhaps students perceive mobile devices as a personal, social tool rather than a formalised learning tool and are, therefore, resentful of the 'requirement' to use a device for their course rather than due to personal choice.

Each student may rationalise their dislike of a device for any number of reasons and further research needs to be completed into why certain students react in specific ways to the use of mobile learning to help us understand and implement appropriate solutions. However, students' 'learning territory', i.e. the extent to which students engage in learning, is influenced by their background, educational experience and aspirations (Fuller and Unwin, 2004), cannot be ignored as a contributing factor along with the value that the student places on the rationale for, and content of mobile learning.

Self-assessment

All students concurred that the self-assessments were useful; one noted:

> '...when you think about it that's one of the regulations of the GDC, writing your notes you have not to be retrospective and [reflection] need to be done at the time, so if you want a clearer picture of what we are doing it should be at the time because otherwise you do forget things which is why they say do it as and when because otherwise you do forget important things.' Student 9

This clearly illustrates that the student has made a connection between reflective practice as a student and the requirements of the GDC that professionals use reflective practice for lifelong learning. Additionally, the mobile device has enabled the student to record reflection *in* action as opposed to *on* action, thus capturing the immediacy of the learning moment. Other students found the self-assessment useful as it prompted them to think about the communication and interpersonal skills used as well as the quality of the clinical procedure performed, encouraging a greater depth of reflection (Patton, 2002).

> 'I thought they were useful, I did find it useful as a reflection not as a "this is what I did" but as I could have done this ...something else maybe ...' Student 1

The university-based tutors were equally supportive of the reflective nature of the assessments. One tutor commented:

> 'The ALPS Mobile Assessment Suite is helping to enhance learning in clinical placements by re-enforcing reflective practice. The graduate Diploma in Dental Hygiene and Therapy offered at the University of Leeds is very "hands-on" and it can be easy for students to get wrapped up in physical tasks and procedures. By asking students to complete mobile assessments based on common competences such as communication skills, we are encouraging the type of essential reflective learning which will ultimately create more confident and competent professionals.' Tutor 1

Peer-assessment

Dental H & T students are comfortable with peer working and learning principles as they are placed in clinics in pairs; however, the peer-assessment was a change to previous practice as they had not been required to assess each other before. Students were expected to observe a peer performing a child tooth extraction and assess their colleague using the form on the mobile device. This assessment is a combination of tick and open text boxes with questions such as 'Did the student make the service user feel at ease?' and 'Did the student take into account the level of the service user's understanding when explaining the course of action?' These questions have scaled responses. Once the assessment is complete the student or their colleague can submit the assessment, which is then viewable in the assessee's e-portfolio. This produced some interesting and unexpected results. One of the students commented that they felt the device made the peer-assessment less transparent as a process:

> 'And also the bit, giving it to you, you felt like when A was doing my bit because she had to peer assess me it was like I wanted to talk to her, the point of that is so you can say ...you learn to be grown up and you can take the criticism constructively (but to talk) but I felt like she had it "here" so I couldn't ...not on purpose ...' Student 4

The implication here is that because the assessment is completed on a device it is held in the hand of the assessor so not easily viewable by the assessee. It would appear the peer-assessor has made the assumption that the student being reviewed should not see the assessment, which is a contradiction as the student will be able to view the peer assessment in their e-portfolio anyway. This leads us to question the assumptions we make as academics about a shared student and tutor view of formative assessment. As academics we believe that these assessments are for learning and that the dialogue that occurs between peers when completing the assessment is as important, if not more so, than the assessment itself. The students, not used to assessment other than for summative purposes, view the assessment more like an exam. Clearly, work must be done to build a shared understanding of the purpose of formative assessment. From a practical perspective, training should include a demonstration or role-play of the most beneficial way to conduct a peer assessment. This had, in fact, been built into the training package; however, time constraints and technical problems with the devices themselves meant the exercise had to be cut from the programme. Clearly, there is a lesson to be learnt here about balancing the immediate need to ensure students have working devices with the longer-term need of the student to fully understand the philosophy of the task they are being asked to complete.

Lastly, one of the students recognised the benefit of completing multiple assessments both to their performance and their learning:

'...I did find the more I did it the better [I got at performing the task].' Student 6

This is excellent as it demonstrates that once students try the reflective assessments they can see a real value in them. The most challenging task for academics and practice-based educators is to encourage the students to try formative assessment in the first instance, due to the notorious lack of value students (and in some cases educators) put on formative assessment (Black & Wiliam, 1998).

Theme 2: Use of e-portfolio for pastoral support

The e-portfolio served to close Kolb's learning cycle by allowing those students, who returned assessments, to review their reflections more objectively after the event and begin (with or without tutor assistance) to formulate abstract concepts of how they might improve in future.

'When we go on the website it's quite ..., once you've seen what responses you've given you think "oh I should have put more there" or ...so that's good ...' Student 10

Additionally, when asked about tutor feedback one student stated:

'You see it's nice getting the comments from S (tutor) because I don't get to see S a lot in clinic ...and I can see if we'd been doing that from the start that would have been nice because he'd have been able to see how I'd progressed.' Student 7

The ability for tutors to go beyond providing supportive learning material and disjointed or cursory visits to being able to enter into a meaningful and natural dialogue with students significantly enhanced the 'scaffolding' (Vygotsky, 1978) that students could call on in practice; thus pastoralising the student experience.

Discussion and conclusion

Mobile assessment provides university tutors with a unique opportunity to open the black box of placement learning; to both observe and potentially guide the student's individual learning journey from a distance. This can enhance students' learning whilst still on placement, allowing them to work on specific areas of practice according to their individual needs. It provides diversification opportunities for tutors to identify and provide additional support to struggling students, potentially reducing the need for re-sit exams as well as further material to encourage exceptional students. It can provide a pastoral support function, connecting the student to the university, their friends and peers, reducing the feelings of isolation many students report while on placement (Tang, 2003).

However, mobile assessment also generates a number of issues that need to be addressed. There are the apparent concerns of cost, rapid evolution of technology, infrastructure and support to be considered but also other, more pedagogical concerns must not be neglected. As demonstrated in the Dental H & T case study, students need to understand the philosophy and purpose of assessment as well as the practical processes involved to avoid misconceptions around a lack of transparency in assessment. This particular group of students have access to PCs, so for them the assessments will now be completed online with both assessor and assessee present, however this is not an option available to the majority of students who do not have this access.

Large-scale mobile technology projects require a lot of technical support and, inevitably when using emerging technologies, technical problems occur that can have an effect on student and staff motivation. These issues illustrate the need for a flexible and realistic approach to mobile assessment. The use of mobile technology as a gimmick or hook with which to rouse student interest in formative assessment may (or may not) work in the short term. However, long term uptake is based on the students' perception of what added value the technology provides, so a legitimate, pedagogical basis for any work using mobile devices must be evident to staff and students alike.

References

Ally, M. (2009) *Mobile learning: Transforming the delivery of education and training.* AU Press

Billett, S. (2001) *Learning in the workplace: Strategies for effective practice.* Allen & Unwin

Black, P. & Wiliam, D. (1998) *Inside the black box: Raising standards through classroom assessment.* London: Kings College London

Boud, D. (2000) 'Sustainable assessment: rethinking assessment for the learning society.' *Studies in Continuing Education, 22*(2), pp. 151–167

Coulby, C. Hennessey, S. Davies, N., & Fuller, R. (in press) 'The use of mobile technology for work-based assessment: the student experience.' *British Journal of Education Technology*

D'Andrea, V.-M. (2003) 'Organizing teaching and learning: outcomes-based planning.' Fry, H., Ketteridge, S., & Marshall, S. (eds), *A handbook for teaching and learning in higher education – Enhancing academic practice.* 2nd edn. London: Routledge Falmer, pp. 26–41

Dearnley, C., Haigh, J., & Fairhall, J. (2007) 'Using mobile technologies for assessment and learning in practice settings: a case study.' *Nurse Education in Practice 8* (3), pp. 197–204

Department of Health (2009) 'Using mobile phones in hospitals.' DoH online. Available online at <http://www.dh.gov.uk/dr_consum_dh/groups/dh_digitalassers/@dh/@en/documents/digitalasser/dh_092812.pdf> (accessed 15/01/10)

Eraut, M. (1995) 'Schon shock: a case for refraining reflection-in-action?' *Teachers and Teaching 1*(1), pp. 9–22

Evans, E. & Roberts, C. (2006) 'Preparation for practice: how can medical schools better prepare PRHOs?' *Medical Teacher 28*(6), pp. 549–552

Falchikov, N. (1995) 'Peer feedback marking: developing peer assessment.' *Innovations in Education and Teaching International 32* (2), pp. 175–187

Fleming, P. (2009) 'Facilitating and assessing multidisciplinary reflection.' In Bulpitt, H. & Deane, M. (eds) *Connecting reflective learning, teaching and assessment.* Health Sciences and Practice Subject Centre. Occasional Paper 10, pp. 25–34. Available online at <http://www.health.heacademy.ac.uk/publications/occasionalpaper/occp10.pdf> (accessed on 15/01/10)

Fuller, A., & Unwin, L. (2004) 'Expansive learning environments: integrating organisational and personal development.' In Rainbird, H., Fuller, A., & Munro, A. (eds), *Workplace learning in context.* London: Routledge, pp. 126–144

Garrett, B., & Jackson, C. (2006) 'A mobile clinical E-portfolio for nursing and medical students, using wireless personal digital assistants.' *Nurse Education in Practice 6*(6), pp. 339–346

GDC (2002) *The first five years. A framework for undergraduate dental education.* 2nd edn. London: General Dental Council

Goldacre, M., Davidson, J., & Lambert, T. (2003) 'Doctors' views of their first year of medical work and postgraduate training in the UK: questionnaire surveys.' *Medical Education 37*(9), pp. 802–808

Goldacre, M. Lambert, T. Evans, J., & Turner, G. (2003) 'Preregistration house officers' views on whether their experience at medical school prepared them well for their jobs: national questionnaire survey.' *British Medical Journal 326*(7397), pp. 1011–1012

Hall, P. (2005) 'Interprofessional teamwork: professional cultures as barriers.' *Journal of Interprofessional Care 19*(1), pp. 188–196

Kneebone, R., Bello, F., Nestel, D., Mooney, N., Codling, A., Yadollahi, F., et al. (2008) 'Learner-centered feedback using remote assessment of clinical procedures.' *Medical Teacher 30*(8), pp. 795–801

Kneebone, R., & Brenton, H. (2005) 'Training perioperative specialist practitioners.' In Kukulska-Hulme, A., & Traxler, J. (eds), *Mobile learning: A handbook for educators and trainers.* London: Routledge, pp. 106–115

Kolb, D. (1984) *Experiential learning: Experience as the source of learning and development.* Prentice Hall

Kukulska-Hulme, A., & Traxler, J. (2005) (eds) *Mobile learning: A handbook for educators and trainers.* London: Routledge

Lave, J., & Wenger, E. (1991) *Situated learning: Legitimate peripheral participation.* Cambridge: Cambridge University Press

Laxton, J., & Coulby, C. (2009) Mobile learning and assessment: The student perspective. In Pachler, N., & Seipold, J. (eds) *Mobile learning cultures across education, work and leisure.* Book of abstracts 3rd WLE Mobile Learning Symposium, 27 March, pp. 25–29. Available online at <http://www.wlecentre.ac.uk/cms/files/m-learning/m-learning_symposium_2009/3rd_wle_mlearning_symposium_-_book_of_abstracts_single_page_display.pdf> (accessed on 15/01/10)

Norcini, J., & Burch, V. (2007) 'Workplace-based assessment as an educational tool. AMEE Guide No.31.' *Medical Teacher 29*(9), 855–871

Patton, M. (2002) *Qualitative research and evaluation methods.* 3rd edn. London: Sage

Piaget, J. (1950) *The psychology of intelligence.* New York: Routledge

Pitts, J. (2007) *Understanding medical education: Portfolios, personal development and reflective practice.* Association for the Study of Medical Education, Edinburgh

Prensky, M. (2001) 'Digital natives, digital immigrants.' *On the Horizon 9*(5). NCB University Press. Available online at <http://www.marcprensky.com/writing/Prensky%20-%20Digital%20Natives,%20Digital%20Immigrants%20-%20Part1.pdf> (accessed 15/01/10)

Ramanau, R., Sharpe, R., & Benfield, G. (2008) 'Exploring patterns of student learning technology use in their relationship to self-regulation and perceptions of learning community.' Paper at the Sixth International Conference of Networked Learning, Halkidiki, Greece, 5–6 May

Roberts, T. (2009) *Learning responsibility? Exploring doctors' transitions to new levels of medical responsibility.* Full Research Report ESRC End of Award Report, RES-153-25-0084. Swindon: ESRC

Schön, D (1983) *The reflective practitioner: How professionals think in action.* Basic Books

Smith, J., Jarman, M., & Osborne, M. (1999) 'Doing interpretative phenomenological analysis.' In Murray, M., & Chamberlain, K. (eds) *Qualitative health psychology.* London: Sage

Tang, S. (2003) 'Challenge and support: the dynamics of student teachers' professional learning in the field experience.' *Teaching and Teacher Education 19*(5), pp. 483–498

Topping, K. (1998) 'Peer assessment between students in college and universities.' *Review of Educational Research 68*(3), pp. 249–276

Vavoula, G., Pachler, N., and Kukulska-Hulme, A. (2009) (eds) *Researching mobile learning: Frameworks, tools and research designs.* Oxford: Peter Lang

Vygotsky, L. (1978) *Mind in society. The development of higher psychological processes.* Cambridge, MA: Harvard University Press

Waterhouse, P., Maquire, A., Tabari, D., Hind, V., & Lloyd, J. (2008) 'The development of a primary dental care outreach course.' *European Journal of Dental Education 12*, pp. 8–16

Wenger, E. (1999) *Communities of practice: Learning, meaning, and identity.* Cambridge: Cambridge University Press

Wertsch, J. (1997) *Vygotsky and the formation of the mind.* Cambridge, MA: Harvard University Press

LUCY STONE

4 The WoLF project: Work-based Learners in Further Education

Abstract

The WoLF project investigated how a group of work-based learners could use mobile technology to enable them to reflect on their practice and share their experiences with their peers and tutor in face-to-face classes or through online activity on an institutional Virtual Learning Environment (VLE). The working environments of some of work-based learners are not conducive to being able to record moments and experiences at an instant that can be used for reflective practice or portfolio evidence or to access appropriate equipment to capture these moments. In the case of the WoLF project the learners were working as Teaching Assistants (TAs) in very busy, early years' settings including kindergarten, primary school classrooms and special educational needs settings. By issuing the learners a mobile device, a Personal Digital Assistant (PDA), the learners could capture spontaneous moments or aspects of theory they were putting into practice with still images, video files and voice recordings. The learners were able to bring the early year's classroom into the FE Classroom and share their experiences and put their working practice into context with real-life examples. The project found that the learners did use the mobile devices to capture moments to reflect back on; however, the biggest impact was made by the use the of the institutional VLE and in particular the e-tutorial chat room, where students were able to talk to their tutor and peers mid-week, and the online reflective journal, with one student commenting that these online features motivated her to carry on with her course.

Introduction

The Work-based Learners in Further Education (WoLF) project was a JISC-funded collaborative project between Leicester College, a Further Education College (FE), and the Beyond Distance Research Alliance at Leicester University. The project started in April 2007 and concluded in September 2008.

Leicester College has a growing provision of Higher Education (HE) courses, in particular Foundation Degrees (FDs). These courses provide learning opportunities to learners who do not necessarily fit into a 'traditional' learning pattern of GCSEs (General Certificate of Secondary Education), A-Levels and undergraduate degree. Learners who choose to study on FDs have often been outside formal education for a number of years or are studying to pursue an alternative career. The learners participating in the WoLF project all worked as Teaching Assistants (TAs) in various early years' settings: nurseries, primary schools and special educational needs establishments. In 2007 the local Learning and Skills Council (LSC), directed by national Government policy, wanted to ensure that all TAs gain a professional qualification to Level Three of the UK National Qualifications Framework (NQF). As the provider of a Foundation Degree in Educational Studies, Leicester College was able to meet this demand.

The original outline for the WoLF project read: 'WoLF is a Higher Education (HE) in Further Education (FE) project. It investigates how Pocket PCs support portfolio development by teaching assistants (TAs) on foundation degree courses. WoLF develops a model for integrating institutional Virtual Learning Environments (VLEs) and personal mobile devices, for the purpose of learning in work-based settings.'

WoLF addressed two challenges directly concerned with TAs' ability to learn:

Challenge One: Systematic recording of classroom activities and developing a portfolio of evidence are key aspects of TAs' learning which occurs in primary school classrooms. TAs rely on pen and paper because it is too awkward to use laptops in a hectic classroom. WoLF examined how Pocket

PCs can open up new opportunities for TAs to develop their portfolios and thereby promote reflection in practice.

Challenge Two: TAs learn in many different spaces: for example, factual and conceptual learning in weekly face-to-face sessions with tutors; through practice and observation while at work; and private study at home, in the learning resources centre and elsewhere. Varied learning activities occurring in these spaces should knit together so that TAs can map their learning in one space onto their learning in the other spaces. Access to the VLE on a mobile device will help the TAs to have all their learning resources in their 'briefcase', enabling them to integrate learning occurring in all the spaces and to record their classroom observations.

As well as the two key challenges being investigated by the project, another aspect was to meet the learners' needs in a work-based learning environment. The project contributed to creating a personalised learning experience enabling learners to reflect on their practice in a number of locations.

Learner profiles

One of the many approaches to work-based learning is the process of formal learning taking place wholly or predominantly in the work setting. The learners involved in the project all worked in their roles as Teaching Assistants and attended taught classes for four hours per week on a Monday afternoon during a 'twilight' session. Some of the learners were returning to formal education after a long gap. Some had become Teaching Assistants when their own children were at the school and have remained there ever since despite their children moving up to secondary education. Some of the learners in the project could be classified as 'non-traditional'. More traditional learners may follow a route through secondary school to university. A 'traditional' learner would normally take a number of GCSEs at 16. 'Traditional' learners wishing to go to university would need to follow their GCSEs with two years of studying AS and AS2 qualifications (the equivalent of the International Baccalaureate) and then an Honours Degree. An example of a 'non traditional' learner may be someone who did not complete their GCSEs and may pursue an alternative route to these later in life, perhaps achieving the equivalent numeracy and/or literacy qualifications at Level Two (the equivalent of 5 GCSEs at grade A to C including Functional Skills English, maths and ICT) and being credited for experience in the work place or by following a vocational route of NVQ (National Vocational Qualifications).

Prior to the project the learners were using the university's Blackboard site to access documents and resources and they occasionally participated in a forum discussion. Blackboard is a web-based virtual learning environment that supports learning by providing a platform to share resources and access discussion forums, blogs and wikis.

At the beginning of the project it was envisaged that thirty TAs would be available to participate. This was an estimate based on previous recruitment. Ultimately, twenty TAs participated in the research due to lower than anticipated enrolments to the course as well as some individuals dropping out in the initial stages. The TAs on the FD in Educational Studies and participating in the research for the WoLF project consisted of a first cohort of learners who started in April 2007. They were five 3rd Years and five 2nd Years. However, from the first cohort, the 3rd year group did not engage in the project for a number of reasons; they had little contact with their tutor and were already carrying out independent study towards the end of their course. The 3rd year group had received a laptop each as part of a grant scheme at the beginning of their course. The learners in this group viewed the mobile devices as an additional piece of equipment that would not be of any benefit to them at this stage of their studies. Another learner from this cohort had no access to a computer, both at home and in the workplace.

A second cohort started in April 2008 they were ten 1st Years. It was felt engagement with this cohort was more positive. The project was mentioned at interview and had become more embedded in their course structure and delivery from the first day of face-to-face lessons.

As the student numbers with the first cohort were less than expected, a number of mobile devices that had been purchased were available. These were given to a group of five 3rd year learners on the Foundation Degree in Families, Parenting and Communities, another work-based course. An induction on the use of the device was given to this group including the support tutor of a learner who had profound learning needs and was a wheelchair user. This learner found the mobile technology of exceptional help in her learning. In particular the access to wireless networking increased her 'mobility'. She found the mobile device light to carry reduced her need to use a wider range of equipment, for example, her laptop which was bulky to carry around and sometimes inaccessible. The learner used the device to develop a wide range of visual resources for her work place, including images of a group of children making fairy cakes.

Work-based learning and technology use

The TAs often work in hectic classrooms within their chosen early years setting and these classroom environments were observed as part of the research process. The TAs often rely on recording instances that occur with paper and pen or a laptop. As technology enhances, there are many devices that provide the facility to take still images, video recordings, dictaphone recordings or digital note-taking. These pocket-sized devices would be easily accessible to the TAs simply to record a moment that could be used for their portfolio of evidence, to refer to when reflecting on their practice or to share with their tutor or peers in a face-to-face lesson. However, owing to the nature of the workplace the TA does not have access to desk space and storage of available technology and often has to sign out the equipment prior to a lesson or to share the equipment across a number of different classrooms making 'instant' accessibility difficult. Providing the TAs with a pocket sized mobile device that has the capabilities of all four functions seemed like a possible solution to this problem. There are many more opportunities to use mobile technology to compliment other types of peripatetic, work-based learners for example chefs, construction workers, hairdressers and nurses.

Research methodology

The research was carried out by Dr Samuel Nikoi at the Beyond Distance Research Alliance at Leicester University. The WoLF project followed an action research methodology for the following reasons:

- Action Research aims to bring about practical improvement, innovation and change within a social practice (Cohen, Manion & Morrison, 2007).
- Within educational research, action research is seen as an appropriate methodology for investigating learning activities (Meighan & Siraj-Blatchford, 2003).
- As a form of enquiry action research is carried out by practitioners themselves to investigate their own practice and find ways of improving and living full in the direction of their educational values (MacNiff & Whitehead, 2006).
- The evidence and practice-based framework of action research is seen as an ideal approach to the management of change (Nunes & McPherson, 2003).

Qualitative data was gathered via a number of sources including semi-structured interviews, tracking online activity, visits to classrooms and observations of the learners in their workplace, a focus group discussion and analysis of evidence included learner portfolios. Data analysis was carried out using cognitive mapping, a data analysis methodology founded on George Kelly's theory of personal construct to help structure analysis and make sense of accounts of problems. This methodology enabled detailed modelling of the views, experiences and feelings of the learners and provided evidence for making interventions at various stages of the project.

Owing to the sensitive nature of going into an early years setting and the ethical issues of capturing images and sound in these settings, two processes occurred prior to any research interviews taking place or the mobile technology being used. The first was a CRB (Criminal Records Bureaux) check of the researcher. The second was a letter to all the heads of the work-based settings informing them of the nature of the project and whether or not recording of children was permissible and in accordance with their institution's policy.

Mobile technology

The first cohort of learners (September 2007) were provided with a Hewlett Packard (HP) rw6185, a Personal Digital Assistant (PDA) with phone functionality, the facility to write digital notes, take still images and video images, to make digital sound recordings and to synchronise diaries and calendars with a personal or work computer. Also provided was a Hewlett Packard Bluetooth foldable keyboard which the project team thought could be used in a busy classroom environment to type up notes or adjust lesson plans in a minimal amount of space. Mini HD cards with pre-stored module handbooks and course handbook were also inserted into the device ready for use. No testing or evaluation of the keyboards had been carried out prior to purchasing them and unfortunately it was discovered after much rigorous testing and researching on forums that they did not connect to the rw6185. An alternative keyboard was sourced. However, it is unclear how much these were used and they seem inconsequential to the learner's use of the HP rw6185 PDA.

The first cohort received a short induction of forty-five minutes on the use of the devices. Further supporting handouts were developed in light of the technical issues that arose with the use of the devices as well as some tutorials that were recorded using Adobe Captivate and made available on the Moodle Virtual Learning Environment (VLE). Moodle is an 'open source' product that has been predominantly used as a learning platform in Further Education and schools. Leicester College has been using Moodle as their institutional VLE since 2003. More universities are moving over to Moodle owing to the nature of 'open source' software and the developments being made within the educational community by practitioners. The functionality of Moodle allows learners to access resources associated with their course as well as to participate in activities including discussion forums, instant chat rooms, wikis, quizzes and surveys, keeping journals and blogging, developing glossaries and much more. Many of the supporting materials were produced as a result of a request from one of the participating learners, an example being 'How to move a sound or image file and put it into a PowerPoint presentation.' As the cohort started to use the device, technical issues became apparent. One key issue was synchronising the devices on an institutional computer where the ICT policy blocked the installation of ActiveSync. Advice to the learners was to synchronise diaries and calendars only to their own, personal computers.

It was strongly felt by the project team that the first cohort of learners should be allowed to use the mobile device in their own way with little influence or guidance by the tutor. The use of the device was not an integral part of formative and summative assessment activities within the curriculum. The reason was to hear the learner's voice and to ascertain whether the learners would come up with innovative ways of using the device for their own learning. The learners used the device to take still images, videos and sound files.

The first cohort had anxieties about using a piece of equipment provided by the college. This 'fear' factor had to be eliminated for the project to progress. This was achieved by writing to the learners about 'safe keeping of the devices' and ensuring them that should something go wrong, the device would be replaced at no cost to them. Consideration needed to be given to insurance claims and the cost of making one for an institution. It was felt that the cost of replacing the equipment would be less than the cost of making the claim for a relatively nominal amount. No equipment was damaged or lost during the project.

By the time the second cohort of learners started (April 2008) the HP rw6185 was no longer available on the market. This made all the supporting technical materials out of date and new documentation and tutorials had to be produced. This group were issued with an HP500 Voice Messenger.

The device resembled a mobile phone more so than the previous PDA. It still had the three main features that the first cohort had used, still images, video and sound recordings. However, it was felt that the second cohort should receive a more in-depth induction which lasted the full taught session of four hours, with over an hour devoted to the use of the mobile device and at least another hour spent on using the VLE. It is felt that the importance of this induction was key to the successful engagement of the learners with both the mobile technology and VLE and became a project 'lesson learnt'.

As tutor confidence grew the use of the device became more 'embedded' with the assignments issued and assessments given as a method of gathering supporting and additional information. Through classroom observations by the project team subsequent discussions took place as to how the device could be used in different and effective ways. With more opportunities to embed the device within the coursework it was hoped that the learners would use the evidence gathered to reflect on their practice (it may be some days between delivery of a lesson or classroom activity in the workplace to sitting down and writing up their coursework) and the images, video and sound files could be used to remind the learners and provide solid examples of practice.

Much consideration had to be given to the nature of the early years settings were the learners worked. Each establishment has different policies with regards to photos, videos and sound files being taken.

Consideration should be given to different work-based learning settings and whether or not capturing evidence, experiences and encounters is wholly appropriate and ethical, in particular with some work-based learners working in 'sensitive' areas, for example nursing.

Examples of the activities where the cohorts used the mobile devices are: digital voice recordings of observations comparing teacher's scientific vocabulary with children's everyday use, for example 'transparent' with 'see through' and 'melt' and 'dissolve' as well as recordings taken during an interview with children as part of a literacy lesson. One example of a digital voice recording was the 'conservation and decentration' task. This activity refers to the third stage of the psychologist Jean Piaget's cognitive development model. Between the ages of 7 and 11 a child will master this third stage, the ability to logically determine whether or not a quantity stays the same despite adjustments to shape of container or size of the container. One of the most famous conservation tasks is to show a child two identical beakers of the same quantity of liquid. When one beaker is poured into another beaker that is taller and thinner a child who cannot 'conserve' the task will think there is more liquid in the taller, thinner beaker. Photographs were taken of the artwork produced by the pupils for the 'draw a scientist' task. Capturing the outcome of this activity shows that when children are asked to draw an image of a 'scientist' the results usually show a man in a white coat. The images can be used for a discussion about stereotyping and understanding that women can be scientists too. Photographs were also taken of classroom displays created by the TAs and children. Two videos were produced of children carrying out a science modelling task. One video clip showed a group without any supporting resources for building a circuit. The second video clip showed a group carrying out the activity with a work sheet produced by the TA. The two clips show the contrast in outcome between the two groups with one group succeeding in building the circuit quickly and effectively and the other group are slower in producing the output. However, the video show evidence of the conversation between the group and evidence of how they worked as a team and communicated with each other.

On the whole the mobile technology was used as a tool for evidence gathering, information management, as an aid to reflect on learning and experiences occurring in the workplace. For example, capturing moments in the classroom that would help with the writing up of an assignment later. Other uses included time management (the use of the alarm function) and the use of digital notes as a memory aid.

Institutional Virtual Learning Environment (VLE)

Prior to the project, the Foundation Degree in Educational Studies learners accessed resources via Leicester University's Blackboard. Leicester University is the validating institution for this qualification. At the beginning of the project a site was set up using Leicester College's Moodle VLE as a space for the participating learners and tutor to access the supporting information about the device.

As the project progressed, and by the time the second cohort started in April 2008, the VLE was beginning to evolve from a repository of supporting documents and tutorials to a fully functioning, interactive course site. As the tutor received support and development on using Moodle and as the learners began to feedback their needs to the tutor, the functionality of the site grew to include an online 'e-tutorial' carried out in the evening in a chat room, an online reflective journal, discussion forums, online uploading of assignments (often including the images, videos and sound files recorded on the mobile devices) and many more features. These developments had a resounding impact on the learners that had not been initially considered by the project team.

Learners were introduced to the first module of their course which included an online Reflective Journal. Learners were able to take the theory learnt during their once-a-week, four-hour class, implement the theory in the work-based setting and reflect on how it went within the journal. The tutor was able to give weekly feedback. Traditionally this assignment had been set in April and submitted, as a typed, printed portfolio in June. For the tutor, this small development impacted on her methods of assessment, the reduction of her paperwork and more time to focus on the delivery of the curriculum and theory in the face-to-face lesson. By giving weekly feedback, evidence showed that learners felt more motivated.

Integration of Mobile Technology with the institutional VLE

The impact of the use of mobile technology and the VLE on the tutor

As part of the induction the second cohort learners were asked to come to the induction session with written work. They were taught how to participate in the forum discussion using this piece of work, making the induction activity relevant and part of a formative assessment activity. Another induction activity was the learners carrying out a self-assessment of their study skills, highlighting elements that they felt unconfident or confident in using the Feedback Module of Moodle. This provided the tutor with a personal profile of each learner and together with the memory of the learning discussion forum and the online reflective journal the learners kept as part of their first, assessed activity the tutor was able to assess the individuals' levels of literacy, study skills and ability to reference their work very early on in the course and intervene to provide any essential and necessary further support to the learner.

The impact of the use of mobile technology and the VLE on the learners

One development in the project made an impact on the learners. This was the introduction of a tutorial run on a Thursday evening. The chat room was made available to any of the learners within the course, regardless of year. Clear instructions were given to the cohort that conversations would be logged and other members of the group would be able to view or join in. Over the weeks, five learners from the second cohort participated regularly and one learner from the first cohort.

The chat room was used purely to capture instant conversations an example being:

> Tutor: Are you settling in ok?
> Learner: thanx, settling in well thanks i do feel i open my big mouth a bit in class but i find the awkward silences when a course leader asks for a reply and no-one answers so difficult not to fill. My brick wall theory is also the basis of my skipping theory I will explain next week. After a course on 'meaningful movement' my skipping theory was not so daft.
> Tutor: No I really appreciate your responses, the group are great, very supportive. Yes we will be looking at nature specifically gender on Monday. Then the week after half term im going to ask the whole group to bring their tasks to date in and we can work on them and the assignment. i will see you all one to one then. Your theories sound intriguing

One learner commented:

> The online tutorial was a new experience but it was reassuring to know support with instant feedback is available half way through the week. I do think it motivates you because of the set up and makes you want to learn.

The tutor said:

> Moodle is great for storing administration, course material, SEDs, Data, Marking, lesson plans and programme specifications. It is useful for communicating with part time learners during the week particularly work-based learners who are difficult to contact via telephone. Uploads from the device allows 'the early years classroom to be brought into the F.E classroom, seeing practice first hand generates quality discussion and sessions are less abstract and more engaging. Learners can download course material; refer to guidelines either at home, when mobile or at work. Formative feedback is easy to give electronically and can arm the learner with confidence to carry on and complete their assignment, sometimes learners do not wish to ask for help within class time if it is a very individual need. Learners can be reminded of upcoming deadline. The new chat function will be great when learners are preparing collaborative presentations.

Findings

Five major factors shape the use of the mobile technology in the WoLF project:

Competence of the learner

From the research six main user cases emerged. These were:

- 'Innovators': TAs who have found innovative and creative ways of using the mobile devices such as creating scenarios in which the children could role play and this was subsequently recorded. One example of this use was a learner who had done a lesson with her pupils on the sun, earth and moon. The pupils had done some activities and supporting research and the TA thought she would get the pupils to model what they had learnt about the sun, moon and earth using balloons, this spontaneous activity was videoed. One quote from a TA within this user case was 'I record and try to evaluate what I have seen during the lesson'.

- 'Progressive' users were once fearful of technology and have overcome this fear to make good use of the mobile device. One 'progressive' user commented 'Listening back to the recording was completely enlightening, e.g. how children form words and make sounds ...If I took notes I don't think I would have had the same results'.
- 'Independent users' were TAs who had access to other technology for recording purposes, for example digital cameras and dictaphones. One 'Independent' user commented 'There isn't anything that I will imagine I will want to use via my PDA'.
- 'Techno-stressed' users had a general dislike of technology and found using the mobile technology stressful and mentally demanding, one user commented 'I like to think IT makes [life] difficult; I like things simple and I can't be dealing with this. Actually, I don't like it, full stop'. These users showed they had a lack of confidence in their own competence in using the device.
- The 'Traditionalist' user showed a preference for traditional methods of learning with little to no technology involved, commenting 'I think the old fashioned method is the best in many ways'.
- The 'White flagger' user surrendered to not using the mobile device at the first hurdle of experiencing a problem. One user commented 'I have not used the PDA at all ...I cannot switch it on, I don't know what is wrong with it'. There was a perceived idea that a lack of support may have contributed to this; however, support for device usage was offered through face-to-face training, email, telephone and an online technical help discussion forum.

Nature of professional practice learners belong to

One key issue with the WoLF project was the work-based environment the learners were gathering their evidence in. Careful consideration needs to be given to how the mobile technology is being used and whether or not it is wholly appropriate. Constraints with the use of the equipment resulted in additional work to eliminate barriers to using the device in particular the agreement from the work-based settings that images, video and sound files could be recorded.

Pedagogy underpinning the teaching and learning process

Evidence suggested that a more 'structured' and directed approach of device usage impacted on the learning process and learner experience. To introduce more 'structure' the tutor began to advise students as to where and when the device could be used when tackling a summative or formative activity. Some examples include the Tools for Learning Activity: 'Video your work area, identifying health and safety pointers – comment on these using a sound file. Share health and safety issues regarding your space with a Blog on the VLE' and the Numeracy Portfolio Activity: 'Observe a numeracy lesson. In your evaluation record how it was structured, including details of timings, grouping and activities. How were adults involved? What part, if any did ICT play in the lesson? Use video and/or voice recording to capture evidence'. The device was used predominantly as an information-gathering and evidenced-based learning tool. Evidence also showed that formative assessment offered through the reflective journal and e-tutorial chat room helped towards motivation, impacting on retention and achievement.

The environmental conditions where the mobile technology is being used

Evidence suggested that when capturing sound recordings in larger groups the sound quality was poor as a result of picking up background noise and interference. The devices were used more often in smaller groups (up to 6 pupils). The device was found to be of value to a disabled learner through ease of access and size.

Quality of output

Using the technology to capture visual and auditory evidence enabled learners to put into context their written work, adding to existing lesson observations in the workplace. However, the quality of the outputs from the device was commented on with the learners feeling image quality was not sufficient for a summative assessment presentation. Learners commented that they felt a dictaphone and digital camera provide a better quality of output. The learners also encountered problems with synchronising the device with their computers and sending files over the internet or via email to their tutor. These issues were recorded as challenges and may have prevented the more innovative and progressive learners from experiencing the true potential of using mobile technology with the VLE or as a device to aid day-to-day organisation by synchronisation of calendars and tasks.

Conclusion

The following issues and implications were identified as significantly impacting on the success of mobile and work-based learning:

- Structured versus flexible learning design approaches towards inclusion of mobile technology into portfolio development, encouraging tutors to embed the use of mobile technology into curriculum design and assessment activities and to have the ability to 'guide' learners in the potential uses of the technology, will improve engagement. Students and staff engaging with the use of mobile technology and VLEs need to be supported with the use of the technology. Owing to the nature of work-based learners, support needs to be flexible in order to meet the learners and tutors needs. Support should be offered face-to-face, over the telephone, via email and via discussion forums and resources on the VLE thus enabling access to the support at varying times of day and from different locations.

- Mobile technology does have a place in a flexible working environment as mobile learning can occur in various work-based locations including salons, hospitals, kitchens and construction sites. There is a need for ethical policies to be considered when using mobile technology within these environments, in particular the instance of capturing nursing practice in a hospital with patients and in the case presented here, capturing pupils in early years' settings.
- Consideration needs to be given to the context in which the devices are being used, with evidence showing that use of the technology within smaller groups promoted engagement by users and was more appropriate for capturing evidence to support their curriculum activities and their portfolio of evidence.
- Effectiveness of the mobile technology was dependent on the quality of the output and what the output was being used for; for example, it was felt that image files were not of sufficient quality for the summative assessment of a graded PowerPoint presentation.
- There is a need for institutional ICT policies to be changed to ensure that learners are able to plug an external device into a computer and be able to upload sound, video and image files to the VLE to share with their tutor and peers.
- It is possible to use the activities within the VLE to carry out early profiling of learners, for example, using feedback modules for learners to carry out a self-assessment of their study skills giving the tutor a sense of their confidence early on in their course. By using these techniques and activities it is possible for the tutor to instigate appropriate and necessary support for individuals.
- It was felt that engagement with mobile technology may be improved with learners being encouraged to use their own, familiar devices. This would reduce learner anxieties about breaking or losing a device provided by the institution.

Further research

Leicester College

Taking the impact of the VLE on the part-time learners as part of the WoLF project a further project has been funded by JISC. The HELLO (Higher Education Lifelong Learning Opportunities) project involves two hundred HE learners and fourteen staff at Leicester College. This is an action research project involving the development of two online communities; the first is curriculum-based and tutor-led over the College's Moodle VLE, bringing together all HE learners in a Student Community Site. The second is the development of a learner-led social network using Mahara. In this space learners will have opportunities to engage with employers and business experts and other learners from other higher education institutions (currently De Montfort University) to seek the advice and guidance from peer mentors with regards to the transition from FE to HE.[1]

Leicester University

Outcomes from WoLF have been deployed in a new Curriculum Delivery project at the University of Leicester: Duckling.[2]

1   For further information please visit <http://hello.lec.ac.uk> (accessed 10/08/10).
2   <http://www.le.ac.uk/beyonddistance/duckling> (accessed 10/08/10).

References

Cohen, L., Manion, L., & Morrison, K., (2007) *Research methods in education*. London: Routledge

MacNiff, J., & Whitehead, J. (2006) *All you need to know about action research*. London: Sage

Meighan, R., & Siraj-Blatchford, I. (2003) *A sociology of educating*. London: Continuum

Nunes, M., & McPherson, M. (2003) 'Action research in continuing professional distance education.' *Journal of Computer Assisted Learning 19*, pp. 429–437

SELENA CHAN

5   Becoming a baker:
    Using mobile phones to compile e-portfolios

Abstract

This chapter reports on the use of mobile phones as tools for the collation of e-portfolios and the use of this concept to contribute to an understanding of how young people become bakers. The chapter begins with a brief background on the overall project. A discussion on the underlying rationale and educational philosophies based on socio-cultural theories (Vygotsky, 1998) which underpin the project follows. Sub-projects and their evaluation framed by the precepts of Activity Theory (Engestrom, 2001) are then detailed. A discussion of the ramifications of e-portfolio development on apprentices' conceptualisation of occupational/vocational identity formation in bakery communities of practice (Wenger, 1998) as bakers follows. The process of occupation/vocational identity formation as bakers is proposed as a process of belonging to a workplace, becoming and then being a baker (Chan, 2008). Mobile phones offer apprentices the opportunity to collect authentic and timely multimedia evidence of situated learning experiences as skill acquisition develops. Evidence collated on social networking sites provide ready access to apprentices, their teachers, peers, friends, workmates, employers and family. The opportunity to share concrete evidence of skill acquisition, which in the past could not be readily communicated, enhanced apprentices' initial self-recognition and eventual self-acceptance of occupational/vocational identity transformation. The compilation of e-portfolios based on mobile phone-generated multimedia evidence, collected and collated by apprentice learners, affords opportunities for the multimodal expression (Archer, 2006) of occupational/vocational identity using multiliteracies (New London Group, 1996), vernacular and skill-sets which are familiar to young people (Alexander, 2008).

Background to the project

The baking industry in New Zealand, in common with many other craft-based trades exampled by building and manufacturing trades, is based in small and medium enterprises (SMEs) which are defined as workplaces with up to nineteen full-time workers (Department of Statistics, 2001). The primary objective of bakeries is a high rate of productivity directed towards manufacturing a wide range of bakery products. One consequence of this production-focused workplace culture is insufficient support for completion of workplace-based assessments required to complete qualifications in baking (Chan, 2003). The completion rate for bakery apprentices who commenced their apprenticeship in 2002 is 30 per cent after five years of indenture and 32 per cent after six years (Mahoney, 2009). In series of projects reported in this chapter completion rates improved markedly (averaging over 60 per cent) due to simplification of the assessment process by gathering evidence of skill acquisition using mobile phones.

Literature foundation for the project

The various projects reported in this chapter are premised on an understanding of socio-cultural theories proposed by Vygotsky (1998) and extended by many others (Billett, 1996; Engeström, 1999; Hung, 1999; Wertsch, 1998). In particular, this project uses cultural-historical Activity Theory (Engeström, 2001) as a framework to evaluate outcomes from the projects and Vygotsky's approach to identity formation (Penuel & Wertsch, 1995).

Cultural-historical Activity Theory (Engeström, 2001) provides the framework from which to better understand how individuals engage and interact with their work and learning environment. This engagement and interaction produces 'tools' for expressing individuals' understanding and emerging identity transformations. Identity can also be conceptualised as personal or collective or as 'individual level phenomenon' or 'societal-level phenomenon' (Ashmore & Jussim, 1997, p. 5). Phrases exampled by corporate identity, national identity, occupational identity or community identity are examples of societal level phenomenon. In addition, forma-tion of identity is enacted against a background of history, culture and society. These further impinge on individuals' self and identity (Ashmore & Jussim, 1997). Therefore, opportunities to collect evidence of occu-pational/vocational identity formation through collection of real-world artefacts, which demonstrate identity transformation, provides affordances to examine processes of situated learning (Lave & Wenger, 1991) within specific/specialised communities of practices (Wenger,1998); identity for-mation as a process of becoming (Colley, Tedder, James & Diment, 2003; Hodkinson, Biesta & James, 2008); and occupational/vocational identity formation (Skorikov & Vondracek, 1998; Kirpal, 2004). The advent and pervasiveness of technology (Brown & Petitto, 2003) into the social lives of young people (Brown, 2002) also provides affordances for the expression of multiliteracies (New London Group, 1996). The use of multiliteracies, including visual and aural literacies (Williams, 2008) coupled with mobile digital literacies (Uden, 2007), form the background to the construction of e-portfolios which evidence occupational/vocational identity formation. A socio-cultural approach to explaining identity formation views both socio-cultural processes and individual functioning as 'dynamic, irreducible tensions' (Penuel & Wertsch, 1995, p. 84). Using a socio-cultural approach means to firstly allow individuals to persuade others (and themselves) about who they are and what they value. This is addressed to someone who is 'situated culturally and historically and who has particular meaning for individuals' (Penuel & Wertsch, 1995, p. 91). In this project, multimedia evidence collated into e-portfolios, which showcase skill attainment of bakery apprentices, may be viewed as a means by which individuals are able to persuade others about how their occupational/vocational identity as crafts people is progressing and eventually coalescing through processes of becoming a trades person (Chan, 2008).

The use of Activity Theory framework as proposed by Engestrom (2001) and contextualised towards mobile learning (Sharples, Taylor & Vavoula, 2005; Uden, 2007) was used in this project to assist with exploring ramifications of using mobile phones to collect evidence of workplace-based skill acquisition on aspects of identity formation in apprentices as they learn to become bakers. The tenets central to Activity Theory include ways in which the human mind works and can only be understood through a study of human interaction and human activity as socially and culturally determined (Engeström, 1991; Uden, 2007). These two tenets connect well with socio-cultural approaches (Penuel & Wertsch, 1995) described in the preceding paragraph used to study and understand occupational/vocational identity transformation, trajectories and formation in apprentices becoming bakers. Of special interest in this chapter is the use of e-portfolios/social networking sites to collate and share multimedia artefacts, collected using mobile phones, which form a 'narrative trail' (Pachler & Daly, 2009), as apprentices belong to a workplace, become and then be bakers (Chan, 2008). These narratives collated using various multimodal (photos, audio clips, videos and text descriptions) artefacts collected using mobile phones, are an expression of individuals' developmental skill acquisition within a specialised community of practice. Therefore, a means by which the activity of becoming a baker may be presented and validated.

The mobile learning projects

Overview

Since 2005, a series of iterative trials have been undertaken to explore the implementation of mobile learning with workplace-based learners. These various trials and projects have involved two major strands. Trials/projects began with a study to use mobile phones to deliver the knowledge-based content of baking to workplace-based learners. This involved conversion of an existing online course platformed on the content management system (CMS), Moodle. Progressing from these trials, possibilities of leveraging other capabilities afforded by mobile phones were further investigated.

In particular, the need to involve students in creating content instead of teacher-led content delivery was explored. Therefore, an active learning approach (Litchfield, Dyson, Lawson and Zmijewska, 2007) was deployed to involve apprentices in their learning. This led to the second strand of the mobile learning project at Christchurch Polytechnic Institute of Technology (CPIT) which was to utilise mobile phones to collect evidence of skill acquisition at work and to collate this evidence into e-portfolios for purposes of competency-based assessments of skill attainment (Chan, 2006). The high ownership of mobile phones by apprentices assisted in obviating a digital divide evidenced in young apprentices who had recently embarked on independent accommodation arrangements. Young apprentices lost access to their family computer when they moved away from the family home on commencement of indenture. Therefore, familiarity of young apprentices with the use of mobile phones (Uden, 2007; Williams, 2008) was harnessed to provide a ready tool for collecting evidence of skills acquisition in workplaces, collaboration with the project team and sharing contents of e-portfolios with significant people in their lives.

An e-portfolio is a method used to digitally store evidence of a learner's skill and knowledge acquisition. They may be used to collect evidence to support competency-based assessments and to describe or provide a historical narrative and/or showcase a learner's achievement. A literature review by Butler (2006) provides discussion on benefits of portfolios, issues relating to use of portfolios and requirements for implementing and supporting successful learning portfolios. These guidelines present good foundation for mobile e-portfolio projects and include principles that encourage good portfolio production. Butler (2006) also provides a comprehensive discussion on the unique advantages e-portfolios afford. These include e-portfolios as more efficient to search through, retrieve information from, manipulate and organise, thereby reducing effort and time needed to maintain; possibly more comprehensive and rigorous as an assessment support tool; able to support multimedia; cost effective to distribute; and easy to share with other stakeholders including peers, teachers, parents, employers and others.

There are five different levels of e-portfolios (Love, McKean & Gathercool, 2004). Level one revolves around a scrapbook concept and level two provides the structure of curriculum vitae status. However, the authors argue a true web-folio begins at level three whereby there is the ability for both students and faculty to compile a working portfolio which showcases students' work. Progression to level four opens the web-folio for feedback from other parties which may include students' families, employers (current and potential), various mentors and faculty. At level five, web-folios become authentic and authoritative evidence linking contents of the folio to standards, programmes and 'other descriptors including higher order taxonomies' (p. 27).

In this project, there was a need to move beyond level one or two 'show and tell' e-portfolios. Instead, construction of e-portfolios involved input from apprentices in selecting, archiving, describing and preparing material for inclusion. The process required apprentices to think about their skill/knowledge acquisition process when they re-aligned evidence they had collected with standards and learning outcomes expected. Apprentices were also encouraged to provide backup text/audio descriptions of the photos/videos selected. This was to encourage meta-cognition with regards to the e-portfolio construction process. The provision of an easy to use, fully mobile phone accessible interface to support this process was therefore an important part of the project. A movement into a level four portfolio eventuated with using social networking sites to collate and showcase some of the evidence collected by apprentices during the projects. In a sense e-portfolios, with evidence of situated learning collected using a mobile phone and based in social networking sites are manifestations of narratives which provide users with a means of sharing social constructs of their learning with others invited to view and critique their work (Pachler & Daly, 2009).

Using mobile phones to collect evidence for e-portfolios collation

This section of the project involved apprentices collecting evidence of workplace skills acquisition using mobile phones to collect photos, videos, voice recordings and text snippets.

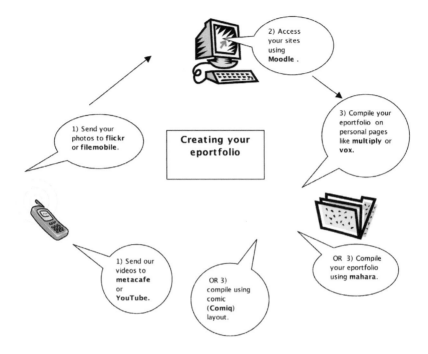

Figure 5.1. Visual representation of CPIT mobile learning e-portfolio pilot project

Figure 5.1 summarises visually the structure, content and connections between various aspects of the projects.

The m-portfolio pilots were to study and evaluate the use of mobile phones to gather evidence and compile evidence into e-portfolios to showcase skills attainment. Several components of the projects, numbered 1 to 3 in Figure 5.1 were enacted. Each of these is now briefly described.

Using mobile phones to collect evidence (No. 1 in Figure 5.1)
and aggregating archives of evidence on Moodle (No.2 in Figure 5.1)

In the project's first iteration, apprentices collected workplace skills evidence using camera and voice recording features on their mobile phones. This component was only used for two iterations of the trials. As social networking platforms matured, it was possible to send photos and videos directly from mobile phones to social networking sites. The use of multimedia archival sites could, therefore, be discontinued.

Complementary to the above, the multimedia sites used by apprentices to archive evidence were hyperlinked to a Moodle site provided to each apprentice. Mobile accessible Moodle sites were constructed through a change in style sheets which minimised amount of data download (Chan & Ford, 2007). Apprentices were then able to view their Moodle site on their mobile phones. Teachers were able to follow progress via apprentices' Moodle sites. Again, this aspect was only used for two iterations of the trials.

Collecting evidence and collating e-portfolios using social networking sites (No. 3 in Figure 5.1)

With the advent of social networking sites and connections between use of social networking sites as a means of archiving and sharing evidence of workplace acquisition, desktop evaluation of over twenty social networking sites was undertaken to evaluate social networking sites' suitability for use as e-portfolios. These e-portfolios would showcase the types of products made by apprentices in their workplaces, archive recipes and detail processes used in manufacturing bakery products. The criteria used to evaluate social networking sites included ease of use; compatibility with a range of mobile phone operating systems; accessibility by mobile phone users in New Zealand; low costs; capabilities for private and public access; visual presentation of the site; capacity to archive photos, videos, voice files and text along with supporting hyperlinks to other archival sites; and structured suitably for collation of e-portfolios. Social networking sites were chosen as e-portfolio repositories as many apprentices already maintained their own social networking sites. The most popular social networking site used by young people in New Zealand is Bebo (<http://www.bebo.com>). However, project evaluation discovered many apprentices were reluctant to share contents of their personal bebo sites with parents, employers and teachers. Therefore, two other social networking sites, Vox (<http://www.vox.com>) and Multiply (<http://www. multiply.com>) were selected for further trialling and evaluation. Most participants preferred Vox due to its user friendliness, clear visual display and natural e-portfolio structure. Other possibilities evaluated included using Comiclife (<http://plasq.com/comiclife>) and Comiqs (<http://www.comiqs.com/>). These provided facilities to caption photos collected of bakery processes. The New Zealand open source e-portfolio platform Mahara (<http://www.mahara.org>) was also evaluated.

Project evaluation

Each cycle of the project was evaluated for overall usability and appropriateness for e-portfolio construction. Data from focus group interviews and completed evaluation questionnaires were organised and analysed based on an Activity Theory framework proposed by Engeström (2001). The visual representation of the framework, showing the nodes (e.g. mediating artifacts, subjects, objects etc.) for categorising and understanding data and the relationships between nodes, is provided in Figure 5.2.

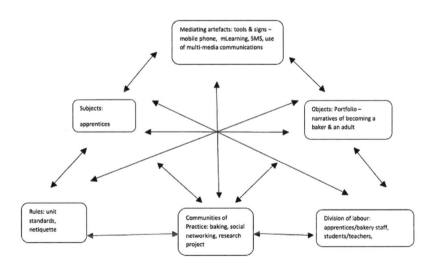

Figure 5.2 Structure of human activity system in the mobile portfolio project. Adapted from Engeström (1999), Sharples, Taylor & Vavoula (2005); Uden (2007).

The project outcomes were evaluated by eliciting student opinions using structured focus groups and structured questionnaires. The questions used in the formative evaluation were based on guidelines informed by an eclectic-mixed-methods-pragmatic paradigm (Reeves & Hedberg, 2003). Questions investigated aspects of usability, relevance, efficiency and cost-effectiveness of the use of mobile phones to gather evidence and ease of use, relevance, efficiency and access issues of utilising social networking sites as e-portfolios. Activity Theory was used to ground the evaluative study and provide structure to data analysis processes. In particular, Activity Theory was used to derive themes (reported in the discussion section) emanating from usage of technology as a tool for communicating skill acquisition attained in a workplace setting. Occupational/vocational identity formation was also traced by examining each node and the inter-relationships between nodes in the activity system.

Activity Theory provides for a method to assist with the description of the structure, development, individuals' contribution and practice which encompasses an activity. In this project, Activity Theory helps to organise various contributors towards the collation of an object: e-portfolios compiled by apprentices who are learning how to become bakers. The subjects of the activity are apprentices. Using mediating artifacts which include mobile phones and protocols for their use, apprentices collect evidence of workplace learning which was governed by rules imposed by workplace pedagogy, workplace organisational culture (workplace communities of practices) and competency-based assessments. The inter-relationships between apprentices (subjects), their workplace learning, the workplace and people from which they learn their trade (communities of practices/division of labour) and eventual collation of e-portfolios (object) to express some of the learning undertaken during apprenticeship make up the structure/framework of the activity system studied. Each node of the activity system is now presented and discussed.

Subject – The apprentices

Apprentices taking part in six iterations of the trials/pilots exhibited a range of digital literacy skills. A total of 72 apprentices participated and 23 of these apprentices followed three years of an apprenticeship. All apprentices owned mobile phones, over 80 per cent owned game consoles but only 15 per cent had ready access to a desktop computer. Therefore, over half the apprentices were not confident with using computer keyboards, navigating through the Windows-based file system and word processing. However, all apprentices were skilled in using their mobile phones to text messages using short message services (SMS). None of the first year apprentices used their phones for web surfing but 20 per cent of third year apprentices used their phones to access the web.

Mediating artefacts – Mobile phones and communication tools

All apprentices used their own phones for the trials. The mobile phone was a crucial element in this project as apprentices had very limited access to desk-top computers. Mobile phones not only simplified the process of collecting evidence of situated learning in workplaces, but were used as the main means of communication with others working on the project including teachers and peers. All apprentices were conversant with SMS and as this was their main means of communication with friends, family and project participants. There was a perception that surfing the web using a mobile phone would be prohibitively expensive, hence many young people were hesitant about experimenting with web access using their mobile phones. Participating apprentices were provided with a voucher across each iteration of the project. This voucher provided sufficient monetary recompense for apprentices to use their own mobile phones to conduct the various activities required to collect evidence for e-portfolios.

Objects – Production of an e-portfolio

Apprentices reported familiarity with portfolio concepts with some having produced portfolios at school. Therefore, extending the concept of a paper-based portfolio into digital portfolios was not difficult. Purposefully initiating and maintaining social networking sites was also straightforward as many apprentices maintained their own personal social networking sites on Bebo. All apprentices who took part in the projects were curious and enthusiastic about the process. Apprentices controlled access to their e-portfolios. They were willing to share their e-portfolios with other apprentices, their employers and teachers and friends and family.

Rules – Imposed by competency-based assessments

Narrow conceptions of competency-based teaching and learning (Hager, 1995) were avoided in this project. A more integrated approach to competence (Hager & Gonczi, 1996) was adopted instead. The integrated approach to competence acknowledges competency as including ability or capabilities to complete tasks along with encompassing attributes related to the more holistic nature of work and learning to do work. Therefore, instead of focusing on individual competency 'unit standards', e-portfolios encouraged a more holistic expression of skill acquisition by allowing collation of suites of competencies. In the case of this project, individual competency 'unit standards' exampled by steps in making bakery products (i.e. weighing, mixing, shaping, baking, finishing etc.) were integrated into e-portfolios as product groups (i.e. breads, biscuits, cakes and pastries). In the first iteration, e-portfolios consisted of photos and some text. Issues of authenticity/authoring of evidence emerged during internal assessment moderation processes. Subsequent trials included short video clips of apprentices performing a task relevant to competencies to be assessed. A hardcopy logbook was used by apprentices to provide a time log of various items of evidence collected. These logbook items were verified by a workplace assessor or supervisor. Currency of evidence could also be documented using the logbook. The reliability of evidence showcased was verified with a final practical challenge test when apprentice attended an off-job training block course.

Division of labour – Roles of participants

Apprentices were the principal collectors of their workplace skill acquisition evidence. As trials progressed, most apprentices became practised and astute with selecting valid and sufficient evidence. Therefore, an increase in understanding of assessment processes by apprentices became evident through the types, quantity and quality of evidence archived and then collated on social networking based sites.

Communities of practice – Three variants

During the course of various trials, three discreet communities of practice (COPs) (Wenger, 1998) were traversed by apprentices. The first community of practice consists of bakeries employing the apprentices and the wider New Zealand and international baking industries. The second encompasses the social networking community. The third was the community of practice of research participants and the researcher. Each of these is now briefly discussed.

COP1: The bakery type of an indenture conferred strong influences on the product skill repertoire afforded to apprentices. Bakery workplaces and the bakery production area are usually staffed with small numbers of people. Therefore, people who work with apprentices were the main sources of craft skills and knowledge (Chan, 2008). This was evident in photos and videos with apprentices showcasing products that they had made, sometimes including their bakery workmates, reinforcing the concept of workplace learning as a product of social activity (Gipps, 2002).

COP 2: The use of social networking sites provided apprentices with opportunities to involve a wider audience for their work. In the past, most of their work would be evidenced in products manufactured at their bakery. The option to use e-portfolios to showcase this work to their friends and family became part of apprentices' motivation to construct e-portfolios. Therefore, e-portfolios were perceived as no longer only an assessment requirement but as a representation of apprentices' growing and maturing skills as bakers.

COP 3: Apprentices contributed many ideas and recommendations towards findings and results of the e-portfolio project. The researcher was able to assume the role of inquisitive but uninformed mobile phone user. Apprentices undertook the task of teaching the researcher various techniques to improve mobile phone use. These included the best methods for using mobile phones to collect photos and videos; evaluating telecommunication providers for the best data plans; utilising the many capabilities of social networking sites; and technical details and capacities related to using various models of mobile phones. A community of sharing practice transpired between apprentices and researcher and an enriched collaborative research process developed.

Narratives of workplace-based skill acquisition

The mobile learning projects presented an opportunity to collect evidence of one aspect of apprentices' development as a tradesperson. In particular, aspects of skill acquisition of a craft and becoming a baker can be partially deduced from the collections of products and videos of processes showcased on social networking sites. In particular, e-portfolios-based on the structural framework of social networking sites may be one avenue for an overt expression of identity formation. As such, they form part of a narrative of identity trajectories. Using social networking sites provides for a 'narrative trail' (Pachler & Daly, 2009) of apprentices' increasing competency as bakers. This identity trajectory included movement of apprentices from 'outsider to insider' via proximal participation (Chan, 2009) and legitimate peripheral participation (Lave & Wenger); from novice to competent practitioner; from dependent learner to co-dependent co-worker; and then independent tradesperson able to teach novices the trade (Chan, 2009).

Evidence of identity formation in the form of photos, videos and text snippets provides artefacts suitable for multi-modal discourse analysis

(Maier, Kampf & Kastber, 2007). The project reported in this chapter is a beginning with indications of possibilities for linking the production of e-portfolios to tracing identity trajectories.

Vocational identity formation in young people

In a separate research project, 13 young apprentices were followed through three and a half years of their apprenticeship journey. Apprentices who participated in this research project were a different cohort to apprentices who participated in the mobile learning e-portfolio pilots. However, both projects were running concurrently across the same time span and profiles of apprentices from both research projects are well matched with regards to age range, gender distribution, ethnicity and types of bakeries in which the apprentices served their indenture. This group of apprentices collected evidence of their skill acquisition using traditional means which included workplace-based assessments and paper based portfolio production.

In the project reported in this section, interviews and participatory observations were carried out over first, second and third years of apprentices' indentures. Interviews and participatory observations were supported by survey questionnaires which gathered demographical and ontological information on apprentices and their workplaces. These methods were used to establish the identity formation trajectory of novices to bakers. Findings from this project include skill acquisition evidenced by increased competency in the production of bakery products accompanied by a transition from being learners dependent on other workers for guidance towards becoming inter-dependent and then independent bakers able to guide and teach newer bakery workers. The identity trajectory from novice to experienced baker was studied under the themes of belonging to a workplace, becoming and then being a baker. Figure 5.3 summarises these progressions. Each of these processes of belonging to a workplace, becoming and being are now discussed with reference to the impact of e-portfolio collation.

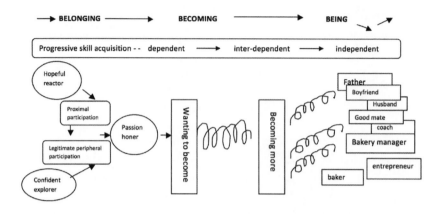

Figure 5.3   Model of belonging, becoming and being.
With identity markers/descriptors from Lave & Wenger (1991) and Vaughan, Roberts
and Gardiner (2006)

Belonging to a workplace

This aspect of identity formation was evidenced through the willingness
with which apprentices showcased their e-portfolios to other apprentices,
their employers and teachers, and to friends and families. Workplaces and
other workers in bakeries featured widely in various multimedia evidence
showcased in apprentice portfolios. This was because belonging to a workplace involves acquiring a sense of belongingness (Levett-Jones, Lathlean,
Higgins & Mcmillan, 2009). Much of belongingness entails the development of strong inter-personal relationships between workers in a workplace
(Chan, 2008) which may be akin to strong friendship bonds described as
'mateship' (Page, 2002).

    Of importance to the assessment process of apprentices' skill acquisi-
tion was opportunities to produce authentic evidence in a vernacular which
is familiar to young people (Armstrong, 2008). Multimedia evidence affords
multimodal means of expression using visual and audio communication
media (Archer, 2006). Evidence gathered using photos, videos and short

text snippets motivates young people who have struggled with written text based assessments.

Becoming a baker

Occupational identity formation in this project was influenced by several factors. These include skill acquisition, personal agency, workplace-based relationships and organisation (social agency) and identity transformation trajectories (Chan 2008, 2009). The use of e-portfolios engaged the wider workplace community in the apprentices' journey from novice to baker. For all participants in the identity formation study there was a need for the occupational identity of a baker to be conferred before eventual inference by individual apprentices. This is described by Penuel & Wertsch (1995) as a form of identity transformation whereby individuals need to be able to persuade others (and themselves) about who they are and what they value. Apprentice-generated e-portfolios may be one avenue to share their journey with not only the other workers in their workplace but with a wider audience. Recognition of competency in skill formation may, therefore, come not only from workplaces but from a wider circle of family, friends, peers and external associations including industry training organisations (ITOs), industry organisations and training establishments.

Being a baker

In the study of identity formation in young people becoming bakers, an awareness of strengths and weaknesses in apprentices' conceptualisation of being a baker was evidenced (Chan 2008, 2009). A concrete platform to record, review and evaluate the apprentice journey was afforded by using e-portfolios. In addition, the competency range of an apprentice may also be assessed remotely or virtually. This allows for a moderation of workplace-based assessment procedures to ensure that fair and reliable assessment processes are completed. The ability to view a range of e-portfolios provided by a cohort of apprentices also allows for moderation of validity of evidence provided.

Discussion

Based on information derived from evaluations undertaken through various iterations of the e-portfolio project and a synthesis with findings from the research project on apprentices' vocational identity formation, several premises for discussion are proposed. These include the need to re-frame competency-based assessments to allow for more holistic representations of workplace-based learning; acknowledgement of multiliteracies which are preferred vernacular of present-day young people; role of social networking sites in re-engaging reluctant learners; and possibilities for utilising social networking-based e-portfolios as research tools for understanding occupational/vocational identity formation.

A need to re-frame competency-based assessments to allow for more holistic representations of workplace-based learning

Much has been written about the impact of competency-based assessments on the overall structure of workplace based training (Hager, 1995; Smith, 1999). It is not the objective of this section to undertake a comprehensive evaluation of advantages and disadvantages inherent in competency-based assessment processes. However, competency-based assessments by virtue of their structure are often focused on assessments of individual skills as opposed to more holistic assessment structures based on recognising capability (Hager & Gonczi, 1996; Robertson, Harford, Strickland, Simons & Harris, 2000). The use of e-portfolios, especially with regard to the pedagogical direction and organisation in this chapter, proposes a more holistic method for aggregation of skills acquisition evidence (Gipps, 2002). In particular, the facility to closely match the visual vernacular preference of young people (Jewitt, 2003; Archer, 2006) by accepting the use of multimedia evidence engages young people more deeply, leading not only to better assessment completion outcomes but improved engagement with the assessment process.

The multiliteracies which are preferred vernacular of present young people

The term multiliteracies (New London Group, 1996; Williams, 2008) is used to describe a proposed pedagogy which provides skills and knowledge for living in a culturally diverse and multi-linguistic world brought about by changes in work, society and private lives. Multiliteracies refer to literacies which are not expressed in traditional forms of reading and writing. Multiliteracies include making meaning out of visual (images, page layouts, screen formats), audio (music, sound effects), gestural (body language) and spatial (environmental and architectural spaces) modalities. Therefore, assessment of multiliteracies requires a re-evaluation of current approaches to assessment practices (Kalantzis, Cope & Harvey, 2003). Assessment methods which are recommended to support assessment of multiliteracies include projects, performance, groups and e-portfolio assessments (Kalantzis et al. 2003). These modes of assessment not only afford opportunities to express a more holistic collation of aspects of identity transformation which distinguishes novices from experts but also provide insight into the formative aspects of learners' skill, knowledge and attitudinal development as processes of occupational/vocational identity formation unfold and progress.

Using social networking sites to re-engage reluctant learners

The extrinsic motivation imposed on apprentices through the need to complete qualifications does not always yield dividends. Evidence of this is provided by continually low bakery apprentice completion rates of National certificates (Mahoney, 2009). There are also considerable barriers imposed by workplace learning with its inherent challenges (Billett, 2001) and workplace assessment issues (Cornford, 1998; Robertson et al., 2000). Yet, apprentices who form the cohort studied on identity formation became bakers despite many not completing formalised recognition in the form of national certificates. These apprentices progressed from total novices, the majority of whom entered into the baking trade with no preconceived planning to become bakers (Chan, 2009). They were then eventually recognised as competent bakers by other workers in the bakery and by themselves as becoming bakers (Chan, 2008).

Therefore, there are significant advantages, in the form of intrinsic motivations for the learner, in utilising mobile phones and employing social networking sites for the collation of e-portfolios. Both the use of mobile phones and social networking sites are familiar means of communication and social expression for young people (Alexander, 2008). Mobile phones provide opportunities to collect salient aspects of apprentices' skill development at the time and place it occurs. The advantages of using social networking sites include ease of access not only for apprentices but also by friends, colleagues and family; an increase in 'traditional' information technology skills; a greater awareness of assessment requirements including aspects of validity, sufficiency and authenticity of evidence; improved confidence in utilising mobile phones to gather photos, videos, voice recordings and text fragments; and better opportunities to obtain formative feedback from assessors and peers as the process of e-portfolio compilation proceeds.

Utilising social networking site based e-portfolios to research workplace-based skill attainment and identity formation

Although the original objective of the mobile phone generated e-portfolios was to provide an alternative approach for workplace-based skill acquisition to be recognised, the aspect of e-portfolios as narratives of vocational identity formation also occurred. This makes available a tool for the collection of user-generated, ethnographical evidence for studying identity formation.

Peng, Su, Chou and Tsai (2009) propose the concept of using mobile tools and the availability of 'cloud computing' to provide learners with opportunities not only to access but also to create knowledge while 'untethered'. Therefore, concepts utilised in this project provide another possible option for workplace-based learners, in this case trades apprentices, with opportunities to contribute their learning, ideas and innovations into their wider industry community of practice. Lehikoinen, Aaltonen, Salminen and Huuskonen (2007) introduce the concept of personal content management (PCM). They posit the growth of PCMs as based on increased mobility of people and their devices along with the growth and increasing importance being placed on personally generated content. Mobile phone access to social network sites based e-portfolios may be one method of utilising precepts of personal PCM to encourage young people to re-engage with learning. The collection and subsequent collation of multimedia based evidence of growing skill acquisition by apprentices provide concrete indications of developing capabilities as skilled crafts practitioners. The added ability to share their e-portfolio with assessors, peers, friends and relatives, afforded by ease of access, provides for another source of affirmation of a consolidating occupational/vocational identity (Gipps, 2002). The simplicity of uploading multimedia evidence using mobile phones directly on to social networking sites, selecting and manipulating evidence to showcase their work and accessibility of social networking sites to an invited audience provides for a positive feedback loop.

Conclusion

Contemporary pedagogy based on present models of teaching and learning which privileged institution-based and predominantly text-based discourse (Kalantzis et al., 2003), rarely afforded learners choices for matching their multi-modal affinities to processes or tools used to optimise learning or assessment processes (Millwood & Terrell, 2005). This was especially the case for workplace-based learning which had specialised agendas and workplace pedagogy which did not always privilege workplace learners (Billett, 2001). Therefore, this chapter has reported on one approach which was technically feasible, utilised communications technology which was readily available to workplace learners (i.e. mobile phones), drawing on learners' existing mobile digital literacies (Uden, 2007) and understanding of social networking, engaging to learners, provided for an alternative but robust form of assessment of workplace skills and underpinned by pedagogical foundations and evaluative research.

This chapter reported on one possibility for harnessing advantages provided by mobile technology and cloud computing to enhance motivation to collect, collate and showcase multimedia evidence of skill acquisition. Mobile phones were key enablers for the projects reported in this chapter. Apprentices' ready access to mobile phones provided incentives, affordances and immediacy for collecting evidence of workplace acquired skills. Then by collating e-portfolios using social networking software, apprentices were also able to construct narratives and showcases of their occupational/vocational identity trajectory from novice to recognised, competent trades practitioner.

References

Alexander, B. (2008) 'Web 2.0 and emergent multiliteracies.' *Theory into Practice 47*, pp. 150–160

Archer, A. (2006) 'A multimodal approach to academic "literacies": Problematising the visual/verbal divide.' *Learning and Education 20*(6), pp. 449–462

Ashmore, R., & Jussim, L. (1997) 'Introduction: Toward a second century of the scientific analysis of self and identity.' In Ashmore, R. & Jussim, L. (eds), *Self and identity: Fundamental issues*. Rutgers series on self and social identity 1. Oxford: Oxford University Press

Billett, S. (1996) 'Situated learning: bridging sociocultural and cognitive theorising.' *Learning and Instruction 6*(3), pp. 263–280

Billett, S. (2001) 'Learning at work: workplace affordances and individual engagement.' *Journal of Workplace Learning 13*(5), pp. 209–214

Billett, S. (2006) 'Work, subjectivity and learning.' In Billett, S., Fenwick, T., & Somerville, M. (eds). *Work, subjectivity and learning: Understanding learning through working life*. Netherlands: Springer

Brown, J. (2002) 'Growing up digital: how the web changes work, education and the say people learn.' *US Distance Learning Association Journal* 16(2)

Brown, D., & Petitto, K. (2003) 'The status of ubiquitous computing.' *Educause Review 38*(3), pp. 25–33

Butler, P. (2006) *A review of the literature on portfolios and electronic portfolios*. A report for the eCDF ePortfolio Project. Massey University, College of Education,

Palmerston North, New Zealand. Available online at <https://eduforge.org/docman/view.php/142/1101/ePortfolio%20Project%20Research%20Report.pdf> (accessed 15/04/10)

Chan, S. (2003) *Becoming a Baker: Factors Contributing to the Successful Completion of National Certificate in Food Production – Baking (level 4) by Apprentices in the New Zealand Baking Industry.* Thesis presented in partial fulfilment of Master in Education (Adult Education). Massey University

Chan, S. (2006) *mLearning for work-based apprentices: A report on trials undertaken to set up mobile portfolios.* mLearn2006, Banff, Canada

Chan, S. (2008) *Belonging, becoming and being: The role of apprenticeship.* ITF 5th Vocational Education Research Forum, Te Papa, Wellington

Chan, S. (2009) *Belonging, becoming & being: The role of 'proximal participation' in apprentices decisions to begin an indenture and its application to preparing young people for work.* HERDSA 2009, Charles Darwin University, Darwin

Chan, S., & Ford, N. (2007) 'mlearning and the workplace learner: Integrating mlearning e-portfolios with Moodle.' *Proceedings of the Mobile Technologies & Applications Conference (MoLTA).* Albany, New Zealand

Colley, H., James, D., Tedder, M., & Diment, K. (2003) 'Learning as becoming in vocational education and training: class, gender and the role of vocational habitus.' *Journal of Vocational Education and Training 55*(3), pp. 471–497

Cornford. I., & Gunn, D. (1998) 'Work-based learning of commercial cookery apprentices in the New South Wales hospitality industry.' *Journal of Vocational Education and Training 50*(4), pp. 549–567

Department of Statistics (2001) *Definition of SME.* Wellington, New Zealand: Department of Statistics

Engeström, Y. (1999) 'Innovative learning in work teams: analysing cycles of knowledge creation in practice.' In Engestrom, Y., Miettinen, R., & Punamaki, R.-L. (eds) *Perspectives on Activity Theory.* Cambridge: Cambridge University Press

Engeström, Y. (2001) 'Expansive learning at work: toward an activity theoretical reconceptualisation.' *Journal of Education and Work 14*(1), pp. 133–156

Gipps, C. (2002) 'Sociocultural perspectives on assessment.' In Wells, G., & Claxton, G. (eds), *Learning for life in the 21st century: Sociocultural perspectives on the future of education* (pp. 73–84). Oxford, UK; Malden, Mass: Blackwell Publishers

Hager, P. (1995) 'Competency standards – A help or a hindrance. An Australian perspective.' *Vocational Aspects of Education 47*(2), pp. 141–151

Hager, P. & Gonczi, A. (1996) 'What is competency?' *Medical Teacher 18*(1), pp. 15–18

Hodkinson, P., Biesta, G., and James, D. (2008) 'Understanding learning culturally: overcoming the dualism between social and individual views of learning.' *Vocation and Learning 1*(1), pp. 27–47

II4   SELENA CHAN

Hung, D. (1999) 'Activity, apprenticeship, and epistemological appropriation: implications from the writings of Michael Polanyi.' *Educational Psychologist 34*(4), pp. 193–205

Jewitt, C. (2003) 'Re-thinking assessment: multimodality, literacy and computer-mediated learning.' *Assessment in Education 10*(1), pp. 83–102

Kalantzis, M., Cope, B., & Harvey, A. (2003) 'Assessing multiliteracies and the new basics.' *Assessment in Education 10*(1), pp. 15–26

Kirpal, S. (2004) 'Researching work identities in a European context.' *Career Development International 9*(3), pp. 199–221

Lave, J., & Wenger, E. (1991) *Situated learning: Legitimate peripheral participation.* Cambridge: Cambridge University Press

Lehikoinen, J., Aaltonen, A., Salminen, I., & Huuskonen, P. (2007) *Personal content experience: Managing digital life in the mobile age.* New Jersey: Wiley-Interscience

Levett-Jones, T., Lathlean, J., Higgins, I., & Mcmillan, M. (2009) 'Staff-student relationships and their impact on nursing students' belongingness and learning.' *Journal of Advanced Nursing 65*(2), pp. 316–324

Litcfield, A., Dyson, L., Lawson, E., & Zmijewska, A. (2007) 'Directions for mlearning research to enhance active learning.' *ASCILITE conference report*, Singapore

Love, D., McKean, G., and Gathercool, P. (2004) 'Portfolios to webfolios and beyond: levels of maturation.' *Educause Quarterly 2*, pp. 24–27

Mahoney, P. (2009) *Modern apprenticeships: Completion analysis.* Ministry of Education, New Zealand

Maier, C., Kampf, C., & Kastberg, P. (2007) 'Multimodal analysis: an Integrative Approach for scientific visualisation on the web.' *Journal of Technical Writing and Communication 37*(4), pp. 453–478

Millwood, R. & Terrell, I. (2005) 'Overview: New technology, learning and assessment in higher education.' *Innovations in Education and Teaching International 42*(3), 195–204

New London Group (1996) 'A pedagogy of multiliteracies: Designing social futures.' *Harvard Educational Review 66*(1), pp. 60–92

Pachler, N., & Daly, C. (2009) 'Narrative and learning with web 2.0 technologies: Towards a research agenda.' *Journal of Computer Assisted Learning 25*(1), pp. 6–18

Page, J. (2002) 'Is mateship a virtue?' *Australian Journal of Social Issues 37*(2), pp. 193–200

Peng, H., Su, Y., Chou, C., & Tsai, C. (2009) 'Ubiquitous knowledge construction: mobile learning re-defined and a conceptual framework.' *Innovations in Education and Teaching International 46*(2), pp. 171–183

Penuel, W., & Wertsch, V. (1995) 'Vygotsky and identity formation: a sociocultural approach.' *Educational Psychologist 30*(2), pp. 83–92

Reeves, T. & Hedberg, J. (2003) *Interactive learning systems evaluation.* Englewood Cliffs, NJ: Education Technology Publications

Robertson, I., Harford, M., Strickland, A., Simons, M., & Harris, R. (2000) *Learning and assessment issues in apprenticeships and traineeships.* AVETRA Conference Report

Skorikov, V., & Vondracek, F. (1998) 'Vocational identity development: its relationship to other identity domains and to overall identity development.' *Journal of Career Assessment 6*(1), pp. 13–35

Sharples, M., Taylor, J. & Vavoula, G. (2005) 'Towards a Theory of Mobile Learning.' *Proceedings of mLearn 2005 Conference*, Cape Town

Smith, E. (1999) 'How competency–based training has changed the role of teachers in the vocational education and training sector in Australia.' *Asia-Pacific Journal of Teacher Education 27*(1), pp. 61–75

Uden, L. (2007) 'Activity theory for designing mobile learning.' *International Journal of Mobile Learning and Organisation 1*(1), pp. 81–102

Vaughan, K., Roberts, J., & Gardiner, B. (2006) *Young people producing careers and identities: A first report from the pathways and prospects project.* Wellington, New Zealand: New Zealand Council for Educational Research

Vygotsky, L. (1998) *Mind in society: The development of higher psychological processes.* Cambridge, MA: Harvard University Press

Wenger, E. (1998) *Communities of practice: Learning, meaning and identity.* Cambridge: University Press

Wertsch, J. (1998) *Mind as action.* New York: Oxford University Press

Williams, B. (2008) '"Tomorrow will not be like today": literacy and identity in a world of multiliteracies.' *Journal of Adolescent and Adult Literacy, 51*(8), pp. 682–686

RUTH WALLACE

6   The affordances of mobile learning that can
engage disenfranchised learner identities in
formal education

Abstract

Mobile technologies have been promoted to improve the participation
and educational outcomes of disengaged learners. The ways that mobile
technologies support the learning of disengaged learners is less well understood. The realisation of mobile learning's potential to enhance learning
experiences is dependent on an implementation framework and underlying
pedagogy that aligns with the ways learners connect with technologies. This
understanding then supports the connection of mobile technologies' use
with teaching and learning systems and practice. Learners' relationships
with and expectations of mobile technologies has changed the ways technologies interact with learning experiences. The use of mobile technologies
is increasing in a range of communities who have been disenfranchised
from formal education provision and its benefits. This chapter considers
the affordances of mobile technologies in recognising and engaging disenfranchised adult learners. The uses of mobile technologies are examined in
the provision of industry-based training in remote Indigenous Australian
communities. Learners' use of mobile technologies provides insights into
provision of education that engages a range of learner identities to achieve
their educational outcomes. The findings provide insights into designing
learning approaches and systems that are: learner-centred, engage Indigenous learners' contexts, negotiate diverse knowledge systems and representations of knowledge and skill. The implications for mobile-learning

pedagogy and implementation are outlined as they relate to improving learner engagement and integration of emerging technologies and applications in vocational education and skill recognition.

Introduction

The use of mobile technologies in work- and home-based learning contexts suggests that there is potential in incorporating new technologies to support learning activities. Integration of mobile technologies in education is of particular interest as they are already embedded in people's daily lives and practices. People who have traditionally been excluded from established institutional knowledge management systems may be distrustful of using institutional resources for learning. They may also be using mobile technologies such as cameras, mobile phones, iPods and so on in other parts of their lives to connect with the world. The challenge is to identify approaches that are engaging, connected to people's lives and encourage people to participate in knowledge exchange for common purposes; purposes that are prioritised and valued by individuals and their communities. Digital technologies have become increasingly intuitive and accessible in remote areas, making the use of ICT more viable. Digitally-based resources have been shown to support people to learn and demonstrate competence across language and knowledge systems. The use of digital technologies is unique as it supports people to communicate and work in different ways. Digital technologies also provide tools for demonstrating the diverse kinds of knowledge, the systems in which it operates and its contexts.

The potential of mobile learning for developing and implementing effective work-based learning programmes is being explored through a current project, funded through the Cooperative Research Centre for Plant Biosecurity. The project is based in Indigenous park ranger enterprises in remote North Australian Indigenous communities that contribute to the sustainability of local workforces. The key to this approach is the role of Indigenous people in the development of the resources, using software and hardware resources within the enterprise and collecting evidence through a range of mobile resources. This chapter explores the affordance of mobile learning and mobile technologies in improving educational outcomes for Indigenous rangers in the project. The use of mobile learning is examined in terms of the cultures represented in its use, its efficacy for engaging learner identities and integration into learners' working lives and traditions. The chapter concludes by reflecting on the challenges of mobile learning. It considers the implications of mobile learning that focuses on the technology rather than the learning, ignoring the cultural bias of mobile learning, learners' and connection to sustainable and interconnected technology use and learning in remote community workplaces.

Digital technologies role in indigenous workplace learning

Participation in education and training is considered vital for a flexible and responsive workforce (OECD, 2001) in a Western society characterized by an emphasis on a learning society, a knowledge economy and lifelong learning (Kearns, 1999; OECD, 2000) yet with a strong connection between global connectedness and the well-being of local and regional communities (Falk, 2001; Hugonnier, 1999). The OECD's examination of 21 OECD countries found a correlation between investment in human capital, including improving engagement in formal education and national productivity (Bassanini & Scarpetta, 2002). The Australian Federal Government and Council of Australian Governments have identified the need to improve productivity through increasing educational participation and outcomes in the tertiary sector (Gillard, 2008).

The National Strategy for Vocational Education and Training (VET) 2004–2010, *Shaping Our Future (ANTA 2004)*, identified that at the core of vocational education in Australia was ensuring Indigenous Australians have the skills for viable jobs, a shared learning culture, increased business development and employment opportunities that lead to greater economic independence with employers and that individuals are at the core of VET.

Indigenous people have identified the essential role of sustainable economic development in community independence, cultural maintenance, self-esteem and economic independence and the importance of engaging Indigenous people in productive economic activity. The *Northern Territory Indigenous Economic Development Strategy* (Indigenous Economic Development Taskforce, 2005) recognises the strength, resilience, diversity and cultural integrity of Indigenous people and also the high levels of disadvantage which impact the capacity of people, families and communities to engage in economic and social development activities. Indigenous enterprise training and development approaches have operated in many cases to meet the aims of Indigenous people and communities. Altman (2001), in a study of sustainable development options on Aboriginal land, suggests that there is a need for a hybrid approach that includes scientific, biological social, commercial viability and 'Indigenous expert assessment of cultural practice' (p. 8). For enterprise development and training this means identifying new ways to understand and develop social, cultural and physical capital in any model. The development of Indigenous enterprises, particularly where there are obvious strengths, such as cultural tourism and land management, are a priority in workforce development and education in Northern Australia. Vocational education and training (VET) has an important role to play in this development that has not been fully realised for a number of reasons.

The European Union's (2003, p. 1) statement about lifelong learning noted the value of digital technologies in knowledge economy 'for promoting digital literacy and thereby contribute to strengthening social cohesion and personal development and fostering intercultural dialogue'.

As Field (2005) notes, disengaged learners are disenfranchised from the knowledge resources that are associated with educational systems including a sense of efficacy as an individual or member of that community. The possibilities of using digital technologies in education have been promoted for creating ways to make better connections and representations to real life and workplaces. Haythornthwaite (2007) notes that the digital divide (related to the access to and competence in use of a range of technologies like computers and high speed internet) impacts on communities' access and, therefore, their engagement in e-learning (including mobile learning). The digital divide can be described in terms of income, education, school connections occupation, ethnicity, region and life stage. Mobile technologies and their use may provide a tool to address the boundaries that are educational and social results of the digital divide. The use of mobile technologies has extended rapidly across a wide range of communities across the globe; including communities that have limited access computer technologies.

The role of mobile learning in improving educational outcomes

The development in mobile technologies have changed the communication, knowledge capture and learning in a range of workplaces and industries. Mobile technologies have been used to expand the geographic footprint of learning experiences (Traxler 2008) to places that were previously isolated from using digital technologies. Mobile devices are characterised by potential for making connections through spontaneous collaboration and communication, location-focused information, being readily available, i.e. within sight, beaming information between devices and providing portable means of collecting and sharing audio and visual information (Kukulska-Hulme & Traxler, 2005). The affordances of mobile technologies have been described by Kukulska-Hulme et al. (2005) as supporting learning that is situated, personal, private and authentic. This is of particular importance when developing approaches to learning with institutionally and historically, disempowered learners:

> new possibilities for how people relate to each other, how knowledge is defined in negotiation between actors and changes our conception of learning environments in which actors make meaning (Erstad, 2008, p. 181).

Technologies cannot be used uncritically, rather they are used within social contexts. It is important to understand the relationships between social, cultural and physical contexts in which learners and mobile technologies operate. Beetham (2007) notes that technologies should not be included in learning situations without understanding participants' competence and confidence in using technologies and ideally extend that competence to build bridges to learning new skills and knowledge. The ways people learn is based on reflecting on their own cultural models of the world that do not denigrate their identities, social connections, strengths and contrast them to new models (Gee, 2003).

Mobile learning is a component of approaches to learning that utilise digital technologies and can be significant in developing approaches that engage educational, personal and workplace experiences. Any definition of mobile learning that refers to a range of personal and mobile hardware and software is limited by the technological advances at time of publication. It also keeps the focus on the technology rather then how people actually use them as the basis of their learning. It may be more useful to describe mobile learning in terms of its use and purpose. The definition used here is that mobile learning is that which draws on mobile technologies used by learners when they are engaged in learning, connecting to the people in their lives and for a range of purposes for communication. As they enable a range of ways to record and represent digital technologies, mobile learning approaches engage diverse people, knowledge, contexts and the relationships between them. Litchfield et al. (2007, p. 587) suggest that 'learners from a wide variety of backgrounds may benefit from mobile technologies because they emphasise activity and interactivity as well as oral communication'.

Mobile learning role in Indigenous education and workforce development

Formal Western educational approaches have systemically failed learners who differ from the mainstream workforce population. Over many years, high numbers of Indigenous Australians have participated in VET training. However, a much lower percentage have had positive results in relation to employment or higher-level qualifications. This outcome questions whether the efficacy of the ways VET has been implemented. For Indigenous Australian learners this is evident in the Australian Bureau of Statistics report (2008) which found that Indigenous people's educational attainments had improved slightly between 2002 and 2008 although non-Indigenous Australians were twice as likely to have a non-school qualification. Indigenous people's employment rates had also improved over the same period although the unemployment rate was over three times that of all Australians. 62 per cent of Indigenous Australians identified with a clan or language group. 11 per cent of Indigenous Australians mainly spoke an Indigenous language at home. In the Northern Territory, where the Aboriginal population is over 25 per cent of the total population, this is considerably higher where, in 2008, 52.7 per cent of the population over 15 years of age spoke an Indigenous language as their main language at home, while 77.7 per cent speak an Indigenous language. This significant population of learners need to have access to educational approaches and systems that recognise and meet their strengths and needs, while also building links to other knowledge systems.

Mobile learning has been utilised to engage disenfranchised learners and explore the different ways learners use mobile learning to communicate in ways that are meaningful to them. The uses of technology have developed with the technological advances and, as Kress & Pachler (2007) note, the incorporation of a range of devices into many peoples' social and cultural practices. As Snyder & Prinsloo (2007) note, the relationships between digital literacy practices in different contexts are complex and differentiated by people's connections to local and global communities. Vosloo, Wilton and Deumert (2009) describe the different usage of mobile technologies by young learners without access to computers outside school, to read and create m-novels. They note that their use is different to that of computers and that is determined by the learners' social context. As they note (2009, p. 208),

> the mere presence of a technology such as a mobile phone or mobile Internet will not shift cultural practices in marginal contexts and make them resemble more highly valued activities in better resourced contexts elsewhere.

The role of digital technologies in improving the educational opportunities for Indigenous learners is dependent on the ways they are used and
connected to people's own lives and purposes. Christie (2006, p. 83), in
discussing the use of digital technologies in Aboriginal contexts, notes that
their use is not 'predetermined, it develops in relation to the context, and
that through use they are reinvented and configured in response to agenda
arising form the context' and are only useful when 'revived on new contexts
of knowledge production in active, creative, situated negotiated encounters'. As Wallace, Curry and Agar (2008) found, improving approaches to
engage Indigenous Australian learners in formal and informal learning are
underpinned by recognition of the diverse knowledge systems that function in learners' worlds of work, learning and community development.
Recognition of the culturally and socially diverse models of learning that
are being utilised by learners has the potential to identify the affordances
of mobile learning that accord with, and differ from existing pedagogies.
They can contribute to an understanding of mobile learning pedagogies
in diverse educational contexts.

Social learning and identities theories

A social theory of practice is used here to understand the practices that
inform educational social systems and institutions and impact on individuals and groups in society. Bourdieu (1990), in describing *habitus*, the social
constructed systems or principles that generate and organize practice and
representations, explored the essentially socially negotiated nature of meaning. *Habitus* is historically produced; individual and group activities and
social practices can be understood in terms of the conditions under which
they are generated and implemented and the interrelationship between the
social worlds that *habitus* performs, while concealing it, in and through
practice (Bourdieu, 1990).

Situatedness is

about the relational character of knowing and learning, about the negotiated character of knowledge, learning, about the negotiated character of meaning, and about the concerned (engaged, dilemma-driven) nature of learning activity for the people involved (Lave & Wenger, 1991, p. 33).

Gee (2003) described the communities of learners first as affinity groups that form around a common endeavour and secondarily about socio-cultural connections; their knowledge is holistic, rather than separated into a specific narrow disciplines and intensive, deep knowledge about matters of importance to the community. Gee (2007, p. 123) asserted the value of learning situations where learning is

situated in the sense that meaning is situated …and in the sense that skills and concepts are learned in an embodied way that leads to real understanding.

The complex nature of learning as a social and mediated practice, the interplay of stakeholders' identities, the institutional or context specific nature of learning and the power relationships that are often hidden or accepted across a number of levels of policy pedagogy, curriculum, knowledges, communities and institutions, demand a level of evidence that recognise these realities. This does not necessarily involve overly complex processes but does imply practitioners need to understand the underpinning theory before using and adapting the processes. Gee (2004) asserts that people learn better through embodied processes, where content is related to activities, discussion and sharing ideas. Embodied knowledge is embedded in educational system elements and interactions (Sharples, Taylor and Vavoula 2007).

Through these interactions and experiences, related to specific contexts, people learn and become partners in creating ways of understanding those elements in that context. The interactions related to learning create connections that are mediated through communities of common interest that may be connected through mobile learning processes across regional, social and workplace boundaries, just to name a few. Gee (2003, p. 51) argues that learning in semiotic domains involves accessing and exploring identities: 'it requires taking on a new identity and forming bridges from one's old identities to the new one'.

Gee asserts that learning is a critical and active process of engagement, knowledge and meaning are developed though multimodalities, learners are active producers and consumers of knowledge and that learners form an 'affinity group' (Gee, 2003, p. 212) connected by their practices and purpose. Falk and Balatti (2003) observe the link that exists between education and identity, that learners are affected by the ways they understand themselves and understand their identity as a learner in relation to education; both formal and informal. 'Deep learning requires the learner being willing and able to take on a new identity in the world, to see the world and act on it in new ways' (Gee, 2007, p. 172). Mendieta (2003, p. 407) described identities as continually

> constituted, constructed, invented, imagined, imposed, projected, suffered, and celebrated. Identities are never univocal, stable, or innocent. They are always an accomplishment and an endless project and empowering forms of ownership of meaning.

Learning opportunities that relate to disenfranchised learners' social practices, group memberships and identities as learners may build bridges between students, educators and communities' understanding of each other's knowledge and learning practices (Wallace, 2008, 2009). These are informed by the different learning identities as they relate to people's worlds, family, local, institution, workplace and global communities. Developing identity affirming learning experiences can support regional students and communities' identities. If the educational system operates from a view that assesses what people coming to learning do not have – a cultural deficit view – their knowledge is not being recognised. The deficit view of students' knowledge actively disempowers teachers and students, reducing their opportunities for learning. If a learner does not identify themselves as a part of a learning experience, its learning practices, knowledge and identities, it is understandable that the learner would reject participation in a learning experience that negates their identity as an individual and in relation to other groups. Workplace and formal learning approaches that were effective for learners were those that recognised people's learner identity and helped learners connect to the learning context. A mobile learning pedagogy that will be successful for disenfranchised learners would, therefore, support the connections to the formal educational context and support the development of an enacted learner identity.

Mobile learning use in a Northern Australian indigenous context

Through a one-year pilot in 2007 and four-year project that commenced in 2008, both funded by the Cooperative Research Centre for National Plant Biosecurity, a learning approach to support Indigenous Australian rangers was developed. The project is being undertaken with five Indigenous rangers based in remote communities and aims to respond to the changing nature of work and economic viability in remote Indigenous communities and the desire for economic, cultural, social and environmental independence. The programme works with existing land management enterprises. Plant biosecurity management-related knowledge and skills are being developed and mapped to improve the management of emerging plants and pests. The pilot found that Indigenous rangers had a priority to have access to a nationally accredited training framework and associated resources that reflect the workforce, community and individual goals and needs of the Indigenous rangers in a rapidly changing market place. Much accepted Western knowledge is codified through long accepted processes, such as qualifications awarded by educational institutions, and formal training system.

The four-year project has worked to develop the systems to recognise Indigenous learners' knowledge and make explicit ways to recognise different ways of understanding or representing knowledge. The project has developed a training framework that maps and identifies the principles for recognising and developing knowledge and skill for plant and pest identification, management and prevention, managing a community-based enterprise and use of digital technologies to access, record and manage the related information in an Indigenous context. The development of the training framework recognises the range of knowledge and skills involved in undertaking biosecurity management through enterprises and the range of stakeholders involved. The resources outline approaches to teach, assess and recognise learners' skills and knowledge related to being an Indigenous park ranger. Some of the areas covered include weed management, chemical mixing, government contract financial management and collating accurate data in the field.

The level of home ownership and access to computers and the internet is minimal for Indigenous rangers in remote communities. Mobile learning provided an opportunity to connect to the devices that are in rangers' pockets and work trucks. There is interested in extending the skill base to using PDAs for data collection on country and developing mobile versions of information websites. The mobile technologies being used are chosen based on the purpose and availability in remote communities. Indigenous rangers using digital cameras and laptops make multilingual digital stories of regular tasks such as mixing chemicals, using the chainsaw, or using safety gear. The digital stories are stored in the rangers' office and being used in the morning briefing before undertaking specific tasks, inducting new staff and refreshing learnings from previous training sessions. The are rangers taking photos of the equipment in their workplace and recording the instructions in the languages that rangers use. Rangers are also recording formal training sessions and developing a bank of refreshers that can be used when they are needed, rather then when trainers are available.

Young women from the park ranger group have developed a range of wildlife-based products to sell at the Darwin markets. They are developing digital stories of the process and practising talking in English to tourists to sell their products. What is different is that the technologies are available in any office in the community, photos can be taken on their own phones and the intuitive nature of the software meant people quickly have taken control of, and are leading the process. The leadership by Indigenous people ensures the respect for cultural leaders and cultural knowledge is maintained throughout the process. Rangers are also developing visual stories for explaining financial management and corporate governance structures. The use of visual images and links allowed the material to be represented in a non-linear way using contextual clues and reflects the learners' ways of connecting knowledge.

I-trackers (Indigenous trackers) are purpose built PDA's using Cyber-Tracker software, that were developed by a team from the North Australian Indigenous Land and Sea Management Alliance to provide 'user friendly tools to facilitate the collection and reporting of ranger patrol data (Jackson et al., 2009). The PDAs are used to record and monitor cultural and environmental and geographic data. They are robust and rangers can collect data in the field. That information is collated to report in accordance with local, state/territory and national contracts. The material is collected using maps and sequences of questions. Rangers are proposing to develop on screen 'How-to' guides that can be accessed in the field to answer their questions about using the equipment when the rangers need to check the sequence.

The challenge was to develop the framework and the resources in terms of Indigenous rangers and senior cultural people's expectations of work, cultural and social relationships and obligations to others and the land, corporate governance of land management contracts with government and non-government agencies. Mobile learning provided a range of tools and approaches that supported Indigenous rangers' learning and demonstration of their strengths. A reflection on the learning approaches that are effective and the role of mobile technologies and mobile learning in this process identifies opportunities and challenges in mobile learning. The use of mobile technologies has become essential in the project as Indigenous rangers identified the need for materials to be presented in a range of Indigenous languages in ways that connect to community contexts and that allowed people to demonstrate their competence, their value as workers in their community and to support the retention of specific knowledge and skills. Mobile learning also provided approaches that support access to information easily in situ and to be able to manage that knowledge for their purposes in the long-term.

Engaging indigenous knowledge through mobile learning

The biosecurity enterprise training framework examines not only the elements of the Australian Qualification Framework (that maps all vocational qualification levels and units) but also the ways people engage with diverse knowledge systems. The framework recognises the governance structures that underpin knowledge utilisation and management in diverse knowledge systems, the impact on representations of knowledge, ways to negotiate and transfer knowledge as well as the social contract between stakeholders in biosecurity management. These diverse knowledge systems operate in bureaucratic, policy, cultural, Western and Indigenous scientific, business, academic and industry-based processes, just to name a few. Management of any biosecurity concept is dependent on the successful engagement of knowledge systems that are diverse, have contradictory bases for their knowledge and competing goals. The stakeholders may have little, superficial or inaccurate knowledge of each other's lives, goals, resources, governance or knowledge sets. There are frequently power differentials which are likely to be protected by the stakeholders at the expense of the shared goal or outcomes. The dominant system in any given situation would tend to advantage one of the existing knowledge systems. For example when working with Indigenous communities, non-Indigenous people will tend to gravitate to the people with best English skills, rather than those with cultural authority. People will respond based on the historical, social and cultural factors which may not be clear to other stakeholders.

Mobile learning is being used to develop a series of context-specific and multilingual teaching resources as described. Mobile learning also provides a means to move away from paper-based assessment conducted in the teaching sessions. By using I-trackers, mobile phones, digital cameras and SMS, rangers are able to collect evidence of their competence in the field. They are then able to organise that information with PowerPoint and digital stories to organise those images and notes into a coherent narrative that explains not only what they did but why. Rangers are able to demonstrate their knowledge in their first language which improves the detail of the description. Previous experience has shown that working in teams, in first language and using images from their own context drastically improves the evidence learners produce and the accuracy of assessment by trainers. This is particularly true for learners who have been shy or reluctant to participate in English only, literacy focussed, linear, formal learning sessions.

Engaging biosecurity knowledge in training and workforce development is underpinned by a preparedness to accept that people think and relate to biosecurity issues differently. The training programme facilitates translation of ideas into local languages and understanding how that knowledge is used in different contexts and the value of seeing an issue from a number of perspectives. The mobile learning tools support rangers to collect information about their country and biosecurity incursions in the field. On returning to the main office and collecting that information, Indigenous rangers are able to manage that knowledge in ways that are empowering rather than embarrassing to senior cultural leaders (by looking like students), people with low level English literacy or oracy skills or learners who prefer to review material often. All of the files are available to the learners at any time. The rangers chose to make all materials so that the rangers' faces are shown, as they want to show how proud they are to do this work. Understanding issues in learners' first language also connects that knowledge to its cultural and social context, an example is a senior cultural ranger defining how work should be done or connecting that knowledge to local priorities. Some concepts are better explained in words, consider showing ratios or pest identification, while others in images that have significance to the learners (that may not be recognised by the trainers). The leadership of senior Indigenous people in establishing the message and its vehicle combined with the use of visual images that can be manipulated by learners is a powerful use of mobile technologies for workplace learning.

Mobile learning that builds bridges to diverse knowledge systems

Mobile learning tools can be used to focus learning on exploring learner contexts, local and global knowledge. By recognising the diverse knowledge systems and contexts of a range of disenfranchised learners, such as youth, regional communities and small enterprise owners, there are opportunities to build bridges between their worlds and that of formal education curriculum. The bridges provide points of connection and sharing, not for one to dominate or denigrate the other, rather to make connections to share ideas, build mutual understanding and extend possibilities for learning. An example has been the use of digital cameras and mobile phones to collect images of workplace tasks (chemical mixing and plant pest incursion reporting), organise the images into a logical procedural digital story and annotate in learners' first, second and third languages. These digital stories look at the learners' own workplace, are organised in ways that reflect their own logic and interpretation of a task (what is important or obvious) and shared in learners' own language and way of expressing an idea. The material is developed with the support and approval of senior cultural leaders who ensure that the images and audio track are culturally appropriate and connected to local community priorities. These are elements that an outsider are unlikely to completely understand and could unintentionally misinterpret.

The use of rangers as the faces and bodies in the digital stories reinforces the profile of Indigenous people in the workplace who have and lead knowledge management and learning. This has an important role in connecting to people's identities. In the workplace Indigenous people have been able to easily make material that represent themselves and their own place in the workplace. This is assumed in non-Indigenous contexts whereas Indigenous people and their contexts are rarely represented positively through learning materials. Using the same processes, learners have been able to make digital stories as evidence of their workplace competence. By showing a video of themselves in their workplace, the learner is seen in a different light by the assessor, as someone confident in their context and provides a discussion point for assessment related to actual experience.

Mobile learning approaches can be implemented to involve disenfranchised learners in positive learning experiences and active construction of knowledge and learner identities. Learners are able to work with and be assessed using material from their worlds as they relate to the worlds of work, community life and lifelong learning, to explore new possibilities and develop strong, empowered learner identities.

By utilising existing and embedded mobile technologies, the mobile learning process does not impose a technology, rather it utilises accepted technologies to build bridges to a wider range of systems and ensure local people are an essential and sustainable part of knowledge transfer processes. An investment in this brokerage role is a crucial part of using mobile technology and mobile learning. Effective processes, then, value and build on individuals' strengths and knowledge. Using mobile telephones, people are already expert in the use of the technologies and are extending their use to a new purpose, reducing anxiety about using new technologies. Mobile technologies also provide a medium through which community members can represent their own tacit and explicit knowledge in ways that they find meaningful for their own purpose and to interact with other educational and work based systems. Learning is then scaffolded to from existing purposes to new purposes. The use of advances in technologies in knowledge management, recognition and learning are bringing new trends in learning and knowledge transfer in a range of often unrecognised workplaces. Our concern is the need to improve formal recognition processes to support the acceptance of digital information and sound processes to incorporate a range of information into formal systems.

The use of mobile technologies in learning environments has been integrated into the workplace to enhance the communication of knowledge and development of ideas between learners, experts and their peers. In this way mobile learning can extend access to 'learning to individuals, communities and countries that were previously too remote, socially or geographically, for other educational initiatives' (Traxler, 2008, p. 9). Depending on the way mobile learning pedagogies are understood and implemented, mobile learning can extend to the socially and educationally excluded. In this way access to mobile technologies and mobile learning pedagogies can provide learners (including trainers) meaningful, context-driven ways to introduce and share their knowledge and worlds. This potential is determined by the ways they are used.

Mobile technologies have provided a tool for people to represent and explore knowledge in people's own languages with the images of community contexts, workplaces, farms and natural heritage areas. The images and information provide manageable files to share with peers and experts to identify pests and diseases, approaches to their management and reporting of the incidence. Rather than being the last person at the end of a communication chain, community people can use mobile technologies to engage in knowledge management with diverse people and systems. The knowledge and its representations is then, in part, owned by and connected to the producer, rather than being imposed externally. This has the potential to increase its effectiveness in introducing plant biosecurity measures and knowledge. Mobile learning had the potential to support Indigenous people to lead the best ways to share cultural, environmental, social and enterprise knowledge, as they are controlled by indigenous people. Trans-generational learning that includes a range of people was important to sharing and negotiating rules about how cultural and other knowledge or images are shared and represented. Mobile learning provided a vehicle for trans-generational teams to work together in the workplace to share cultural, workplace and digital knowledge with each team member demonstrating, and being valued for their strength.

Mobile learning building bridges to learner identities and their contexts

Knowledge management through mobile learning or any other approach is not benign or unproblematic. It is influenced by learners, trainers, workplace, industry and educational systems' social, cultural and historical structures. As mobile technologies and their use are a product of and a part of social and cultural practices, the issues related to social purpose are worth considering in developing their use for educational purposes, i.e. for mobile learning. Field (2005, pp. 115–116) discusses the impact of emerging technologies on social capital, the trust and reciprocal relationships between people in society and the development of communities and places in cyberspace 'where people actively construct their identities as parts of wider sets of shared relationships'. The use of mobile learning approaches presents opportunities to engage with a range of knowledge sets, constructs and contexts beyond those found in many formal or desk-based educational settings. This might include multimedia-based representations of diverse home life and beliefs systems, representations of knowledge as constructed by different social and cultural constructs. Though educational experiences, learners can use mobile learning to make connections between learners' worlds, make unfamiliar contexts more accessible and create ways of interpreting knowledge that reflect different ways of knowing. This also had the benefit of making visible the knowledge that could be invisible to external trainers and ensure learner is context driven.

> Digital tools create new possibilities for getting access to information, for producing sharing and reusing ...The main point is more and more people in our culture can take part on these remixing activities; not only elite or specific groups. Everyone engages in remix in this general sense of the idea ...what id ne is, of course, the impact of digital technologies. The possibilities of remixing all kinds of textual expressions and artefacts have thereby changed. (Erstad, 2008, p. 185)

People were engaged in accessing, capturing, interpreting, remixing and presenting information about their own and other's worlds in multimedia formats. They used their own and available devices to participate in the production and sharing of resources about their own lives without being restricted by extensive and expensive infrastructure. The opportunities for engagement of a range of people whose distance from major centres, economic realities or language background differ from the mainstream and have limited opportunities should not be underestimated. Mobile learning (learning that utilises mobile technologies) tools extended the ways information can be collected, formatted, mixed and shared, particularly as learners can use readily available technologies in socially approved and recognised ways. For example, young people taking photographs with mobile phones, creating digital stories about their lives or recording elders' oral histories.

Mobile technologies are frequently connected to people's lives, are used for people's own purposes for recording and communication information. These uses of mobile technologies focus on making meaning and connection beyond the educational to the social. Mobile devices provide opportunities for a wider group of people to create and share new forms of information using multimedia forms for their own purposes. By focussing on learners' strengths in audio and visual communication and spatial relations, rather then on a deficit technical English language written literacy, mobile learning was a point of connection for learners to demonstrating their own knowledge and learning new knowledge. Participating teams of learners have used the mobile learning approach to work by making and annotate videos on mobile devices about their work. The mobile technologies provided a point of reference to help assessors understand learners' perspective and skills in the workplace. While this has not been a huge issue in this project, it has potential for making connection in the future to trainers in less familiar areas. This can lead to a better assessment of learners' abilities and needs and development of a refined training programme.

Recognising learners' knowledge through mobile learning

The Recognition of Prior Learning (RPL) process recognises and records the knowledge and skills individuals have as it relates to their contexts and experience. One of the challenges in Aboriginal contexts is the recognition of community competence, that a group of rangers can undertake work as a team, each knowing parts of the process and know who and how to access the knowledge they need. Training plans can then be targeted to individual's actual needs and can then focus training time on their actual priority areas. The training framework includes mapping work-based tasks to training modules and the types of evidence that is collected on the job. This process recognises the valuable informal training that occurs when teams work together over time and develop confidence in their work-focussed competence. Mobile technologies provide a range of tools to collect evidence using written, visual and audio means. These technologies mean people can demonstrate their skills in their own context, language and time.

Portable, accessible mobile learning devices and software provided the powerful tools for people to share and interpret their knowledge in ways that are meaningful to them rather than only in relation to curriculum-based contexts. The use of technology in relation to Aboriginal people's work contexts incorporated ways of presenting ideas in visual, audio and written forms and for people at basic entry level of skill and technology to remix those forms as they understand it. Mobile technologies that utilise existing infrastructure reduced the reliance on expensive and site-specific connection technologies that are expensive to maintain such as satellites, wireless connections or laptop networks. Accessing SMS, GPS and digital cameras embedded in mobile telephones which are cheap and readily accessible, supports individuals' engagement in communication networks. That the technology is in people's pockets while they are engaged in daily work and learning activities increases the connectivity between that knowledge and people's own worlds. SMS and user familiar technologies are simple and cheap. They utilise language that is familiar and draws on simple language in people's own dialects. The images are of people's own worlds, representing people's experience accurately, providing a window to often unrecognised competence and realities. The information is shared in two ways that reciprocate the accountability to local communities and broader systems. One challenge is to ensure the ways information is shared back to community members retains its authenticity, accuracy and simple language or images.

The social contracts that manage the associated knowledge processes need to be negotiated in ways that recognise community based governance structures and the expectations of those who are collecting, assessing, analysing and reporting relevant information. This social contract might include differentiated roles for all participants, if so, the important issue is how the partnerships around using mobile technologies and managing knowledge are negotiated, understood and adhered to.

Considerations in the development of a mobile learning pedagogy

Pachler and Seipold (2009, p. 153) reject transmission and productivity-based concepts of mobile learning, noting that mobile learning definitions

> are often reductive in nature and foreground the delivery of content to mobile devices in small micro-units …instead we see mobile learning as concerning the processes of coming to know, and of being able to operate successfully in and across, new and ever changing contexts and learning spaces with and through the use of mobile devices.

A reflection on the experiences with Indigenous rangers leads to a number of observations that have moderated use of mobile learning. The impact of mobile technologies in learning experiences is connected to the way they are used. It is important to ensure that their use challenges, rather than replicates exclusionary processes and approaches. For example assuming that a non-hierarchical structure of knowledge is preferred by learners, connecting knowledge through images and allowing students to define the ways knowledge can be related and communicated. The introduction of single-use mobile technologies that do not address interoperability issues can be disconnected from learners' worlds and ongoing practice. The risk associated with this approach is that mobile technologies have a high cost as they are not used continually and connected to daily practice. As a consequence, the technologies are part of disenfranchising experiences of learning and will be rejected by learners, rather than recognising learners' strengths and building new skills.

The introduction of mobile technologies may be improved by focusing on learners' purposes and potential engagement in positive learning experiences. The technologies can reinforce the advantage of learning concepts in learners' first language and in relation to their own known contexts. The technologies that meet that need may not be the most exciting technologically, they are more likely be stable, simple to use and do not need the ongoing input of a facilitator. They can be owned and controlled by the learners in the workplace and the rest of their lives in the long term. When learning to use the mobile technology interferes with learning as it is frustrating to learn and relearn each time it is used, doesn't work when needed, takes longer than a non-technological solution, i.e. asking someone, learners will reject its use. It is important for mobile learning facilitators to invest themselves more in the learning outcomes and the learners needs than the introduction of a certain technology.

Improving learning outcomes for disenfranchised learners can be enhanced by mobile technologies. This is dependent on drawing on the affordances of mobile learning; that learners can incorporate and relate to their own contexts, use learning tools to which they already have a strong positive connection, learners own language, non-linear knowledge systems are accurately represented learners actively control their learning and assessment. Mobile learning opens opportunities to immediately incorporate the unexpected. The unexpected includes learners suggesting an approach to managing and interacting with knowledge that reflects their own and their workplaces knowledge structures or no using mobile technologies at all at that time. The evaluation of mobile learning approaches needs to differentiate between the attraction of a new technology and the impact on learning in the long term. As a consequence this project will be evaluated over several years allowing the technology to become backgrounded and learning outcomes to be fore-grounded.

Conclusion

Mobile technologies can operate outside a formal and often disenfranchising learning situation and move the learning space to where a learner is expert; for Indigenous rangers, this is in the field. Mobile technologies provide a vehicle for disenfranchised learners to take a leadership role in designing the way knowledge is collected, represented, organised, and protected in its context. That is, decisions can be made while in the field or undertaking sensitive work and institutions where Indigenous people are in control. Mobile learning supports learners to connect to their own learning and identity as an empowered learner. Learners are able to make their context, the centre of their learning experience and then provide a point of connection and recognition to industry-based recognition systems. Industry-based recognition might include nationally accredited qualifications, certificates or promotion. For Australian Indigenous rangers this includes units from the whole qualification in the Certificate II, III, IV or Diploma in Conservation Land Management, Business Management, Information Technology or Tourism based on their experience or moving from being a park ranger to a senior park ranger or a supervisor. This recognition is currently being undertaken with rangers in their workplace using their work-based and personal mobile technologies (i.e. iTracker and mobile phones). This is particularly important in communities with low levels of computer ownership and access to the internet. Mobile learning provides a platform for learners to actively engage in learning production and co-production in different languages, contexts in relation to their cultural governance structures. Mobile learning, then, can support the bridge between formal workplace learning and disenfranchised learners. The efficacy of mobile learning is based on a critical examination of the ways mobile technologies are used and the engagement of learning structures and connection to learners' own lives and purposes. The affordance of mobile learning, therefore, is its two-way process that provides ways for learners and institutions to interact and negotiate knowledge in ways that are meaningful, support the development of learner identities and connect learners, industry and formal educational systems (see also Pachler, Bachmair and Cook, 2010).

References

Altman, J. (2001) *Sustainable development options on Aboriginal land: The hybrid economy in the twenty-first century*. Canberra: Centre for Aboriginal Economic Policy Research, ANU

Australian Bureau of Statistics (2008) *Australian Social Trends, 4102.0* Canberra: ABS

Australian National Training Authority (2004) *Shaping our Future: Australia's National Strategy for VET 2004–2010*. Brisbane: ANTA

Bassanini, A. & Scarpetta, S. (2002) 'Does human capital matter for growth in OECD countries? A pooled mean-group approach.' *Economics Letters 74*(3), pp. 399–405

Beetham, H. (2007) 'An approach to learning activity design.' In Beetham, H. & Sharpe, R. (eds) *Rethinking pedagogy for a digital age: Designing and delivering e-learning*. Oxon: Routledge

Bourdieu, P. (1990) *The logic of practice*. Stanford: Stanford University Press (English translation of *Le Sens Pratique*. Paris: Taurus, 1980)

Christie, M. (2006) 'Traditional research and Aboriginal knowledge.' *Australian Journal of Indigenous Education 35*

Erstad, O. (2008) 'Trajectories of remixing: digital literacies, media production, and schooling.' In Lankshear, C. & Knobel, M. (eds), *Digital literacies* (pp. 177–202). New York: Peter Lang

European Union (2003) Decision No 2318/2003/EC of the European Parliament and of the Council of 5 December 2003 adopting a multiannual programme (2004 to 2006) for the effective integration of information and communication technologies (ICT) in education and training systems in Europe (eLearning Programme) (European Union) Official Journal of the European Union OJ L 345 of 31.12.2003 Available online at <http://europa.eu/eur-lex/pri/en/oj/dat /2003/l_34520031231en00090016.pdf> (accessed 01/06/08)

Falk, I. (2001) *Sleight of hand: Jobs myths, learning and social capital*. Report for the Centre for Research and Learning in Regional Australia (Launceston)

Falk, I. &. Balatti, J (2003) *Role of identity in VET learning*. Paper presented at the 11th Annual International Conference on Post-compulsory Education and Training, Gold Coast, Centre for Learning Research, Griffith University

Field, J. (2005) *Social capital and lifelong learning*. Bristol: The Policy Press

Gee, J. (2007) *Good video games + good learning: collected essays on video games, learning and literacy*. New York: Peter Lang

Gee, J. (2004) *Situated language and learning: A critique of traditional schooling*. New York: Routledge

Gee, J. (2003). *What video games have to teach us about learning and literacy*. New York: Palgrave Macmillan

Gillard, J. (2008) *A higher education revolution: Creating a productive, prosperous, modern Australia*. Report for Speech in Parliament House (Canberra)

Haythornthwaite, C. (2007) 'Digital divide and e-learning' In Andrews, R. & Haythornthwaite, C. (eds), *The Sage Handbook of E-learning Research* (pp. 97–118). London: Sage

Hugonnier, B. (1999) *Regional development tendencies in OECD countries*. Report for
    Keynote address to Regional Australia Summit, Parliament House (Canberra)
    Indigenous Economic Development Taskforce (2005) *Northern Territory Indigenous
    Economic Development Strategy*. Darwin: Northern Territory Government:
Jackson, M., Burton, D., & Kennett, R. (2009) *The I-tracker report: A review of the
    I-tracker data collection and management program across north Australia*. Darwin:
    North Australian Indigenous Land and Sea Management Alliance
Kearns, P. (1999) *Lifelong learning: implications for VET*. Adelaide: National Centre
    for Vocational Education Research
Kress & Pachler (2007) 'Thinking about the "m" in m-learning.' In Pachler, N. (ed.),
    Mobile learning: towards a research agenda. London: WLE Centre, IoE. Available
    online at <http://www.wlecentre.ac.uk/cms/files/occasionalpapers/mobilelearn-
    ing_pachler_2007.pdf>
Kukulska-Hulme, A., & Traxler, J. (2005) 'Mobile teaching and learning.' In Kukulska-
    Hulme, A. & Traxler, J. (eds), *Mobile Learning: A handbook for educators and
    trainers*. Oxon: Routledge, pp. 25–44
Lave, J., & Wenger, E. (1991) *Situated learning: Legitimate peripheral participation*.
    Cambridge, UK: Cambridge University Press
Litchfield, A., Dyson, L., Lawrence, E., & Zmijewska, A. (2007) 'Directions for
    m-learning research to enhance active learning.' *Proceedings ascilite Singapore*
Mendieta, E. (2003). 'Afterword. Identities: postcolonial and global'. In Alcoff, L. &
    Mendiata, E. (eds), *Identities: race, class, gender and nationality* (pp. 407–416).
    Oxford: Blackwell
Organisation for Economic Co-Operation and Development (2001) *The Well-being
    of nations: The role of human and social capital*. Paris: Report for Organisation
    for Economic Co-operation and Development
Pachler, N., Bachmair, B., & Cook, J. (2010) *Mobile learning: Structures, agency,
    practices*. New York: Springer
Pachler, N., & Seipold, J. (2009) 'Harnessing mobile devices to connect learning in
    formal and informal settings: the role of digital narratives and discontinuous
    text production for narratives and discontinuous text production for mean-
    ing making.' *Proceedings of the 8th World Conference on Mobile and Contextual
    Learning*, Orlando, Florida
Sharples, M., Taylor, J., & Vavoula, G. (2007) 'A theory of learning for the mobile age.'
    In Andrews, R., & Haythornthwaite, C. (eds), *The Sage Handbook of E-learning
    Research* (pp. 221–247). London: Sage
Snyder I. & Prinsloo M. (eds) (2007) 'The digital literacy practices of young people
    in marginal contexts.' *Language & Education: An international journal 21*(3),
    pp. 171–270

Traxler, J. (2008) *From text to context. Proceedings of the mLearn 2008 conference: The Bridge from Text to Context.* Ironbridge, UK

Voosloo S., Wilton, M. & Deumert, A. (2009) 'm4Lit: A Teen M-novel Project in South Africa.' *Proceedings of the 8th World Conference on Mobile and Contextual Learning,* Orlando, Florida

Wallace, R. (2008) *Identities of reluctant students: Constructions of learners' identity against educational institutions' best intentions.* Research monograph. Adelaide: NCVER

Wallace, R. (2009) 'Social partnerships in learning: Working across identity and learning boundaries.' *Proceedings of the Australian Vocational Education and Training Research Association,* Sydney, Australia

Wallace, R., Curry, C., & Agar, R. (2008) 'Working from our strengths: indigenous enterprise and training in action and research.' *Proceedings of the Australian Vocational Education and Training Research Association,* Adelaide, Australia

Learning and work processes:
Providing information on demand

CLAUDIA DE WITT, SONJA GANGUIN, MACIEJ KUSZPA
AND SANDRO MENGEL

7 Mobile learning in the process of work: Participation, knowledge and experience for professional development[1]

Abstract

Today's workforce is increasingly required to learn continuously and within a flexible timeframe. At present, however, there exists little research on the potential benefits of mobile learning in the process of work. Nevertheless, we can draw on experiences in the field of e-learning and professional development. With its technical features, mobile learning offers new didactical potentials. In this chapter some scenarios for the use of mobile learning are presented. Two target groups, professional drivers and apprentice electronics engineers, are characterised. Mobile learning scenarios are developed, implemented and evaluated within a research project for these occupational groups. Starting points for the design of didactic scenarios are learning practices and requirements, strategies as well as media use of the target groups. On the basis of this data concrete conclusions are drawn for the didactic and methodological realisation of the project. The evaluation design of the research process is explained with respect to the phases of planning, implementation and execution. Initial results support the view that, comparable to e-learning, the conceptual design strongly depends on the needs analysis of target groups; in addition, mobile learning in the process of work has to be aligned with the specifics of the respective work situation.

1   This chapter was translated from German into English by the editors.

Introduction

This chapter is based on initial results from a research project that focuses on mobile learning in the process of work. It presents the comprehensive evaluation concept of the project and focuses on how to conceptualise didactic scenarios for mobile learning in such situations. For example, how much text should be displayed on a mobile device? Which content is suitable for which mobile scenarios? How can contextual, cooperative and participatory learning be put into practice? What do concrete learning situations look like? The challenge lies in finding out whether the hypothesis which prevail in the literature, namely that learning takes place independently of time and location, align with practices of mobile learning in the process of work.

Mobile learning can be viewed as a specific form of e-learning through the extended context of mobility. This is the view taken in this chapter and findings from the field of e-learning are taken into account. Theoretical approaches, didactic requirements and evaluation measures which are relevant for e-learning should, therefore, be considered in the development of mobile learning scenarios in the process of work. However, due to the technical particularities of mobile devices and in view of the extended mobile context of use it is necessary to adapt existing didactic scenarios. The ambition is to raise potential benefits of mobility for activities and professional development.

Mobile learning can be of value for all types of occupational groups. Various companies are obliged to train their employees on a regular basis, for example in the field of occupational health and safety regulated by the German Occupational Health and Safety Act. These instructions are mainly classroom training at the company's headquarters and should guarantee safe and health-conscious behaviour of employees at work. Employees who travel a lot and work at constantly changing locations with a flexible agenda also have to participate in compliance training. Professional drivers constitute an occupational group where it is hard to agree on a fixed training schedule. In many cases this training is, therefore, conducted on weekends usually in people's free time. For long-distance lorry drivers flexible training and the independence of time and location appear to be a promising alternative to traditional professional development.

Despite a considerable number of examples of mobile learning (see e.g. Vavoula, Pachler and Kukulska-Hulme, 2009) not much knowledge about mobile learning in the process of work exists at present. This suggests the need for the development of a number of different didactic concepts for learning in professional environments. Mobile learning does not replace any of the existing didactic concepts but extends the possibilities of media and, thereby, also the didactic dissemination of knowledge, competences and experiences in the process of work.

In the following sections a couple of scenarios are characterised which appear to be suitable for mobile learning in the field of professional development. We describe a comprehensive evaluation concept which is based on different phases and methods (quantitative online survey, qualitative interviews, learning diaries, knowledge tests etc.). We present initial results from the research project on learning with mobile devices in the fields of professional drivers and electronics engineer apprentices (e.g. socio-demographic data, media use, learning requirements and strategies). Finally, the consequences for the didactic design of mobile learning for these target groups are discussed.

Mobile learning in professional development

The expansion of the internet has changed work practices and structures in production, trade, services and administration; these new practices have been well established by now in these fields. The internet has become an integral element of socio-cultural as well as work-related information and communication structures. Cheap and powerful mobile devices with ubiquitous access to the internet and simple applications allow the production and sharing of content for everyone. That progress has already led to significant changes in user habits and learning cultures. In the debate on lifelong learning the linkage of knowledge acquisition and work is of great importance for individuals.

The model of learning in the process of work integrates learning and work, they exist in parallel. 'Informal, activity-orientated and experience-based learning processes are linked with organised learning in decentralised learning spaces at work' (Dehnbostel, 1997, p. 5; translated from German). In this context, the methodological concept of a workprocess-orientated approach to teaching and learning is seen as the future concept for professional development (cf. Rogalla, 2007, p. 22). This point of view extends traditional instructional perspectives of learning with constructivist approaches. It takes current didactic development strands in professional development into account that are based on the principles of authenticity, situatedness and social inclusion (see Reinmann-Rothmeier & Mandl, 1998; de Witt & Czerwionka, 2007).

The close relationship of learning and work and real tasks constitute the framework of learning processes. 'Situated and mostly subconscious learning at work is, however, not left to chance but consciously designed. Formal and informal learning are linked .... Autonomous, self-directed learning in holistic and comprehensive work tasks encourages up-to-date subject and workprocess knowledge as well as the skills required' (BMBF, 2007, p. 14; cf. Dehnbostel, 1997; translated from German).

Both the model of activity-orientated learning (see Babel & Hackl, 2004) and the model of workprocess-orientated learning (see Dehnbostel, 2007) are based on similar principles. They are currently used in traditional as well as in innovative scenarios including the deployment of digital media in professional development (see Treichel & Mayer, 2004; Bremer, 2005). If a rapid change of learning content is required, the sole use of traditional media is insufficient. Supported by modern digital information and communication technologies, learning content can be prepared and structured on demand and at short notice. They can be integrated in learning processes relatively easily according to situational requirements. Through learning forms such as e-learning and mobile learning, content can be accessed in a manner that is situation-specific, personalised and independent of location and time. Informal, activity-orientated and experience-based learning processes are enabled at decentralised places at work. In order to increasingly implement mobile learning scenarios in professional development and in the learning cultures of the companies tailored concepts are needed which are aligned to the specifics of the respective industry.

In some industries mobile learning pilot projects are already in evidence. However, there is certainly potential for further educational opportunities involving mobile phones. Learning modules that can serve as reference work as well as for the training of subject knowledge en route might be used in manufacturing industries such as arts and crafts, for example in the area of material science for metal-workers and carpenters. Due to occupational safety hazards the issue of accident prevention is of continuous importance in the construction industry. In such a context, access to material on occupational safety based on mobile devices can provide additional value. Therefore, mobile learning can be used to offer codes of behaviour on occupational safety. It can provide information on demand, e.g. in case of unexpected problems such as accidents with hazardous material or in order to avoid long-term damage through unnatural posture.

Mobile learning devices are already used in medicine. The content deals with prevention, identification and treatment of human injuries and diseases. For example, the innovation network 'PflegeWissen' (<http://www.projekt-pflegewissen.de>) aims to provide self-directed, work-related learning for care professionals through multimedia learning modules. The systematic integration of these qualification measures in work processes is crucial as is their anchoring as fixed elements in professional development. Learning modules on critical, practice-orientated content accessible through mobile phones by ambulant care professionals have already been developed. In addition to traditional professional development provision the Helios Academy (<http://www.helios-akademie.de>) offers short learning videos, which can be accessed on mobile devices. The videos on anatomic and therapeutic issues, which were specifically adapted for mobile phones, are not only available to doctors but also to care professionals and even to patients.

If the content is adequately adapted to the medium then the use of mobile learning can be applied in many other industries or fields of knowledge. Mobile learning is suitable for all occupational groups that require a certain degree of mobility. This does not, however, exclude office workers who, for example, can practise technical terminology through mobile phones to improve their knowledge on their way to work.

Didactic implementation of mobile learning in occupational practice

The scope of our research project 'mobile learning process-related information seeking and learning in changing work-contexts' at the Institut für Bildungswissenschaft und Medienforschung (IfBM) at the FernUniversität in Hagen includes the development, implementation and evaluation of mobile learning applications for different target groups in the context of their work and professional development (project length: 3 years). The target groups are professional drivers and apprentice electronics engineers. In this chapter, we discuss implementation examples from these occupational groups that can be included in concrete didactic conceptualisations of mobile learning scenarios.

Example 1: Mobile learning for professional drivers

The work of professional truck drivers operating in national and international markets is characterised by changing work schedules and places. This leads to a particular demand for professional development because the group cannot easily participate in classroom training. Nevertheless, even this highly mobile group is subject to lifelong learning needs and, as part of the legal obligations of freight service companies, requires ongoing training in occupational safety. Topics include securing of loads with consideration of safety regulations and the prevention of health-related harm.

Volume and complexity of relevant content make them perfectly suitable for implementation as mobile learning. Besides text-based instruction and access to regulations relevant to occupational safety and accident prevention, learning modules that show risks of road traffic and the correct behaviour in cases of emergency can be also used. Therefore, a target group-orientated design of audiovisual learning modules in the form of videos of 3 to 5 minutes is planned; these videos can be accessed on demand by learners through self-study. Furthermore, learning results can be tracked and integrated in a central learning management platform with the help of mobile radio transmission. This helps to encourage a better understanding of learning content with the assistance of skilled personnel at the head office. The automatic tracking of learning progress provides opportunities to close knowledge gaps with additional learning modules. Interactive knowledge games that are embedded in learning modules offer learners control over their learning progress.

Technical pre-requisites for learning 'on the road' often exist in the driver cabins. Navigation and mobile devices are often standard issue, particularly for long-distance truck drivers, so that ideally no further expense for mobile learning is incurred. Consequently, knowledge and skills are acquired directly at work through familiar media. The outcome can be applied immediately after the learning phases. On the basis of the given infrastructure the advantages, namely the reduction of training costs and the temporal variability of learning, can also be transferred to related areas in the freight industry. This can include modules for gaining and strengthening language skills, but also foreign transport law or topics around motor vehicle maintenance and cleaning.

Example 2: Mobile learning for the training of apprentice electronics engineers

Electronics engineers are a state-recognised, skilled occupation in Germany. A three-year period of training in the so-called 'dual system' is required. The apprentices are educated at the workplace and at a vocational school. In view of the fact that mainly young people start such vocational training after their compulsory education, on the one hand a technically highly skilled group is targeted with mobile learning; on the other hand, the learners are confronted with content on power- and building-engineering or machine- and drive-technology in many situations outside their vocational training. So the deployment of mobile technologies makes sense for this occupational group.

Curriculum subjects such as mathematics or physics appear to be appropriate for implementation on comparably small devices. Calculations of mathematical formulas or the meaning of graphical symbols can be trained through multiple choice tasks in short learning sequences of 5 to 10 minutes. The matching of graphical symbols and the correct use of technical vocabulary can be improved and deepened through glossaries and appropriate tests.

The use of mobile learning by apprentice electronics engineers allows individualised learning demands of heterogeneous target groups to be addressed better. Apprentice electronics engineers include learners with different educational backgrounds comprising a range of school types. In addition to the provision of classroom-based training, self-directed learning is used to achieve the mastery and application of basic knowledge by the comparatively young and professionally inexperienced target group. Learning is based on frequent repetition of content. It is conceivable that, given appropriate levels of motivation, learners engage in practice outside school using familiar media – mobile phones – for example on their way to school or at the workplace and particularly in their free time.

Learning 'on the road' should not be limited to mobile phones but should also encourage social interaction. Prompt support by the teacher can be provided through the creation of a micro-blogging feature. Such a system can also encourage exchanges between apprentices and allow the formation of virtual learning groups. The involvement of teachers in such a system can enable manual and automated assessment and learners can receive prompt and comprehensive feedback. In addition to the transmission of text-based messages, learners can take pictures with their mobile phones in situations in which they don't know how to proceed in order to discuss their uncertainties with others. In order to document the learning situation in more detail, the deployment of QR or barcodes is also conceivable with which the mobile device can identify objects and machines automatically and be linked to learning content.

The technical realisation of mobile learning does not only require standard mobile phones; in addition, a server-based infrastructure has to be set up in order to respond to the mobility of learners. Learners have to commute between school, company and, optionally, also between different work sites. Furthermore, teachers need administration and communication tools to address individual needs as well as to conduct the coaching of groups of learners. If mobile learning is employed on a production site or in the field, the robustness of the devices also has to be taken into account. Humid and dusty environments of workplaces can impact on electronic and mechanical parts and can result in contamination and physical damage of the devices.

Factors with impact on the didactic and methodological design
of a mobile learning platform

For the didactic and methodological design of mobile learning the following factors have to be considered (see Figure 7.1).

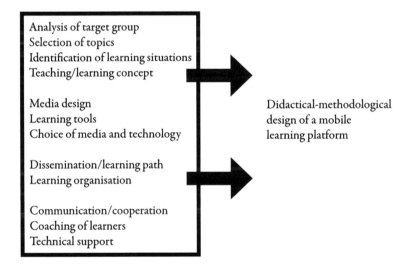

Figure 7.1 Elements of a didactical-methodological design

Learning strategies, practices and requirements of target groups form the basis of the didactic and methodological design of a mobile learning platform. The use of different didactic methods, such as quizzes or the integration of multimedia and augmented reality but as well as virtual coaching,

156   C. DE WITT, S. GANGUIN, M. KUSZPA AND S. MENGEL

will be piloted in this project. In addition to short learning sequences, features supporting communication and cooperation will be implemented in order to address problems that arise in work processes and to facilitate activity-orientated decision-making. In this context not only the expertise of teachers but also the experiences and knowledge of peers should be accessed; in the process they experience appreciation. Moreover, the opportunity to participate in problem-solving with one's own experiences and ideas is very important. It contributes to the feeling of joint responsibility.

Multiple choice questions and cloze tests are frequently used to support the learning process. For this research project, methods for activity-orientated knowledge and sustained professional competences (e.g. network graphs) will be developed for use in employees' own work-processes through mobile learning. The aim is to meet the practical requirements of the target groups. Learning practices, media competence and characteristics of the professional context of learners are all crucial for the selection of appropriate didactic methods with mobile devices.

Evaluation design

A particular challenge is evaluation or, more specifically, the question of what should be evaluated. Here our focus is firstly on technology for mobile learning and secondly on the mobile learning process. The evaluation process is centred on the one hand on didactic scenarios suitable for mobile learning in the process of work; on the other hand we concentrate on the question of how motivation for, and acceptance of mobile learning by different occupational groups can reach a sustainable level. The potential, the requirements and the didactic methods for participatory, cooperative learning on mobile platforms are explored as well as changes in learning efficiency through the use of audio and video material on mobile devices. This implies a dual challenge. In order to clarify both perspectives and their associated requirements, the overall approach is briefly explained here before the individual phases are illustrated.

The research accompanying the project places great importance on the consideration of different didactic approaches. Also, the development of their own initiative by employees through their professional development is taken into account. And, opportunities offered by social networks through Web 2.0 technologies in terms of didactic advice are considered. Upon the identification of suitable learning content for the target groups of the respective companies, didactic scenarios are developed and tested. The needs of the target groups determine the specification of hardware requirements and selection.

The evaluation design of the project takes into account that evaluation methods vary and that methodical usage differs across different occupational contexts and target-groups. Due to the different work-contexts of the target groups involved the evaluation of the three-year project was based on specific occupational baseline conditions. Despite the varying phases of the evaluation process and the different methods used in the individual phases, we propose a general framework which provides the basis for individual projects. The research design of the overall evaluation can be seen as a starting point for the projects and offers a frame of reference for individual evaluations.

The evaluation process can be divided in three phases. The first phase can be understood as the planning phase. The associated analytical perspective, which follows an active, process-orientated and constructive approach, can be considered as ex ante. This is followed by the implementation phase centred on the ongoing adaption and optimisation of learning content, didactic scenarios and the technical infrastructure. Finally, in the execution phase, the implemented educational scenario is researched, for example with respect to attainment or acceptance by users, in order to create generalisable recommendations (see Figure 7.2).[2]

---

2   By-and-large these three phases of the evaluation process draw on the dimensions of the evaluation research according to Stockmann (2007).

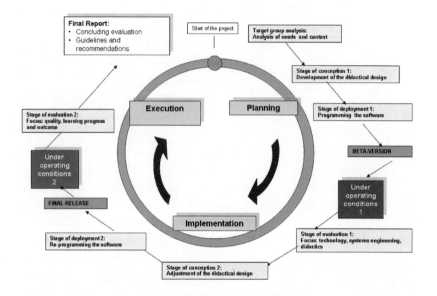

Figure 7.2 Phases of the three-year evaluation process of the mobile learning project

Planning phase

The planning phase is necessary for the development of the mobile learning proposal. The focus is on the conceptual design of the mobile learning application in order to identify important parameters of the framework and 'to contribute to the development of the program design' (Stockmann, 2007, p. 33; see also Brandtstädter, 1990, p. 217; translated from German).

Due to the involvement of diverse occupational groups in this research project (maintenance employees, professional drivers, apprentice electronics engineers) an analysis of the respective target groups has to be conducted first. The intention of the initial survey becomes apparent when taking the different conditions of the workplaces into account. Moreover, the different occupational groups imply different socio-demographic, social- and media-ecological characteristics. In a first step, therefore, the different conditions concerning the conceptual design of the learning application must be accommodated. This means to identify (a) the relevant learning content, (b) the most suitable technological infrastructure (devices) and (c) to analyse learning conditions and requirements of the different occupational groups. These three aspects are relevant to develop a didactically sound mobile learning scenario for the respective target group.

For this purpose, talks with the respective cooperation partners were conducted. The research team approached the contact persons in the field of professional development for expert interviews. This exchange provided first insight into the institutions taking part, their conditions for work and professional development. The findings of these interviews were documented and served as a starting point for the design of a quantitative online questionnaire.[3]

Secondly, a base-line survey was conducted with the target groups. All participants of the projects were asked to complete online questionnaires. The online questionnaires – a separate questionnaire was designed for each target group – comprised the following aspects: (a) socio-demographic data, (b) information on media use and media competence, (c) information on learning behaviours, demands, strategies and experiences, and (d) personal views on mobile learning. In addition to the online survey, preferences concerning didactic and technical devices as well as expected disadvantages and potential advantages were identified.

To begin with the evaluation was primarily centred on univariate analysis, aiming at the provision of a general overview of the conditions, practices and requirements of the respective target group. The analysis addressed, for example, the question of learning practices or media preferences of the average professional driver and the average apprentice electronics engineer. Afterwards the individual data sets were brought together to a combined data set in relation to corresponding variables. This allowed the research team to gauge group-specific characteristics as well as general characteristics and compare them with each other. The findings and results are necessary

---

3   The online questionnaire was based on the program 'Limesurvey'.

to develop a didactic design for the respective occupational groups and to implement it at a programming level on the mobile devices.

For this purpose teaching content has to be defined. The content has to be geared to the required or the desired themes for professional development of the different target groups. Seven mobile learning episodes within the umbrella topic 'health and work protection' were implemented on mobile devices for the group of truck drivers. The selected learning content is methodically and didactically prepared by means of a storyboard.

Initially different didactic approaches were contrasted and tested in terms of their practicability. Methodical and didactic aspects, which respond to the specific work and learning conditions of each occupational group, were developed on the basis of scientific research and the policy objectives of an evolving innovative qualification within the work process. Therefore, a concrete didactic concept for all partners involved in the project does not exist, which is subsequently evaluated. Based on the respective target group the following components are taken into account:

(a) varying work environments and sites for learning;
(b) extent and manner of how the learning content is represented;
(c) didactic methods;
(d) acceptance of mobile devices;
(e) enhancement of the motivation to learn; and
(f) interaction and communication factors.

Completion of the beta version of the learning software for the different target groups represents the end of the first phase of testing.

Implementation phase

After the learning software is available as a beta version, the first trial phase will be carried out. For this purpose, criteria were developed, the results of which are documented in an evaluation catalogue. Test persons and the project partners from individual co-operating institutions will take the tests. In this way, the beta version is evaluated in the framework of a holistic evaluation design by means of oral and written interviews with the respective target groups and the teachers. Existing evaluation tools are used and, if necessary, amended. For the first round of implementation under operating conditions a time span of three to four months is envisaged. On the basis of the results of the beta tests and their interpretation bug-fixing of the learning software is carried out. The resulting pre-release is then tested against errors. Further errors, which might occur, will be fixed and the software will be released as version 1.0.

Execution phase

After the release of version 1.0 the second trial under operating conditions of the learning software and the didactic scenario will be realised. The attendant evaluation will implement oral and written interviews of the target groups. The aims of the evaluation are quality assurance, examination of the comprehensibility of the learning content in terms of the applicability what is learnt as part of daily job routines as well as the examination of usability of the learning scenarios and software that have been developed. In addition, large-scale assessments are carried out analysing the completed interactive knowledge questions which are asked at the end of each learning unit. Furthermore, data for the analysis and interpretation are based on the analysis of log-files and learning diaries. The result of the evaluation allows conclusions about the efficiency and acceptance of this kind of training in comparison with traditional methods. The whole process is scientifically supported and the evaluation results are analysed from a scientific perspective. The final report marks the end of this phase. It will include substantiated statements regarding the applicability of the chosen didactic scenarios, about acceptance, about efficiency of learning compared with conventional professional development schemes and software usability. Furthermore, recommendations for sustainable activities for vocational training practice for the target groups in question are provided.

In the following key results of the analysis of the target group as part of the planning phase are introduced.

How professional truck drivers and apprentice electronics engineers want to learn whilst being mobile

Random sampling

The professional truck drivers

The data collection was carried out during October 2009. Data was collected from a total of 27 people from a German truck company using standardised online questionnaires. All participants in the survey were male. Their average age was 43 (SD [standard deviation] = 9.00); the youngest participant being 23 year old, the oldest 61. The majority of the professional truck drivers (i.e. 17 persons) held formal general secondary education (ISCED IIa; i.e. 'Realschulabschluss'). A middle to lower level of education of the professional truck drivers interviewed can be assumed. Furthermore, the majority of interviewees had completed their professional education as professional truck driver (59.3 per cent); 37 per cent are career changers who originally graduated from different apprenticeships, e.g. painter, farmer or metalworker. Analogous to their age there are differences to the duration of practising the job. The minimum duration of their professional life is two years, the maximum 42 years (i.e. range = 40 years); the average is 19 years (SD = 9.2). Furthermore, most of the professional truck drivers interviewed are appointed to work in the area of long-distance transport (81.5 per cent), the rest in long- as well as in short-distance transportation (18.5 per cent). In conclusion, the 'average' professional truck driver interviewed can be characterised as male, about 43 years old, with a middle level of education and with more than 19 years experience as truck driver.

Apprentice electronics engineers

The second phase of data collection was realised during January 2010 at a German vocational school for metalworking / electronic engineering. A total of 41 vocational electronic engineering students were interviewed by using a standardised online-questionnaire. 40 of them were male, one female. Analogous to the gender ratio of the professional truck drivers the profession of electronics engineers can also be described as male dominated. Whilst in general 55 per cent of males and 45 per cent of females are holding down employment, only 3 per cent of females choose the professional career of an electronics engineer, 13 per cent of an electrical device constructor (see Bundesagentur für Arbeit 2008, p. 6). The age average of the apprentices interviewed was 18 years (SD = 2.00); the youngest participant in the survey was 16 years old, the oldest 22. The majority of apprentices (i.e. 32 people) have a formal general secondary education (ISCED IIa; i.e. 'Realschulabschluss'). The respondents were asked about their precise professional training: 43.9 per cent are completing an apprenticeship as electrician with specialisation in power engineering and building services engineering; 56.1 per cent had chosen a specialisation in information and communication technology. When asked for their main operational area, 39 per cent indicated construction sites, 17.1 per cent homes, 22 per cent company and further 22 per cent 'other'. By way of summary, the 'average' apprentice electronics engineer can be characterised as being male, about 18 years old and having a middle educational level.

Initial results of the target group analysis

Initial experiences with new media

Within the scope of the analysis of the socio-demographic data of the target groups as well as details of their media use, media literacy, needs for learning content and issues as well as learning habits were identified. It became clear that the target groups had little to no experience with mobile learning and only some experience with self-directed learning. But according to their statements their motivation for mobile learning within their working processes is very high.

Comparing the target groups interviewed one can observe definite trends in their experiences with new media which seem to correlate with the participants' age. For example, 37 per cent of the interviewed professional truck drivers assess their ICT knowledge as being 'low' or 'very low', whereas this applies to only 5 per cent of the apprentice electronics engineers. Answers to the question about them coping with different computer applications are similar with the younger target group having more advanced skills. By putting the focus of the analysis on frequency of use of different technical devices it is interesting to observe a certain 'professional socialisation' which indicates profession-specific media use. Figure 7.3 evidences this. Whilst professional truck drivers, who are permanently en route, are using the mobile phone as well as other portable devices (e.g. portable DVD player, laptop) frequently for work-related purposes, the teenage apprentice electronics engineers are more advanced in terms of the non-portable medium of PC and in particular in relation to modern entertainment media (e.g. portable gaming consoles).

Frequency of different media use

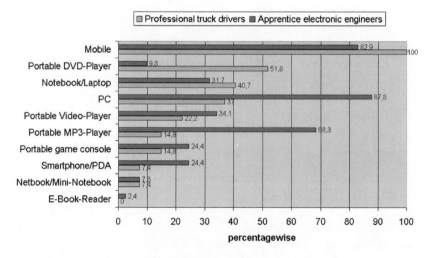

Figure 7.3 Frequency of using different technological devices.
Categories 'very often' and 'often' are merged; n = 68.

Learning strategies and learning needs

In relation to the learning mode favoured by both professional guilds, data indicate that respondents are trying out things on the basis of personal motivation. This subjective need corresponds to the general attitude towards professional development in Germany as evaluated by the Federal Ministry of Education and Research. According to the report *Berichtssystem Weiterbildung IX*, learning through observation and trial-and-error at the workplace is in first place with 84 per cent as most popular further education mode (BMBF, 2006, p. 277). Whilst Figure 7.3 indicates clear differences between the different professional guilds interviewed, Figure 7.4 shows that the professional truck drivers and the apprentice electronics engineers differ in matters of learning strategies only in specific areas.

Professional truck drivers lead the category 'playful learning' which, according to the details provided, is linked to the fact that the game-versed electricians don't want their leisure time activities to be misappropriated for other purposes. According to this finding, the so-called 'digital natives' (Prensky, 2001) do not seem to be specifically attached to game-based learning. Therefore, Prensky's demand to conceptionalise a new learning approach for pupils, students and apprentices of today, who want to learn by using computer games and who suspend the difference between gaming and work, seems empirically disputable.

The clear lead of electronics engineers within the category 'internet-assisted learning' could have several reasons: one could be a generation-specific phenomenon whereby the young apprentices are more used to the internet as knowledge and information resource. On the other hand it is possible that the mobile professional truck drivers – due to their work-patterns – are rarely able to access the internet in order to retrieve information as required. This assumption is underpinned by the following data: when asked for the frequency of using the internet, 87.8 per cent of the apprentices indicate that they use the world wide web 'very often', whereas this applies only to 25.9 per cent of the professional truck drivers.

According to Figure 7.4, both occupational groups differ only a little in relation to the other categories (except for 'learning in groups'). In both groups learning strategies and learning needs, which support self-

166   C. DE WITT, S. GANGUIN, M. KUSZPA AND S. MENGEL

determination, prevail. They prefer to deal with specific tasks and opportunities and to try things out. This could be captured by the notion of
'learning-by-doing' – a learning strategy that is well accepted by both professional groups. Flexibility of time and place for learning is more important
for professional truck drivers than for apprentice electronic engineers.
However, notes as reminders are relevant for both target groups.

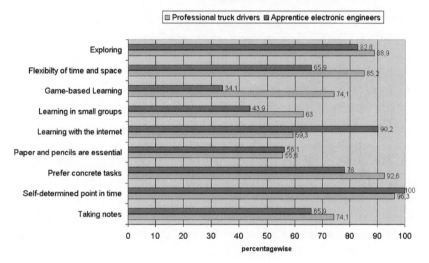

Figure 7.4 Learning strategies and needs.
Categories 'I fully agree' and 'I rather agree' are merged, n = 68.

Problems encountered during learning

If the professional truck drivers or the apprentice electrical engineers
encounter problems during their learning, they seek support from their
colleagues or mainly solve comprehension problems on their own. Figure
7.5 shows – as did Figure 7.4 – that there are no serious differences between
the professional groups, except for the category 'if I encounter problems, I
seek for help from my instructor' respectively 'training staff'. The difference
in this category probably relates to specific experiences with the current
instructor and cannot, by implication, be generalised.

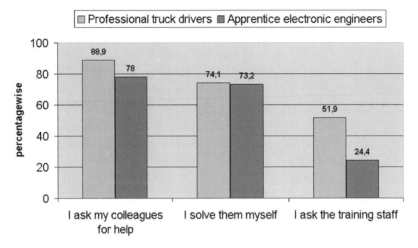

Figure 7.5 Problems encountered during learning.
Categories 'I fully agree' and 'I rather agree' are merged; *n* = 68.

Experiences in the field of online learning

On the one hand, online learning is practised rather rarely (especially by professional truck drivers); the answer 'I don't agree' has the highest consent in both professional groups. On the other hand, the wide difference between the two professional groups of truck drivers and electronic engineers is evident. This could again derive from age-related differences in the general use of the internet. But it would also be plausible that the work-related low use of the internet by mobile truck drivers has consequences for online learning.

How do we learn best

The data suggest that the target groups learn best if they undertake practical tasks and if they appropriate knowledge with the help of case studies. Furthermore, Figure 7.6 clearly shows a structural difference between these two professional groups that has consequences for their learning. Electricians do not prefer discussions with colleagues as a favourite learning mode. This is different in the case of professional truck drivers, who are a very communicative occupational group. For truck drivers the exchange with others is essential, be it recreational activities with colleagues, information exchange relating to stop-and-search operations or assistance in the case of breakdowns and accidents. These differences between the professional drivers and the apprentices are reflected in the answers: 'I learn best independently without instructions' and 'through discussions with colleagues'. These results clarify the different demands of heterogeneous target groups. For example truck driver need more and other possibilities to communicate and cooperate with colleagues in learning processes than electricians do. These findings have to be considered by deploying the different didactical scenarios for the target groups.

I learn best...

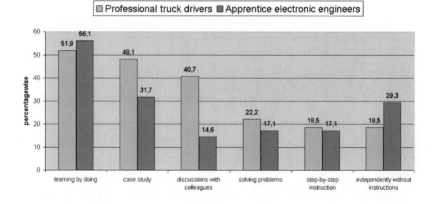

Figure 7.6 'I learn best ...' Category 'I fully agree'; *n* = 68.

Didactic implications and future steps

Initial results on mobile learning during work processes, which are available, suggest – as did the requirement analyses related to the implementation of e-learning measures – that each professional group has specific conditions, work situations and learning cultures. For this reason a unified approach to mobile learning for work process in general is not adequate. It is also evident that self-determined and application-orientated learning as well as flexibility of time and place are favoured across professional groups. The didactic and methodical design has to relate to specific challenges. Contextual learning can be realised through anytime and ubiquitous information and knowledge. Making notes and engaging in case study work is part of a mobile learning situation as is participating in the practice-related know-how and the work experience of colleagues. For this reason, applications which integrate communicative exchange are an important element during mobile learning time. For the methodical implementation the need for balance between free exploration of learning content and step-by-step instructions emerges.

However, theoretical models are an important basis for describing parameters that can be an incentive for the successful integration of mobile learning into working processes of specific professional groups. The socio-ecological approach of mobile learning by Pachler (2010) and Pachler, Bachmair and Cook (2010) as well as the theory of mobile learning for a mobile society by Sharples, Taylor and Vavoula (2007) emphasise the communicative interaction and participation in a mobile learning culture. Inspired by this, one of the next challenges within our research is the development of a didactic framework model for mobile learning within working processes which accommodates the work-related competence and the knowledge gained by experience of those involved. A further goal is to introduce certification for professional development to be gained through mobile learning.

References

Babel, H., & Hackl, B. (2004) 'Handlungsorientierter Unterricht – Dirigierter Aktionismus oder partizipative Kooperation.' In Treichel, D., & Mayer, H. (eds) *Handlungsorientiertes Lernen und eLearning* (pp. 11–35). München: Oldenbourg

Brandtstädter, J. (1990) 'Evaluationsforschung. Probleme der wissenschaftlichen Bewertung von Interviews – und Reformprojekten.' *Zeitschrift für Pädagogische Psychologie 4 (4)*, pp. 215–228

Bremer, C. (2005) 'Handlungsorientiertes Lernen mit Neuen Medien.' In Lehmann, B. & Bloh, E. (eds), *Online-Pädagogik – Band 2 – Methodik und Content-Management*. Baltmannsweiler. Available online at <http://www.bremer.cx/paper24/bremer_online_paedagogik2005.pdf> (accessed 01/03/10)

Bundesagentur für Arbeit (2008) *Elektro. Weiterbildung und Beruf. Informationen für Arbeitnehmer/innen.* Ausgabe 2007/2008. Nürnberg. Available online at http://infobub.arbeitsagentur.de/bbz/hefte/BBZ_14_Elektro.pdf (accessed 11/02/10)

Bundesministerium für Bildung und Forschung (BMBF) (2006) *Berichtssystem Weiterbildung IX. Integrierter Gesamtbericht zur Weiterbildungssituation in Deutschland.* Berlin. Available online at <http://www.bmbf.de/pub/berichtssystem_weiterbildung_neun.pdf> (accessed 01/03/10)

Bundesministerium für Bildung und Forschung (BMBF) (2007) *Neue Medien in der beruflichen Bildung. Digitale Medien eröffnen der beruflichen Aus- und Weiterbildung neue Chancen.* Bonn, pp. 6–7

de Witt, C., & Czerwionka, T. (2007) *Mediendidaktik.* Studientexte für Erwachsenenbildung. Bielefeld: Bertelsmann

Dehnbostel, P. (1997) 'Erweiterte didaktisch-methodische Ansätze in der betrieblichen Berufsbildung.' In Leonardo da Vinci, *Aktionsprogramm zur Durchführung einer Berufsbildungspolitik der europäischen Gemeinschaft* (pp. 3–6). Pilot. Heft 2. Thema: Didaktisch-methodische Ansätze in der Ausbildung

Dehnbostel, P. (2007) *Lernen im Prozess der Arbeit.* Münster: Waxmann

Pachler, N. (2010) 'The socio-cultural ecological approach to mobile learning.' In Bachmair, B. (ed.), *Medienbildung in neuen Kulturräumen* (pp. 153–167). Wiesbaden: VS Verlag

Pachler, N., Bachmair, B., & Cook, J. (2010) *Mobile learning: Structures, agency, practices.* New York: Springer

Prensky, M. (2001) *Digital game-based learning.* New York: McGraw-Hill

Reinmann-Rothmeier, G., & Mandl, H. (1998) 'Lernen in Unternehmen. Von einer gemeinsamen Vision zu einer effektiven Förderung des Lernens.' In Dehnbostel, P., Erbe, H.-H., & Novak, H. (eds), *Berufliche Bildung im lernenden Unternehmen: Zum Zusammenhang von betrieblicher Reorganisation, neuen Lernkonzepten und Persönlichkeitsentwicklung* (pp. 195–216). Berlin: Edition Sigma

Rogalla, I. (2007) 'Das Konzept der Zukunft. Arbeitsprozessorientierte Weiterbildung.' In BMBF: *Neue Medien in der beruflichen Bildung. Digitale Medien eröffnen der beruflichen Aus- und Weiterbildung neue Chancen* (p. 22). Berlin

Sharples, M., Taylor, J., & Vavoula, G. (2007) 'A theory of learning for the mobile age.' In Andrews, R. & Haythornthwaite, C. (eds), *The Sage Handbook of E-Learning Research* (pp. 221–247). London: Sage

Stockmann, R. (2007) 'Einführung in die Evaluation.' In ibid. (ed.), *Handbuch zur Evaluation. Eine praktische Handlungsanleitung* (pp. 24–70). Münster: Waxmann

Vavoula, G., Pachler, N., & Kukulska-Hulme, A. (eds) (2009) *Researching mobile learning*. Oxford: Peter Lang

GEOFF STEAD AND MARTIN GOOD

8 Mobile learning in vocational settings: Lessons from the E-Ten BLOOM project

Abstract

The BLOOM project (Bite-sized Learning Opportunities On Mobiles) ran from 2007 to 2009 in Austria, Germany and the UK, supported by the EU. It aimed to find out whether mobile learning was a fit-for-purpose and commercially viable solution for the passenger transport and logistics (PTL) industries in Europe. The rationale was that the PTL workforce is mobile by definition and cannot easily rely on face-to-face training or even e-learning. However, it faces a constant stream of legislation; the technology is constantly changing; 'green' issues demand new skills; many drivers need support with literacy, numeracy or foreign languages; skills such as customer service have increased importance. The PTL sector was chosen partly because its drivers already use mobile technology in lorries, buses and taxis, so the 'learning journey' would probably be easier for them. Did all that mean that employers and employees would be interested in mobile learning? In all three countries the response was positive: stakeholders saw benefits in using existing content, adapting and customising it locally and even in generating their own content using mobile authoring tools. Many topics, e.g. driving regulations, customer service, literacy, numeracy, IT skills and health and safety were relevant in all countries. Mobile learning showed itself to be a useful component within a wider blend of methods and media.

Introduction

The BLOOM project (Bite-sized Learning Opportunities On Mobiles) explored the pedagogical validity and commercial potential of mobile learning to address common learning needs in the PTL and communication sectors in Austria, Germany and the UK and its ability to cross the physical, linguistic and cultural frontiers of the EU. For the purpose of the project, mobile learning was defined as 'the use of small digital devices such as phones, Smartphones, PDAs and small notebook computers to support vocational learning'. We recognise there are other definitions that encompass a wider range of technologies,[1] but this was beyond the remit of the BLOOM project.

The rationale for working across several countries was that a significant proportion of the PTL sector is inherently transnational, integral to all EU economies and critical to European economic performance. Its scale of operation is growing but it is facing massive changes, including those that arise from 'green' issues. As a result the industry is subject to increasing amounts of EU engagement[2] and regulation which drives the need for ongoing training in issues such as drivers' professional competence. This includes health and safety, vehicle maintenance and use, route planning

[1]   e.g. 'the exploitation of ubiquitous handheld technologies, together with wireless and mobile phone networks, to facilitate, support, enhance and extend the reach of teaching and learning' in *The Impact of Mobile Learning*, Attewell, J. et al. (2009), 'The impact of mobile learning: Examining what it means for teaching and learning', LSN London. Available online at <http://www.molenet.org.uk/pubs/> (accessed 24/08/10).

[2]   See e.g. 'Comprehensive sectoral analysis of emerging competences and economic activities in the European Union: Transport and Logistics.' Employment, Social Affairs and Equal Opportunities, European Commission. Available online at <http://ec.europa.eu/social/main.jsp?langId=en&catId=89&newsId=569&furtherNews=yes> (accessed 29/07/09).

and maximising environmental performance,[3] improved customer service, cultural understanding and 'survival' second language acquisition.

In all partner countries there are barriers of access to PTL training owing to the mobile nature of the work and its often unsocial hours. There clearly is a need to develop practical training methods that are fit for purpose. Would the use of mobile devices help to address this? A transnational approach provided the opportunity to compare and contrast the project rationale in related but different situations with different training traditions, systems, cultures and coverage but sharing many common challenges facing the workforce.

Underpinning assumptions: Work-based learning and mobile devices?

Over the last 50 years many philosophical and pedagogical perspectives on work-based learning have appeared; learning has acquired a central position in economic policy at national and regional levels and in corporate strategy and planning. There are many models: problem-based learning, the use of 'learning sets', competence-based learning, learning organisation and culture, generic skills, situated learning, game-based approaches, simulation and so on.

The problem for BLOOM, and for many practitioners seeking to maximise the impact of technology on learning, is that the use of a 'machine' can add value or not, across almost any learning model, depending on how it us used. Content and process are transformed both by and through use. A mobile device is a resource for many different kinds of learning and can rarely take the sole credit for being the cause of success or failure.

---

3   On 'green' issues see e.g. 'Commission challenges road industry to "get green"', European Commission. Available online at <http://ec.europa.eu/research/transport/news/article_8729_en.html> (30/01/09).

Mobiles add convenience, flexibility, availability, privacy and many other well-documented features, but they are media not curricula. They can be used alone or in, and by teams; across many different learning 'styles'; for both rote-learning and problem-solving; as tools for either exclusion or inclusion. They support scaffolding and also unsupported knowledge-testing. The BLOOM project focused on what employers and employees articulated as their learning priorities within the PTL sector, and the ways they could see themselves using mobile learning. In most cases the view was that it would form part of a wider, 'blended' strategy for workforce skills and would principally be a mechanism for rehearsing knowledge and practising for tests. However, more adventurous uses may well emerge as people become more familiar with the power and capability of devices in the ever-growing m-family. Valiathan[4] has a useful overview of the way blended learning slots into many different modes and models, an analysis that extends nicely to cover mobile learning.

Methodology and summary results

To collect a sensible mix of qualitative and quantitative data the project adopted a mixture of:

- background contextual research;
- workplace questionnaires;
- focus groups and;
- real workplace trials managed by local training providers in each country.

A total of 135 organisations and companies completed workplace question-naires. In the UK, trials were conducted with organisations and companies

---

4   See Purnima Valiathan, 'Blended Learning Models.' American Society for Training and Development. Available online at <http://www.astd.org/LC/2002/0802_vali-athan.htm> (02/08/02).

such as Royal Mail, First Bus, O2 and with health and safety representatives from the communication industry and taxi companies. They were accessed via the relevant sector skills council (GoSkills) and trade union (CWU). In Austria, trial sites included large-scale logistics enterprises, such as Interdean International, Schenker and Österreichische Post; passenger transport companies such as Airport Transfer Service Vienna, Wiener Linien and SME taxi companies; and network operators such as T-Mobile Austria and Mobilkom Austria. In Germany the focus was on major bus services such as BRN Mannheim, Verkehrsbetriebe Heilbronn, WBO Böblingen, RNV Heidelberg, SWEG Wiesloch and Hoffmann Reisen.

In addition to the partner countries, there was informal information and knowledge exchange with providers and stakeholders from other countries including Sweden, Spain, Romania, Bulgaria, Turkey, Norway, France, Italy, Belgium, Netherlands, Finland, Greece, Portugal, Slovenia, Poland, and Latvia, as well as with EU-wide network providers such as Telefonica, O2, Vodaphone and Orange.

Workplace trials

Because of the great variety of languages and workplace settings, mobile learning trial sites did not all trial the same content, though most adopted similar approaches:

- existing, pre-made English mobile learning content was selected for its relevance and then translated into the local language and context;
- new content was created to fill gaps by Tribal in the UK and by local training providers in Austria and Germany using the MyLearning Author;[5]

---

5   See 'Mobile content authoring,' Tribal. Available online at <http://www.m-learning.org/m-learning-solutions/mobile-content-authoring> (accessed 24/08/10).

- learners were loaned mobile devices with pre-loaded content for the duration of their trials. Tracking and scores were preserved on the devices and collated later.

The sample screens of content in Figure 8.1 show a mix of languages, subject matter and interactivity.

Figure 8.1 Sample contents

Summary of results

There was an interesting mix of similarities and contrasts in the three countries in areas such as funding mechanisms for vocational education and training and preferred modes of delivery. However, these differences did not appear to be a material factor in the way the market perceived the potential of mobile learning. Most training in all three countries is face-to-face, with the UK showing significantly more experience than the others in the flexible use of the internet.

It is worth noting that the country with the lowest use of classroom training also has the lowest use of online learning. The UK, with its major investments in e-learning and more recently in mobile learning, has the highest take-up in all learning modes. However, taken with the other information acquired in the market-testing exercise, it appears likely that the provision of training in the sector is inadequate in all three countries and that the opportunity to address this through mobile technology is equally strong in all of them. This proposition is supported by the extent to which all PTL actors in our surveys, after initial doubts, were attracted to the idea of using mobile learning as a component in their training strategies.

Adult literacy and numeracy: Basic skills

In the UK, basic skills training (in literacy and numeracy) is becoming a 'mature' element of education and training provision for adults. It is seen as integral to many vocational pathways rather than as a stigmatised barrier to entry. There is evidence of a widespread need for 20 per cent of the workforce[6] and this has been accepted both by government and by a growing number of major employers and trade unions. As a result, modern basic skills practice seeks to 'embed' literacy and numeracy into vocational curricula rather than treat them separately. This approach is not widespread elsewhere in the EU, where basic skills are often seen as a separate problem that employers do not expect to be involved in addressing. However, much of the content on which there was significant agreement in our survey included 'embedded' basic skills, such as oral communication for customer service, ability to work out costs and mileage and the ability to

---

6   See e.g. Peter Kingston, '"Dismal picture" of adult literacy in UK,' The Guardian. Available online at <http://www.guardian.co.uk/education/2009/jan/29/literacy-numeracy-skills> (accessed 29/01/09).

read maps. These are recognised as belonging to the vocational curriculum and therefore relevant. The convenience of mobile devices, combined with the pedagogy of 'small steps' to which they lend themselves, is well suited to this type of curriculum.

Regulatory requirements

The PTL sector is highly regulated at both EU and member state levels.[7] Much of it is concerned with health and safety (e.g. the requirement for tachometer monitoring). Not surprisingly, health and safety was one of the most common topics for training in all partner countries (see Figure 8.2). More recently, a new training requirement for drivers – called the Driver Certificate of Professional Competence (Driver CPC) – has been intro-duced (from September 2008 for the passenger transport sector; and from September 2009 for the logistics sector). At the time of writing this imposes compulsory face-to-face training for seven hours a year for five years. Many employers believe that the prescribed approach is outmoded and there is considerable pressure for a more flexible approach which would lend itself to mobile learning very well. More EU regulation is likely and, although this will place a burden on employers, it is also an opportunity to offer flexible, cost-effective training using mobile devices (see Figure 8.3).

7   See e.g. 'Freight transport logistics in Europe,' European Commission. Available
     online at <http://europa.eu/legislation_summaries/environment/tackling_cli-
     mate_change/l24456_en.htm> (accessed 15/11/06).

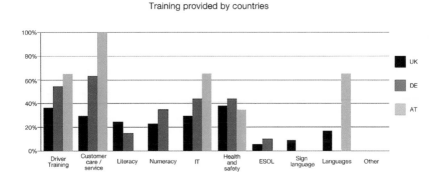

Figure 8.2 Current training actually delivered into PTL sector in each country

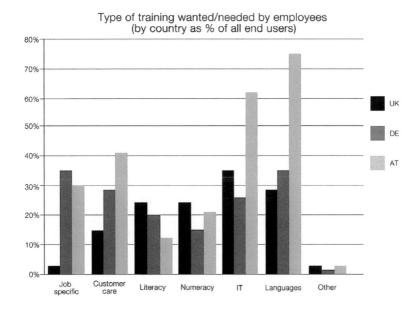

Figure 8.3 Training that employees / learners themselves felt they needed

Subject areas that were common to all three countries included job-specific issues (driving, regulations etc.), customer care, literacy, numeracy, IT skills, health and safety and second/other language support. If centralised content were to be created and shared across this industry, these would be good subjects to cover.

Top priorities cited by employers and learners were also similar:

- Germany: languages, job-specific (driver training), customer care;
- Austria: languages, IT, customer care;
- UK: IT, languages, literacy and numeracy.

Broadly speaking, there appears to be a match between the training currently delivered by employers and that required by employees with the possible exception of language skills.

How attractive is mobile learning?

The research showed that, in the PTL sectors, mobile learning has the potential to support skills development and enhance learning outcomes that are critical for job competence. About 60 per cent of the employers and 80 per cent of employees were keen to use mobile learning. Key reasons included increased flexibility and time-effectiveness (more employees trained faster), quality assurance through learner tracking and fast feedback, motivation to learn in a way that is new, exciting, interesting and convenient and the ability to add value to conventional training methods.

The main perceived barriers were technical: Is it difficult to learn to use the devices, e.g. are there compatibility issues? The issue of cost was also seen as significant: Are costs lower than conventional training? One interesting example of crossed perspective was the difference between what employers thought employees would think and vice versa:

- employer perception: 'we are keen, but our employees are not motivated';
- employee perception: 'we are keen, but our employer is unlikely to invest'.

This type of unsubstantiated mutual misunderstanding may be a factor in decision-making that needs to be challenged. Where there is no conflict in reality there is surely no need to invent one!

Motivation and engagement

Users were engaged by mobile learning and this was not related to confidence or experience of using IT. Most were used to using computers or mobile devices at home, at work or both. Only 11 per cent were not. Eighty-three per cent of the youngest age group (18–30 years old) were familiar with PCs and/or PDAs. Seventy per cent of the over 50s also had prior experience. Users' self-assessment of their 'IT-friendliness' had little bearing on their enthusiasm or willingness to engage with mobile learning: only 20 per cent had tried a smartphone before, of whom 64 per cent considered themselves 'IT friendly', and 86 per cent wanted to use them again.

Also:

- 87 per cent thought the training was relevant because the material was customised to suit them;
- 86 per cent would like to do this type of training again; the method of delivery was appropriate;
- 92 per cent would recommend BLOOM training; the overall concept is valid.

Typical user comments included:

- 'Fast checks, mistakes are shown straightaway.'
- 'Everything can be repeated, you can work anywhere, independent study is possible.'
- 'Relevant to my job, helps in studying for driving licence exam.'
- 'I got new information.'
- 'Useful, fun exercises.'
- 'It got me thinking.'
- 'Good menu, easy access.'

Training providers saw the relevance of BLOOM materials to support their delivery. Key messages from this group focused on the need for added services that could help learners learn faster and differentiate them from their competitors. Overall findings were:

- eighty-five per cent of tutors would recommend using mobile devices but saw a need for initial support for themselves in choosing and using technology and learning design.
- potential competitive advantage in responding to e.g. national tenders from government departments.
- the potential added-value of authoring tools to tailor new packages and customise existing courses.
- excitement about selling mobile learning products as a part of a vocational learning package deal incorporating mobile learning with their existing services, training and materials.

Tutors reported that learners felt the BLOOM materials added value to their learning experience. In particular, they specified many motivational benefits, including independent learning at one's own pace, privacy and flexibility (the ability to learn anywhere for short or long periods, in privacy); convenience with 'the teacher in your pocket'; the use of modern technology and innovative materials supporting skills and knowledge practice; interactivity and feedback and the use of different media to target different senses; fun, 'game-type' exercises to 'spice up' quizzes and tests; a different 'feel' from conventional delivery methods; the ability to author or adapt content for specific target groups (e.g. those with low literacy).

Employers supported the use of BLOOM materials in their training provision. Eighty-six per cent of employers who expressed an opinion confirmed that such use of mobile devices would be suitable for their learning needs. The main reasons were:

- getting training to more employees more quickly (47 per cent);
- flexibility of delivery in terms of time (47 per cent);
- flexibility of delivery in terms of location (43 per cent);
- wider access provision for shift workers and others with non-standard work patterns (33 per cent);
- ability to brand and customise learning for specific learners and using the authoring tools.

Additional findings suggest favourable deployment conditions because of the wide variation in access to learning centres: 71 per cent (UK), 78 per cent (Germany) and 14 per cent (Austria). Even where there is access, not all learning centres are on site or conveniently located; access to on-site learning centres was not offered by 31 per cent of employers in the UK, 100 per cent in Austria and 14 per cent in Germany.

The need for customisability

The analysis showed that many tutors and learners wanted a much larger variety of exercises than the original BLOOM project could offer. For example, they wanted the materials to:

- be more job-specific (e.g. specialised topics such as automotive technology for drivers);

- be individually gradeable so users choose the time and difficulty level that suits their needs;
- use different languages to provide better support for immigrant learners.

This indicates a need to provide the capability to adapt, customise and create materials rather than relying on centrally produced content. Mobile learning is not necessarily or solely a simple publishing activity. However, trainers, and tutors' experience of authoring e-learning suggested that they see it as a specialised activity not widely used by frontline practitioners, who have insufficient time and skill to develop new multimedia materials. This suggests a requirement for generic content that is easy to customise with authoring tools that are simple enough to use with a minimum of training and capable of producing useful resources quickly.

Specific trials with Tribal's MyLearning Authoring tool[8] with learners, tutors and training providers showed that

- there is a need to customise and adapt to an employer's specific requirements, e.g. for basic skills and/or second language learning;
- customising materials for different levels allowed learners to use them with little support;
- the tools provided were easy to use, e.g. tutors were able to make content for the German BKRFQG (professional drivers' qualification) using the authoring tool with no support after the initial introduction.

The authoring tool would definitely be a good thing for us when it comes to customising learning materials specifically for people in our company. (A national bus company in Germany)

Most of our drivers cannot participate in regular courses due to time constraints. Using BLOOM they could improve their skills in a more flexible way, such as while waiting for their customers. (Airport Transfer Service Vienna, Austria)

8   See 'Mobile content authoring,' Tribal. Available online at <http://www.m-learning. org/m-learning-solutions/mobile-content-authoring> (accessed 24/08/10).

Although there were differences between partner countries, there was a sufficient overlap for a generic approach that addressed all three provided that authoring tools were included in the package. Cultural and methodological differences did not seem to be a significant barrier to the idea of introducing a new, highly flexible delivery medium into wider training strategies, often designed to address the learning required by regulatory frameworks. Although mobile learning was seen as potentially saving money, the general view was that it was only fit for purpose for some aspects of the curriculum and would not provide a 'complete solution' addressing the full curriculum.

Some examples and case studies

Given the fact that mobile learning is perceived as suitable for specific parts of the curriculum it seems useful to consider some of the examples of its potential use as identified in the discussions with employers and employees.

Suggestions for future usage

Example 1: Accident prevention: Face-to-face plus mobile learning

Step 1: Driver attends a face-to-face health-and-safety briefing on accident prevention.
Step 2: Driver uses mobile device to access follow-up self-testing to prepare for a formal test.
Step 3: Driver attends formal test.
Step 4: Driver continues to use mobile content as a reference.

Example 2: Survival language: Mobile learning on its own

> Step 1: Driver uses mobile device before leaving to learn key phrases related to:
>
> - traffic regulation;
> - communicating with the police;
> - communicating with the public (can you tell me the way to ...?).
>
> Step 2: During overnight and other suitable breaks, driver uses mobile to check and practise pronunciation.
> Step 3: Driver progresses and requests more challenging content.

Note: Some of these resources are available in an audio-only mode for listening while driving.

Example 3: E-learning plus mobile learning for portfolio-building

> Step 1: Driver and tutor identify areas where practice is required for progress in a competence-based vocational qualification.
> Step 2: Driver goes through practice tests of underpinning knowledge.
> Step 3: Driver sends test scores and progress data to online portfolio and alerts online tutor via MMS.

Specific BLOOM case studies

BLOOM partners were focussing on different sub-sectors of the PTL industry. Two of the specific case studies were:

Case study 1: Using the MyLearning authoring tool in Germany (IVT)

Institut für angewandte Verkehrs- und Tourismusforschung –
Passenger Transport Research Institute

The organisation

IVT is a research and consulting institute that works closely with freight transport and passenger transport companies in Germany. It has a national and international reputation for work on the movement of passengers and goods and is particularly interested in innovative ways of up-skilling the workforce.

Purpose

The purpose was to document feedback on the use of the authoring tools with freight transport/logistic and the passenger transport sector.

Methodology

IVT research staff received training in how to use the authoring tools covering the basics of the hardware and software, the use of smartphones and how to program learning sequences. They then developed customised content which they used with a selection of potential end-users.

A key focus was the ability of mobile learning to stimulate interest and confidence in handling smartphones and the extent that key decision-makers in the companies saw benefits in mobile learning. The trials included functions within the smartphone (such as cameras) that help with customisation and adaptation to meet specific learners' needs.

Use of the authoring tool by IVT researchers:
How material was developed

IVT developed content that reflected the different educational levels of prospective users by including graphical material and developing questions of various levels of difficulty.

It took twelve weeks to establish the first test version. The use of current photos of signs, buses and local streets etc. kept the material as close to reality as possible. The team used the authoring tools without difficulty with no additional training or support.

How the material was received by participants

No participant had difficulties in using the devices and working with the materials. The time spent customising and localising the learning sequences was meaningful to end-users and, therefore, beneficial in the field study.

Developing content to help professional drivers meet German and EU regulations

A key consideration was to focus on content that was relevant for one segment of the target client group, namely bus drivers. Course content was developed based on the German BKRFQG (professional driver's qualification law) and the curriculum framework 'Education of Professional Drivers'. All professional drivers must be familiar with this knowledge and it will become be increasingly critical because of the Europe-wide Driver Certificate of Professional Competence (CPC).

How the material was received by companies

There was strong interest at both company and drivers' level. Mobile learning was seen as an alternative method of delivering aspects of vocationally targeted further education, particularly in the role of support material that is engaging, easy-to-use and which can be customised to the users' educational level.

Martin Sokoup of Interdean International said:

> The MyLearning Authoring tool would definitely be a good thing for us when it comes to customising learning materials specifically for people in our company. I appreciate that this way of learning can take place at any time and place people choose to.

Mohammed Aziz of AirportTransferService Vienna agreed:

> Most of our drivers cannot participate in regular courses due to time constraints. Using m-learning, however, they could improve their skills in a much more flexible way, for example while waiting for their customers.

Conclusion

This case study demonstrates successful use of an authoring tool to develop materials for clients in the passenger and transport sector in Germany and Austria and their enthusiasm and need for this kind of service to meet current national and EU requirements for drivers.

Case study 2: Taxi drivers in the Liverpool city region – GoSkills

The organisation

Tony Norbury is a transport learning support worker and a union learning representative working in the Training and Development Team Merseylearn, at Merseytravel, the local provider.[9]

---

9   For more on Merseytravel see <http://www.merseytravel.gov.uk/> (accessed 24/08/10).

Carl is a self-employed taxi driver and union learning representative operating in the Liverpool area.

Purpose

The purpose was to demonstrate the potential for using BLOOM as a learning resource for taxi drivers in the Liverpool city region.

Requirement

As self-employed people, taxi drivers are isolated, operating on their own as a skilled micro-business with little preparatory training in areas such as customer service, local area knowledge, legislation, and key business skills, e.g. finance, time management etc. Many drivers left school at the earliest possibility and only 11 per cent of the workforce is qualified to Level 2 of the National Qualifications Framework (NQF).[10] Their isolation contributes to a lack of confidence in many aspects of operating their businesses.

The new Level 2 National Vocational Qualification (NVQ) in Road Passenger Vehicle Driving aims to:

- raise the profile and image of the industry;
- achieve consistency of skills throughout the 343 licensing authorities in England and Wales;
- help to retain existing drivers and encourage new entrants;
- improve the experience of service users;
- ensure service sustainability;
- provide a pathway for skills development in the industry;
- integrate basic skills as component of the NVQs.

10   For an explanation of the NQF see 'Animation introducing the QCF,' Qualifications and Curriculum Development Agency. Available online at <http://www.qcda.gov.uk/qualifications/60.aspx>. Last modified 12/04/10 (accessed 24/08/10).

A key delivery issue is that when drivers are not driving, they are not earning, so time and place for learning needs to accommodate the business imperatives of drivers. Training must also be relevant to their work; therefore, it is essential to show it can be applied in the workplace.

The case study

Tony and Carl are strong advocates of using mobile devices to 'deliver' learning for taxi drivers to use in their 'down time', waiting for the next client. As part of his work supporting drivers to gain their NVQ, Carl lends out mobile devices to let them see how they get on with this method of learning. No pressure is applied; users can engage in their own time and space.

Tony became an advocate for mobile learning as a way to help drivers get familiar with technology, update skills and knowledge, increase confidence in the ability to learn and pass official tests. For Carl, mobility, accessibility, 'any-time, any-place' and the absence of being judged are key success features.

Conclusion

Mobile learning is ideally placed within a blend. It motivates learners to begin their learning journey, provides experience with learning and assessment materials, enables drill and practice, and increases confidence in the process of learning, handling technology and individual skill levels.[11]

11   For an online interview with Carl and Tony, see 'Bloom Liverpool Project – M-learning in a taxi,' Tribal Education. Available online at <http://www.youtube.com/watch?v=jUvoFgkFKdY> (accessed 11/07/09).

Looking ahead: Other vocational applications for mobile learning

Since BLOOM, mobile learning has become more popular in schools and adult education and is slowly appearing in vocational learning. Interesting examples of current projects include the following:

TATRC/US Department of Defense

Tribal is working with medical training experts in the US Department of Defense to create mobile health micro-courses, based on existing emergency medical training. They cover how to deal with crisis situations. All learning is available on the phone, over the air. Trialling is planned with civilian and military learners across 30 different countries and the final courses will be given to any agency and organisation working with the US for disaster relief.

UK Ministry of Defence

A very successful low-tech mobile learning project has sent soldiers into Iraq with language learning 'flash cards' on their iPods.[12]

---

12   For further information, see Major Roy Evans, 'Learning Pool Presentation.' Available online at <http://www.slideshare.net/JMHarkin/roy-evans-mlearning-in-the-army> (accessed 20/05/09).

MoLeNET

MoLeNET is an umbrella project, funded by the LSC in England, that provides partial funding for mobile learning to over 30,000 college-based learners and tutors. Over 50 per cent of MoLeNET projects in 2007/8 looked at work-based learning. Most were partnerships between colleges and employers, covering hairdressing, motor vehicle, engineering, electrical engineering, industrial services, care, construction and plumbing. An overview study found the main advantages of mobile learning for work-based learning to be:

• convenience, due to size and portability;
• improved access to learning and reference, including internet access;
• improved communication;
• just-in-time, any-location, access to video and video recording;
• support for evidence-gathering, portfolio-building and assessment.[13]

ESOL for migrant workers in the UK

Despite efforts to teach English to migrant workers, many fall through the net because of access issues. A project to address this distributed mobile courses to over 1000 learners.[14] An innovative dimension was the inclusion of integrated audio recording and playback to support speaking and listening.

13   For further information, see MoLeNET website, <http://www.molenet.org.uk/> (accessed 24/08/10).
14   For further information, see 'ESOL Materials for Migrant Workers,' Learning and Skills Improvement Service. Available online at <http://www.excellencegateway.org.uk/page.aspx?o=196280> (accessed 24/08/10).

Medical training

Roundpoint worked with Reed Elsevier, publishers of *The Lancet* and other medical journals, to develop mobile revision courses for aspiring doctors to refresh their knowledge. Group activity was encouraged through a 'challenge a friend' feature where students challenge others to beat their score.

The Crash Course was based on a mixture of questions including multiple choice, multiple selection and plain text. Users register and complete sets of test questions. Initially not all questions are visible to users but more become available on a daily basis as they visit the website.

Overall conclusion

Mobile learning has a potentially significant role in work-based learning in the PTL sector as long as it remains easy to customise in different contexts. On its own it is unlikely to provide a complete solution; it needs to be seen as part of a wider solution and has particular strengths where there is a need for personalisation, flexibility and ease of access.

LIZA WOHLFART, SIMONE MARTINETZ AND
ALEXANDER SCHLETZ

9 From know-how to knowledge: Exploring Web 2.0 concepts for sharing hands-on service expertise[1]

Abstract

Many German mechanical engineering companies involved in machine building and plant construction today send their service technicians on complex installation and repair tasks to customers as far afield as China and India. The technicians' on-site contribution to the customers' satisfaction cannot be overestimated. They are the main face of the company, demonstrating its reliability and technical excellence – if they perform their job well. This, however, depends on the availability of ad-hoc support whenever they encounter problems. The best way to get this support today is to either call a colleague or a helpdesk support engineer for practical advice. The tacit knowledge on products and processes shared in these interactions is an important yet not fully explored corporate asset, as it still essentially resides within the individuals involved. The German 'eColleagues' research project tries to make better use of the support processes by capturing and distributing the knowledge exchanged for later reference. Is this a challenge Web 2.0 can master?

1   We would like to thank the companies involved in the eColleagues project – Oerlikon Barmag, HOMAG, Tooltechnic Systems and Infoman – as well as the project's supporters VDMA (German Engineering Federation) and VermIT (Association of Medium-Sized Industrial Training centres of Baden-Württemberg). Special thanks also to the BMBF (German Federal Ministry of Education and Research) as well as the ESF (European Social Fund) for co-funding the project. The project is coordinated by the DLR (German Research Centre for Aeronautics and Space).

Training 'to go' – The idea of mobile, work-embedded support for service technicians

Companies have always offered some sort of service along with their products. However, this service was often not specifically labelled as such, nor nurtured with dedicated care as part of a corporate 'solution package'. The growing importance of product-related services in the past number of years is largely due to the increasingly complex nature of products, particularly in machine building, where installations and maintenance tasks call for expertise in areas as diverse as engineering, electronics and IT.

In the machine-building and plant construction industries, in particular, the expertise of a company's service personnel is key to a company's service quality. They are the main interface with the customer, both as experienced technicians performing installations and as fast problem-solvers on site to take care of machine breakdowns. Another service task of increasing importance is the consulting of customers, for example on how upgrades can increase a machine's productivity and service life (Gestmann, 2005).

But not only clients benefit from the hands-on expertise of a company's service staff. Internal departments likewise need their feedback for machine improvements and innovations. The service technicians have practical experience in the use of the machines on site; they talk to those working with the machines as well as to those investing in them, and are on the receiving end for both complaints and ideas.

Keeping service technicians well trained is one of the core tasks of any company in order to maintain their reputation and market success. This is not an easy task, however. As maintenance and repair times are extremely costly for customers, they need to be fast and smooth. At the same time, the complexity of the machines is constantly increasing, calling for more specific service expertise.

HOMAG Group – Wood processing systems and machinery

With an installed base of 35,000 machines, HOMAG Holzbear-beitungssysteme AG, a company of the HOMAG Group AG, is the world market leader in the development, production and engineering of systems and machinery for wood processing. Customer segments include the furniture and building components industries. HOMAG Group AG employs around 5,000 workers worldwide, with 1,500 staff working at HOMAG Holzbearbeitungssysteme AG. In 2008, the HOMAG Group reported earnings of €830 million, with exports accounting for roughly 85 per cent of all revenue.

HOMAG Holzbearbeitungssysteme AG realized the importance of new services in machine and plant manufacturing at an early stage and has designed an innovative service portfolio in their service centre in Schopfloch. Currently about 16% of revenue at HOMAG Holz-bearbeitungssysteme AG is generated through services. The high complexity and increasing pace of innovation in machine and plant development, however, make it more and more difficult to maintain quality services worldwide.

<http://www.homag.de/cms/en>

Training this expertise is a real challenge as the service technicians' life on the road and the abrupt nature of their job assignments sit ill-at-ease with traditional training schemes. Formal training formats such as face-to-face seminars and e-learning are still an important part of the companies' training programs. However, they cannot provide all the help travelling service technicians need given the time and distance constraints, and also because such programmes cannot cover all problems encountered, and certainly not the most recent ones.

What is needed is fast on-demand support right when and where it is required, i.e. during the actual work processes (Regnet & Hofman, 2003). The main tools used by service technicians on job assignments at distant customer sites are laptops and mobile phones. An additional requirement with respect to suitable work-embedded learning concepts thus will involve focusing applications on these key devices.

As far as learning contents are concerned, an important source of knowledge resides in the experiences gained within individual problem-solving processes. Each technician is an expert in some fields and constantly increases his/her expertise with each new assignment. This knowledge, often created within informal discussions with the helpdesk or colleagues, is mostly lost for later reference.

Oerlikon Barmag – Spinning and texturing machines

Oerlikon Barmag, a member of the Oerlikon Textile GmbH & Co. KG group, has more than 1,600 employees worldwide. The company, whose history goes back to 1866, is the world's leading manufacturer of spinning and texturing machines for man-made fibres such as polyester, nylon and polypropylene. An extensive after-sales service complements their product range. Customers include clients in East and West Asia, Europe, the U.S. and the Middle East. Oerlikon Barmag's headquarters are in Remscheid, Germany, while its production, sales and service networks within the Oerlikon group cover all their customers' regions.

Due to the increasing complexity of Oerlikon Barmag's products, which not only include mechanical, but also electronic and software elements, the company's service technicians need a broad range of skills and up-to-date information along with fast on-demand support usually provided by the headquarters' service helpdesks or internal colleagues.

<http://www.barmag.oerlikontextile.com/en>

In order to better leverage the information shared through informal channels, companies today have installed various tools and methods, such as weekly or monthly team meetings, reports, knowledge databases and so on. However, these concepts are often perceived as unproductive. Service technicians have to travel to the company's headquarters and spend time filling out reports in addition to their actual task of installing and fixing machines, advising clients and the like. Effective ways of communicating the experiences of individual service technicians on a global scale have yet to be identified.

With the rise of the Internet and especially today's Web 2.0 concepts, connecting people worldwide looks easy. But several questions still need to be answered: How can a person's expertise be formalised for large-scale exchange? What kind of technology is best for capturing, storing and sharing it on a global scale? And what are key incentives for people to share their knowledge gained in days, months, years, or even decades 'in the field'?

This paper presents the interim results of an ongoing German research project entitled eColleagues (www.eColleagues.de) aimed at providing fast and high-quality support for service technicians of machine-building and plant-construction companies. The project was initiated within the BMBF 'New media in education' support programme, which aims at expanding current concepts and technologies of further education in professional training, especially with respect to the emerging possibilities of mobile communication technologies and innovative concepts of knowledge exchange.

To ensure the solutions developed can be successfully translated to other companies on completion of the project, the eColleagues research and development consortium comprises different pilot companies that are typical of their industry. Two of the three companies are presented in more detail in this paper, as eColleagues' analysis of their experiences and ideas has largely been finalised: Oerlikon Textile GmbH & Co. KG (man-made fibre spinning and texturing) and HOMAG Holzbearbeitungssysteme AG (wood processing). The third industrial partner, TTS Tooltechnic Systems AG & Co. KG, is from a slightly different sector (a tools provider).

The company side is supported by a well established IT partner from the field (Infoman AG) and a scientific partner (the Institute for Human Factors and Technology Management (IAT) at the University of Stuttgart). Furthermore, two inter-trade organisations are represented in the consortium that can provide input from company practice to the solution development phase (and vice versa): the German Engineering Federation (VDMA), one of the key lobby groups of, and a service provider to, the German engineering industry, and the Association of Medium-Sized Industrial Training Centres of Baden-Württemberg (VERMIT), a training association that is mainly active in the south of Germany.

The project started in July 2008 and will end in June 2011. Currently, the first pilots of the on-demand learning system are being conceptualised and implemented in the companies.

From 'Googleitis' to 'Wikimania': Theoretical building blocks of the eColleagues concept

eColleagues started out with the idea of trying to make the best possible use of Web 2.0 concepts as well as current learning and IT trends. All in all, four major building blocks were defined as the core of the project's theoretical concept:

- merging learning and knowledge management concepts;
- enabling bottom-up emergence of knowledge;
- supporting international structures;
- ensuring ease of application within natural work processes.

Merging learning and knowledge management concepts

Learning and knowledge management (KM) are usually treated as two separate domains, each with its own methods, tools and guidelines. The increase in informal learning, however, has increasingly blurred this distinction, as employees do not simply rely on formal training alone to extend their expertise, but also chat with colleagues or use the Internet to browse for ad-hoc knowledge needed. The concept of self-constructed, explorative learning is growing in importance in markets such as the machine-building industry, calling for specific expertise and excellent skills.

Enabling the bottom-up emergence of knowledge

Many Web 2.0 applications benefit from the collaboration of multiple users for gathering and structuring knowledge. Applications such as Wikipedia have demonstrated the power of bottom-up emergent databases, continually edited and re-edited with a view to up-to-date accuracy. These concepts also change the roles of those involved: users are authors are users – true peer-to-peer support, just as that intended by eColleagues (see also Hron et al., 2002).

The German ministry co-funding the eColleagues project, the Federal Ministry of Education and Research (BMBF), stresses the importance of expert communities in a set of recommendations for work-embedded learning concepts. 'Task-oriented didactical concepts aim at the support and maintenance of cooperative, self-organized learning in Communities of Practice' (BMBF, 2004, p. 8).

Supporting international structures

Many machine-building companies today have an international focus. The exchange of knowledge and experience in worldwide corporate networks is one of the key challenges they have to tackle in the face of globalisation. Barriers not only include differences in language, but also in culture (see also Prokop, 2000) – an aspect often underestimated. eColleagues aims at supporting the exchange of experiences beyond national, cultural and language borders – a difficult venture considering the various regions to be covered.

Ensuring ease of application within natural work processes

Traditional e-learning applications have often failed due to their focus on technical aspects, resulting in sophisticated, highly complex tools users refrained from deploying. By contrast, many KM tools of recent years, such as Google and Skype, have managed to harmonise complex background functionalities with simple user interfaces. The eColleagues consortium similarly puts pedagogical aspects and the users' work processes first when designing the project solution, and then thinks about appropriate IT structures to support it. 'E-learning', as the German Ministry for Education and Research puts it, 'is above all a pedagogic process, although information and communication technologies play a significant role as supporting medium' (BMBF, 2004, p. 8).

To meet this aim, the collaborative, on-demand training to be provided in the end will have to be both work-embedded and, as such, mobile. The concept of 'work-embedded learning', as defined by Reuther (2006), means learning that both takes place in the real work processes of the learners and makes the best possible use of the tools and methods used in the processes. A related concept is the idea of 'situated learning', established, for instance, by Lave & Wenger: 'Situated learning [...] takes as its focus the relationship between learning and the social situations in which it occurs. [...] Lave and Wenger situate learning in certain forms of social co-participation [...], they ask what kinds of social engagements provide the proper context for learning to take place' (Hanks, 1991).

To a large degree, work-embedded learning in eColleagues will also mean 'informal learning', i.e. learning that does not make use of formal structures such as face-to-face seminars or online courses. As a 1999 study illustrated (Overwien, 2001), it is one of the main forms of training used by adult learners, and the form experiencing the biggest growth in popularity. All survey participants, who were currently or soon-to-be employed, indicated an average of six hours of informal learning each week for their current or future job. Topics ranked as most significant included job-related knowledge (75 per cent) and computer skills (66 per cent). 66 per cent of survey participants said that they use informal learning to develop problem-solving and communication skills.

The recent report on adult learning published by Eurostat, the statistical office of the European Union, stresses the importance of informal learning in work contexts today. It highlights that 'over 80 percent of the non-formal [learning] activities are job-related' and finds that 'the main reasons for participation are to do a better job and improve career prospects' (Eurostat 44/2009). The two most important obstacles to adult participation in education and training mentioned by the Eurostat report are work schedules and family responsibilities. Other barriers mentioned include the cost of participation and the lack of facilities within a reachable distance.

The mobile aspect of eColleagues will mainly focus on providing training independent of the current location of the user. For instance, this could include the provision of e-learning on new products via the Internet, stimulating online chats on current problems at hand and relaying up-to-date information on technical problems with a specific machine type to the technician's mobile phones by text message.

eColleagues requirements analysis – A multi-perspective and process-oriented approach

The actual design of the eColleagues concept started with an extensive assessment of practical user needs and ideas. In a mixed 'top-down' and 'bottom-up' approach, both the management's and the service staff's perspectives were analysed, the latter including in-house units as well as service technicians working in the field (see Figure 9.1).

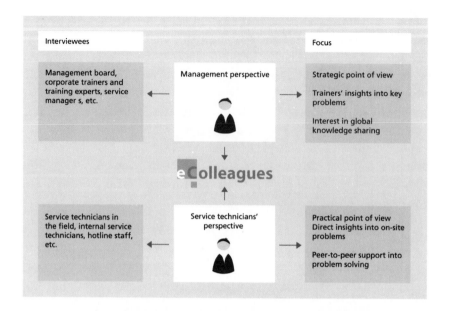

Figure 9.1 eColleagues approach: Top-down and bottom-up

Method 1 Focus group interviews

The analyses were mainly conducted by means of interviews with semi-standardised questionnaires and took place in the respective headquarters of the industrial partners. The project's scientific partner, IAT, initially also considered holding workshops with some of the service technicians to initiate multi-perspective discussions on key problems and ideas for future solutions; this however could not be realised due to the tight work and travel schedules of the companies' service staffs.

IAT's alternative solution was to hold single and focus group interviews, the latter usually involving two to four people. The sessions included both managers (including the heads of service and training) as well as service technicians [external and internal (hotline) staff], totalling nearly 50 people in all. On average, each interview took about 90 minutes. The questionnaire included questions on the interviewees' professional background, the service technicians' experience and working history within the company, their training schemes and the service processes within the company. Another cluster of questions was devoted to problems in daily operations, as well as suggestions for improvements, for example with respect to financial, process-related, IT, infrastructural, work-life balance and incentive issues.

Since a semi-standardised questionnaire was used, the results of the interviews at the respective companies can be compared to identify common characteristics within the real working environments of mobile service technicians. The findings will, in due course, serve for the development of a general concept for collaborative on-demand training that can be transferred to other companies. The project's two inter-trade organisations will play a key role in this respect by providing feedback and disseminating project results, as well as other companies involved in the project's Community of Interest (CoI). Further discussions will be held with experts contacted through scientific publications, project events and presentations.

Method 2   Service blueprints

An additional tool employed in the design of the eColleagues concept was the method of service blueprinting. A service blueprint is a concept for illustrating service processes step-by-step in a kind of visual map. The various service steps are separated by what are known as 'lines of interaction and visibility'. The key perspective taken is that of the customer.

- The *line of external interaction* marks the point where customers and service staff come into contact. Actions above that line are performed by the customer alone and are not visible for the service personnel. Activities below that line are service tasks done in direct contact with the customer.
- The *line of visibility* separates service tasks that are visible for the customers from those that are not visible for them, i.e. performed internally.

- The *line of internal interaction* separates internal service activities of the staff members from supporting processes and tools, such as the use of common databases, collaboration with other internal departments etc.

eColleagues uses service blueprints to gain a better understanding of the service processes of the industrial partners involved. The maps help the team to find suitable points in the process where support by the future tool is needed and to make sure that this support will neatly fit into the natural service processes performed. A key advantage of applying the method of blueprints in eColleagues is that they make it possible to distinguish tasks performed by the external service staff at the customers' sites from those done in cooperation with internal service teams. The blueprints show the chronology of events, potential waiting times and support documents used in the process.

Selected findings

The interviews and blueprints have highlighted some of the main challenges and success factors eColleagues will have to respond to. In general, the external service technicians work in a very decentralised fashion. In many cases, 50 technicians cover an area as large as Germany or even larger. Therefore, it is very likely that such service technicians hardly meet most of their colleagues. Each and every one of them might face a similar if not the same problem thinking they have an entirely new problem to solve. A way to efficiently collect and share the experiences of all service technicians is urgently needed.

The future on-demand support to be provided will need to be both mobile (i.e. location-independent) and work-embedded (i.e. provided within the actual work processes). Preferred devices include laptops and mobile phones, i.e. the standard equipment used by service technicians at customers' sites. This last aspect is especially interesting for eColleagues, given the fact that information access can be quick and easy with decently fast mobile data transfer rates, and considering the options provided by QR-Codes and camera functionalities. Mobile telecommunication infrastructure is available almost on a worldwide level.

The *HOMAG* service technicians currently report problems with machinery to the headquarters via 'service tickets', i.e. online reports. Headquarter units scan these tickets in order to identify common problems. This information is used both to improve the machinery and to train the staff. Since there is a huge variety of machinery in the field, it is, however, next to impossible to train each service technician on every typical problem. Thus the service technicians often call HOMAG's hotline to get assistance. A fast and easy problem-solving process – in the majority of cases. However, calling the hotline takes time, as capacities are limited, and service technicians have to call the same hotline as the customers. Answers are documented, but not in a structured way, nor in a centralised system.

The company's hotline is also often the first choice of *Oerlikon Barmag's* external service staff. Depending on the problem at hand, the technicians sometimes also contact other internal experts directly, e.g. from the mechanical construction or software development units. In addition, the service staff members themselves provide support for each other. After all, they are the true experts on their machines. This peer-to-peer knowledge exchange is strongly encouraged by the company's management who would like to try and leverage the expertise of their travelling specialists. For the German service technicians, this concept does, however, represent a challenge. Large parts of the service are already handled by service staff units within the respective markets for much lower wages. The only way the German team feels they can compete is through excelling in professional know-how.

The obstacles mentioned (by both companies) with respect to traditional training schemes mainly result from the specific nature of the service technicians' jobs. Assignments of several weeks or even months at far-off places make traditional face-to-face seminars hard to implement. This is further aggravated by the fact that projects, especially those related to repair tasks, often have an ad-hoc start and undetermined end date. With the rise of the internet, e-learning modules and instructional videos may be accessed virtually from everywhere in the world. However, as the interviews showed, service technicians hardly have the time to watch them during their on-site work processes. In addition, traditional ways of producing instructional videos are time-consuming and expensive.

Web 2.0 technologies may provide faster and less expensive possibilities. Service technicians could generate short videos (or photo sequences) themselves, using their mobile phones, to document current problems. These documentations of problems and corresponding solutions could then be used to train others later on.

> The phone is important. In addition, the Internet is a great help. For example, faulty diagrams can be corrected quickly and sent back to the construction site. This way we can continue with our work rapidly and don't have to wait very long. But this is also true the other way round. If we have a problem on the construction site, we can take a digital photograph, and ask a helpdesk colleague for a solution. (Statement of service technician in the eColleagues interviews)

The problem with this idea emerging in the interviews, however, is the aspect of liability: Companies have to make sure that all instructional material, including that provided by service technicians themselves, is in line with the company's safety regulations. Systematically analysing service reports – another potential solution – is a very difficult and complex task. Capturing informal interactions between internal and external service staff during phone discussions is even more challenging as both teams lack the time to write up detailed reports.

Another finding of the eColleagues requirements analyses is that the service technicians have to stay up-to-date for their jobs, and the companies' back offices need to work as efficiently as possible to ensure the optimum provision of service. To this end, it is crucial to smoothly interconnect R&D departments, construction departments and service units.

Outline of the eColleagues concept

Both the scientific background ideas and the findings within the analysis phase have provided the information base for the eColleagues concepts to be implemented by HOMAG and Oerlikon Barmag. The two concepts differ in some respects while pursuing similar aims:

(a) Providing fast on-demand support during practical work processes.
(b) Enabling some sort of pre-qualification on potential problems to be encountered including a pre-assessment of available competencies.

Fast on-demand support

The concept of 'on-demand support' in eColleagues will mean fast, mobile and work-embedded access to different kinds of information needed within the work processes of service technicians. This information could, for example, include product and customer data, contact details of colleagues with specific expertise or documentations of hands-on solutions for emerging problems. As service technicians at customers' sites cannot spend a lot of time browsing through information, eColleagues will have to be complemented by an excellent search function.

> We always have the customer on our back. They keep asking whether we have found an answer and how it will go on. (Statement of service technician in the eColleagues interviews)

As stated in the interviews, service technicians almost always prefer calling a hotline colleague to other means of support. The hotline phone support, however, is not always available for external staff and cannot always provide suitable solutions straight away. This could be a big advantage for an IT solution.

> If I know a colleague who already solved this particular problem, I can certainly call and ask him. Provided I get him on the phone. The time difference is a real problem in this respect. If he is on an assignment at the other end of the world, he may not be available at this particular point in time. (Statement of service technician in the eColleagues interviews)

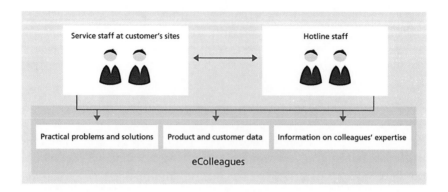

Figure 9.2 Fast on-demand support for internal and external service staff

The usefulness of an online IT tool will depend on the quality and quantity of the material provided. Major input for the online collection could be gained within the phone discussions between external and internal staff, a key source of informal knowledge not yet fully exploited. Considering the constraints of the service technicians on the road, documenting these processes will, however, have to be fast and easy.

The quality of the online database will also need to tackle the international nature of the company's service tasks today. This could mean providing the material either in a language common to most technicians (e.g. English) or several languages, for example. Supportive visual material such as photos, illustrations or short video clips could also be helpful. HOMAG will place specific emphasis on capturing practical problems and solutions in eColleagues, for example by analysing service reports ('service tickets'). Oerlikon Barmag focuses on providing fast access to product and customer data (e.g. product catalogues), contact details of colleagues and the exchange of practical experiences (e.g. via blogs or wikis).

Pre-qualification/pre-assessment

eColleagues will not only have to provide immediate support to emerging problems. Another challenge will be enabling suitable training on recurring problems, such as clients' machine operating mistakes or gaps in expertise of the service technicians with respect to installations.

Dealing with these problems could include alerting technicians on the road by e-mail or text message, providing e-learning material or including new aspects in traditional seminars, for example.

HOMAG is particularly interested in developing some sort of mechanism for identifying and classifying the main problems emerging ('Top-Ten List') to then provide the right kind of information/training for each type of problem ('Early warning system'). A key challenge here will be setting up useful classification schemes for identifying the right kind of training for each type of problem. For example, while some may require immediate information via e-mail, others may need to be tackled by instructional films provided online to all technicians concerned.

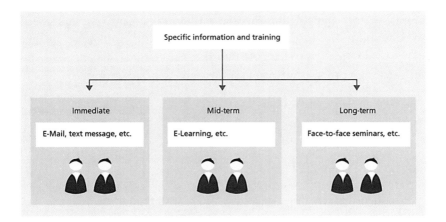

Figure 9.3   Training on recurrent problems and solutions

Oerlikon Barmag is working on a 'qualification matrix' that will help to assess the available and required skills of every service technician out in the field. The information on available skills could be used to identify technicians with a specific expertise when planning service tasks or trying to solve a specific problem. The match between available versus required skills could also form the basis to the company's training schemes.

Conclusions and next steps

A particularly interesting aspect of eColleagues will be the leveraging of informal knowledge exchanges. Making the service technicians' tacit knowledge available to each other is, apparently, one of the success factors for effective mobile, work-based support. The interconnection of field units, in-house units, R&D departments and IT managers collecting, storing, and sharing their expertise is a key factor here. This concept, however, challenges or even weakens the position of each single service technician, or so it seems.

An interesting aspect to be explored in eColleagues could thus be how to secure the expert status of individual experts (along with their jobs), despite their exchanging information with others. Incentive systems need to be established to further boost information-sharing and the acceptance of new communication channels. Besides these cultural challenges, several technical and process-related questions need to be addressed:

- How to gather the knowledge exchanged in informal discussions without disturbing the support processes? Is it possible to substitute the phone as the key medium with reports or text-based chats? Or should speech-to-text applications be explored?
- How to structure the knowledge collected in a systematic way? How to identify recurring problems? And how to present them in a proper way either to internal units for required machine improvements or to customers and technicians for future avoidance?
- How to successfully identify issues to be included in the company's formal training schemes, i.e. seminars or e-learning? How to decide on which form of training to use for the specific issues to be addressed?
- How to enable the editing of problem-solving documents to ensure the high quality of the emergent database? And, how to manage the accuracy of the contents?

eColleagues will explore the usefulness of the various technologies at hand for this in the specific setting of mobile, work-embedded learning in complex problem-solving processes. The resulting practical prototypes and scientific insights will not only benefit the German machine-building and plant-construction industries, but service-intensive industries as a whole.

References

Boateng, S. (2009) 'Population and social conditions – Significant country differences in adult learning.' In *Eurostat Statistics in focus* 44. Available online at <http://epp.eurostat.ec.europa.eu/cache/ITY_OFFPUB/KS-SF-09–044/EN/KS-SF-09–044-EN.PDF> (accessed 25/05/10)

Bundesministerium für Bildung und Forschung (ed) (2003) *Förderprogramm Neue Medien in der Bildung – Auditempfehlungen zum Förderbereich 'Neue Medien in der beruflichen Bildung'*. Available online at <http://www.dlr.de/pt/Portaldata/45/Resources/dokumente/BMBF-neue_medien_in_der_beruflichen_bildung.pdf> (accessed 25/05/10)

Gestmann, M. (2005) 'So wird der Service-Mann zum Kundenberater.' *Industrieanzeiger* 26. Available online at <http://www.steinbeis-beratung.de/public/dtab_files/ia-6–05Zeitung.pdf> (accessed 25/05/10)

Hanks, W. (1991) 'Foreword.' In Lave, J., & Wenger, E. *Situated learning. Legitimate peripheral participation* (p. 14). Cambridge: Cambridge University Press

Hron, A., et al. (2002) 'Gemeinsam lernt es sich besser – Kooperatives Lernen und kognitive Prozesse in netzbasierten Szenarien.' In Scheffer, U., and Hesse, F. (eds), *E-Learning – Die Revolution des Lernens gewinnbringend einsetzen*. Stuttgart: Klett-Cotta

Innovation & Technologietransfer (2004) *Allein auf weiter Flur?* Available online at <http://cordis.europa.eu/itt/itt-de/04–4/dossier01.htm> (accessed 15/04/10)

Overwien, B. (2004) 'Internationale Sichtweisen auf "informelles Lernen" am Übergang zum 21. Jahrhundert.' In Otto, H., & Coelen, T. (eds), *Ganztagsbildung in der Wissensgesellschaft*. Wiesbaden, pp. 51–73

Prokop, E. (2000) 'Weiterbildung in globalen Kontexten.' In Götz, K. (ed.), *Interkulturelles Lernen – Interkulturelles Training*. München: Hampp Verlag

Regnet, E., & Hofman, M. (2003) *Innovative Weiterbildungskonzepte*. Göttingen: Hogrefe

Reuther, U. (2006) 'Der Programmbereich Lernen im Prozess der Arbeit.' In Arbeitsgemeinschaft Betriebliche Weiterbildungsforschung e.V., Projekt QUEM: *Kompetenzentwicklung 2006 – Ergebnisse – Erfahrungen – Einsichten*. Münster: Waxmann

Mobile simulations and laboratories: Preparing learners for work

MICHAEL E. AUER, ARTHUR EDWARDS AND
DANILO GARBI ZUTIN

10 Online laboratories in interactive mobile learning environments

Abstract

Work-based mobile learning is increasingly becoming one of the most important means of providing knowledge, skills and competencies to the workforce. Traditionally, on-the-job training has been *the* educational 'delivery' choice over many years. Recently, however, the increased capacity of the internet and wireless communication has changed the focus from learning while on the job to the assistance of a person providing constant support to a system where wireless mobile technologies can provide this assistance both in the workplace, or just about any other location the learner chooses. This flexibility takes learning from a traditionally one-on-one experience, where a worker serves to train a coworker, to a situation where individuals can, in large part, train themselves, without the constraints of having a trainer present or having to be physically present in the workplace itself. This chapter provides a discussion of online laboratories and moves into a discussion of work-based mobile learning based on theories that substantiate the use of this modality. It concludes by providing technical details of an online learning environment to provide remote or mobile work-based experimental practice in the area of engineering.

Introduction

Work-based education, in its most rudimentary form, was primarily used in apprenticeship programs. In these programs, the role of the artisan was to personally teach one or more persons wishing to learn a craft. These persons were expected to learn by observation, imitation, practice and feedback provided by the artisan. This system, which has been in place for millennia, has proved to be very effective, primarily because new knowledge, skills and instrumentation evolved at a relatively slow pace, thus allowing for a slower and more predictable learning process.

However, as human progress has developed at a greater pace, this method is somewhat losing its importance. This is in large part because the time required to learn a skill has greatly increased and the knowledge, skills and competencies needed have become more complex. Also, workers no longer tend to dedicate an entire lifetime to one job and the present job market permits workers to move freely from one job requiring one set of job skills to another job that requires a completely different set of job skills, etc.

Traditionally, work-based training has been viewed as a formal process that begins in an educational setting, such as a school, that is complemented by additional learning experiences and training in a workplace setting. Work-based leaning, therefore, has traditionally been seen as a collaborative effort of schools that provide semi-polished human resources and the workplace environment which fine tunes the worker with additional and job-specific training.

However, learning cannot be seen as only a formal process that occurs entirely within the physical confines of school and work. We should focus more on the workplace as a learning environment that concentrates 'on the interaction between the affordances and constraints of the social setting, on the one hand, and the agents and biography of the individual participant, on the other' (Billett, 2004).

Workplaces have specific expectations of their workforce, which are largely based on organisational policies, objectives and goals. Consequently, they impose their real or perceived needs based on the perceived prosperity and survival of the enterprise. However, individual workers have their own perceived or real needs that do not necessarily coincide with the organisation.

Learners, for example, tend to act according to their own perceived interests, preferences and goals (Harris et at., 2005). This makes the workplace an area in which these differences must be minimised and exploited, when possible, for the benefit of both the worker and the workplace. Therefore, work-based training entails possessing knowledge about how knowledge is used (operationally), as well as institutional and personal roles, procedural knowledge and restrictions and the expected participation of the individual worker (Tuttas & Wagner, 2001).

Consequently, success for both the organisation and the individual depends on leaning and adapting to quickly evolving situations. In today's marketplace, the only thing that is certain is change, and change comes quickly, requiring both organisations and individuals to change the way they train and work. That is why the premises and modalities of work-based education are constantly subject to change. One important fundamental change is the introduction of work-based mobile learning. Work-based mobile learning has developed primarily to meet a traditional workplace need – the need to develop personnel who can function optimally in the workplace. Work-based mobile learning has also developed because of the enhanced delivery of educational services through technological innovations and socio-economic factors which have redefined the physical and temporal boundaries of the workplace. Critically, however, for online laboratories to be successful, they still need to meet psychological, educational and technological principles. An important point to take into account is the additional life experience more mature workers possess. The workplace often involves real-world knowledge and experience. Repeated exposure to different experiences over time tends to prepare mature workers to react to novel experiences that can be related to previous experiences. However, it is also important to mention that mature learners can be more 'set in their ways'. This 'fossilisation' can create circumstances where older learners feel more threatened by new circumstances. Therefore, theoretically, learning in workplace environments should be continuous, stimulating and enjoyable in order to create the habit of learning.

Importantly, not all experience can be gained within the physical confines of the workplace. Mobile learning systems, and specifically remote engineering platforms, can permit workers to learn and experience situations they might not commonly come across at work.

Learning in online laboratory environments

Synchronous active interaction with experiments and problem-solving helps individual or collaborative learners directly acquire applicable knowledge that can be used in practical situations, which is why pedagogical theory and practice considers laboratory experimentation an essential part of the educational process, particularly in the sciences and engineering. Synchronous interaction is also important because it provides immediate feedback so that students can interact with experiments in real-time, thus obtaining numerous potential results, instead of running one experiment and waiting for the results at a later time.

Online (Remote) laboratories make all this shared use available via the internet and are becoming increasingly important applications in the new domain of Online Engineering. Online Engineering can be defined as an interdisciplinary field utilising the areas of engineering, computing and telematics, where specific engineering activities like programming, design, control, observation, measuring, sensing, and maintenance are provided to both remote and local users in a live interactive setting over a distributed, physically dispersed network (for example: an intranet or the internet).

The availability of high bandwidth internet connections world-wide and other derivative capabilities in the areas of real-time communication, control, teleconferencing, video streaming and others have made multi-site collaborative work, utilising state-of-the art equipment in remote laboratories across the globe a current reality.

Learning situations in laboratories can be highly complex, although they have the advantage of usually being well structured. How the particular experiments and learning strategies of specific practices provided in laboratories must be tailored to the knowledge students possess in the theoretical realm and in function of the abilities and competences that are explicitly stated in educational objectives of each individual practice. Although self-directed learning is the most common learning strategy used, a mix of self-directed and collaborative learning is also very common. It is important to mention that this mix in learning strategies is important as it favors both field independent and field dependent learning styles respectively. On the other hand, the communication skills and the skills used in collaborative learning are also well trained in an online laboratory situation (Euan et al., 2005). Splitting the communication channels in such a complex situation stresses a learning process that must handle this more complex multilateral communicative task, emphasising communicative skills, including negotiating meaning and the use of pragmatics to communicate with team-partners over various channels. When designing online experiments, the developer has to model these situations because students must learn to effectively participate in collaborative and teamwork learning environments in teleworking situations, plus receive specific training in the experiment itself.

The emphasis on work in laboratories has varied over the years. While much attention has been paid to curriculum and teaching methods, relatively little has been written about laboratory instruction. For example, in surveys of the articles published in the Journal of Engineering Education from 1993 to 1997, only 6.5 per cent of the papers used laboratory as a keyword. From 1998 to 2002, the percentage was even lower at 5.2 per cent (Wankat, 2004).

One reason for the limited research on instructional laboratories may be a lack of consensus on the basic objectives of the laboratory experience. While there seems to be general agreement that laboratories are necessary, relatively little has been written about what they are expected to accomplish, although some commonly articulated goals include gaining a better understanding of scientific concepts, increasing interest and motivation, providing practical skills and developing problem solving abilities (Hofstein & Lunetta, 2004). Within the discussion of these goals, however, in most papers about laboratories, no course objectives or outcomes are listed, even though it is not unusual for the author to state in the conclusion that the objectives of the course were met. An accepted set of fundamental objectives for laboratories, as set out in this chapter, would help engineering educators focus their efforts and evaluate the effectiveness of laboratory experiences.

It is useful to distinguish among three basic types of engineering laboratories: development, research and educational. While they have many characteristics in common, there are some fundamental differences. These differences must be understood if the instructional laboratory experience is to be well-structured and to provide actual learning experiences that meet educational objectives.

Practicing engineers go to the development laboratory for two reasons. Firstly, they often need experimental data to guide them in designing and developing a product. The development laboratory is used to answer specific questions about nature that must be answered before a design and development process can continue. The second reason is to determine whether a particular design performs as intended. Performance measurements are compared to specifications and these comparisons either demonstrate compliance or indicate where, if not how, changes need to be made.

While a development laboratory is intended to answer specific questions of immediate importance, research laboratories are used to seek broader knowledge that can be generalised and systematised, often without any specific use in mind. The output of a research laboratory is generally seen as an addition to the overall knowledge that we have of the world, be it natural or human made.

However, when students, especially undergraduates, go to the laboratory, it is not generally to extract some data necessary for a design, to evaluate a new device or to discover a new addition to our knowledge of the world. Each of these functions involves determining something that no one else knows or is not generally available. Students go to an instructional laboratory to learn something that practicing engineers are assumed to already know. That 'something' needs to be better defined through carefully designed learning objectives and well-structured practices if the considerable effort devoted to laboratories is to produce a concomitant benefit.

In a laboratory environment, we have an experimenter (researchers, students) who is performing an experiment. Both the experimenter as well as the experiment can be local or remote. Therefore, we have a classification of laboratories as shown in Figure 10.1, where we distinguish between local, remote and virtual labs.

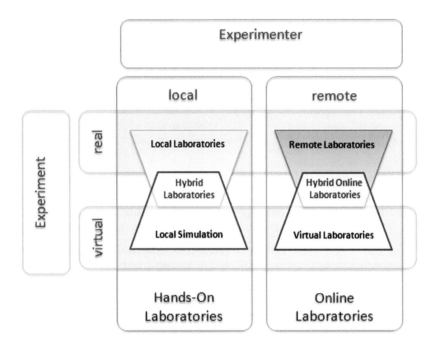

Figure 10.1 Classification of online laboratories

The internet and mobile devices

The internet was first used in 1994 as a tele-control medium and subsequently applied in educational contexts in 1996, when web-based laboratories were first introduced by universities worldwide in undergraduate engineering courses (Aktan et al., 1996). The evidence that the field of remote engineering has matured are overwhelming, particularly as indicated by the number of remote laboratories in operation today. Furthermore, the range of disciplines being taught continues to grow and collaborations between universities all over the world are becoming increasingly common (Euan et al., 2005). The opportunity to provide students with remote access to experimental hardware and the ability to offer flexibility in the time and place in which laboratory practices are conducted are becoming powerful motivations for the field (Euan et al., 2005). However, as online education continues to grow, new and innovative ways to more optimally integrate the practical knowledge gained from online laboratory experiences are needed as interaction models between educational institutions and learners evolve.

Mobile learning technology is portable and, as the name suggests, it is wireless. Thus, any developed learning platform must be able to move with a handheld device and accompany the learner throughout the day, regardless of his/her actual location. Learning using mobile devices is important because the learner is no longer limited by the constraints of time or location. Anytime and anyplace learning is presently revolutionising learning in the workplace as it provides access to on-demand learning content for users (Khaddage, 2009).

Recent advances in mobile technologies have led to a substantial increase in the number of internet users accessing information via mobile devices and the number of applications designed for such devices is growing and becoming increasingly popular. There has been substantial progress in the development of network protocols and hardware technologies that enable these devices to achieve better performance. Mobile devices have advanced considerably in the last decade. Early devices were merely able to render text strings (Lavín-Mera et al., 2009), which represented a major barrier that basically limited mobile learning to a simple message exchange service. In this context, mobile devices considerably increased their processing capabilities and performance. Today, mobile devices go far beyond simple text-based input possibilities and make use of high quality displays, faster wireless interfaces that enable faster internet connections and very affordable prices. Again, mobile technologies expand the concept of traditional laboratories and even the 'extended' online laboratory that is accessed by fixed computer stations. These trend became stronger with the release of Visual Studio .NET 2003 as it became possible to create applications to run on resource-constrained devices in almost the same way Windows application are created. These applications are built for the .NET Compact Framework that includes a large selection of Framework classes and is optimised for the small-screen resolutions of handheld devices. From a pedagogical point of view, student expectations on how and when they learn are also creating increasingly heavier demands upon all aspects of technology. Presently, students are increasingly making mobile devices an extension of their personal space as they become more fundamental to their daily lives. In response, educational and research institutions are moving very rapidly to engage their students and researchers in the expanded opportunities and flexibility offered by mobile technologies.

Mobile learning environments

Mobile remote solutions may represent attractive tools to enhance access to practical experiments because they offer many different possible applications in industry and educations, including online simulations, remote control of real hardware, and industrial application. Also, importantly, they offer the additional advantage of not being subject to the limitations imposed by time and location, as persons can synchronously collaborate, experience, and obtain results in a collaborative synchronous manner. This, along with expanded access to broadband internet, is transforming the way e-learning is carried out, allowing increased levels of interactivity and providing virtual environments closer to real ones. Virtual environments provide the opportunity for students to freely practice various scenarios in quick succession without the fear of actually damaging resources, which often hinders real-life practice. This 'safe' way of gaining practice also encourages initiative, experimentation and creativity as students do not have to face real-world practical restraints. Hence, mobile remote systems can be very useful when applied to situations involving high equipment or personnel costs, particularly with regard to downtime due to transportation and equipment installation. Expanded use of existing laboratory equipment is becoming increasingly important as its acquisition is becoming increasingly expensive. This expense, in part, can be defrayed by universities and institutions sharing laboratory resources by means of a cooperative network of remote systems.

In sum, however, the technology and equipment used in either conventional or online laboratories is only effective to the degree that it respects and conforms to the manner in which people learn. In this case, it is important to note that older learners are significantly different to their younger peers and that success in teaching older learners using work-based learning hinges on recognising these differences and adhering to both, general learning theories and theories specifically pertaining to adult learners.

Generalities about learners and mobile learning

Mobile learning at universities is still in its infancy and several different possibilities need to be explored. New models and methods are necessary and need to be developed to successfully integrate mobile learning with the current practices used in education (Khaddage et al., 2009). Collaboration is certainly a strong point toward the use of mobile devices for education, as these devices are almost ubiquitously present in most students' daily lives. This is an area still to be explored and studies must be carried out before universities or enterprises can fully embrace mobile learning (Khaddage et al., 2009).

Online laboratories and online engineering

Online laboratories are necessary for distance or mobile learning for the same reason laboratory practices are important in traditional educational settings. Persons can acquire theoretical knowledge, but experience that creates significant learning often involves manipulating or viewing the behavior of objects in order to see how they behave in the real world.

Online engineering laboratory practice is delivered by mobile devices that permit workers to access knowledge and experience from remote colleagues or institutions who share similar problems. In this way, an individual problem can become a shared problem to be resolved with the experience of homologues for different places. Among other things, remote laboratories are important because they provide real-world results, not simply knowledge or resources. Persons using remote lab resources can view how objects actually behave under a certain set of circumstances, providing them with a better insight as to what needs to be done. Online engineering in the workplace is becoming increasingly important because of the growing complexity of engineering tasks, the need to share resources among different companies (equipment, simulators etc), especially for short-term trouble shooting that does not warrant the purchase of equipment, the potential collaboration among workers in different companies who share the same problems and can contribute to collaborative solutions, the increased linkage among SMEs and larger enterprises, etc.

Considerations about the learners and learning theories

To be successful in dealing with adult learners, persons in charge of developing online laboratories to be used in work-place learning, above all, need to consider the learner. Thus, adult learning theories become critical in the design and implementation aspects of online laboratories. There are three learning theories primarily related to adult learning. This, of course, does not exclude the contribution of many other learning theories that also apply to learning, in general, but as the focus of this chapter is adult learning in a work-based environment, we will focus on these adult learning theories.

Experiential Learning Theory (Rogers, 1969), as we now know it, was first developed by Charles Rogers in 1969. In many of his works, Rogers discusses what he considers 'significant' learning. Significant learning, he believes, occurs when people actually do things. Cognitive learning is often meaningless and is employed in basic operations, according to Bloom's Taxonomy (Bloom, 1956) (Pohl, 2000). Most learning, according to Bloom is 'cognitive'. Cognitive learning is basically knowledge or encyclopedic in nature. According to him, most knowledge becomes irrelevant if it is not complemented by an affective and psychomotor component. Significantly, according to sensory stimulation theory (Laird, 1985), the more senses instruction incorporates, the more consolidated learning will be. This means that by involving sight and sound, persons can greatly improve leaning because more than 80 per cent of learning involves these two channels. In laboratory practices, kinesthetic learning, often referred to as 'learning by doing' or tactile learning, involves movement and active manipulation of objects. In kinesthetic learning, which is greatly stimulated in laboratory environments is added, the having to actually do or experience something consolidates learning even more. The basis of action learning and action research, where individuals study and analyze their actions in order to improve the performance of specific actions, is akin to 'leaning by doing' or teaching by ways of exemplification and repetition of actions (observational learning) (Revans, 1982).

Experiential leaning theory maintains that adult learners bring experiences (both positive and negative) to leaning activities. Therefore, learning experiences need to be non-threatening, especially if the adult learner has had a previous negative experience or the learning experience is completely novel. Importantly, whatever the learning activity happens to be, it needs to be highly relevant. While younger learners can be easily coerced by grades, adults learn to cope with the demands of life. As far as the workplace is concerned, they learn because they perhaps have recently been hired to a new job. A couple of generations ago, adults could work their entire adult lives in one place. However, modern society often requires adults change jobs several times over a lifetime as new jobs evolve and older jobs disappear. Adults, seeking work-based learning opportunities primarily to obtain a new job either within or outside the organisation, take advantage of a promotion opportunity or avoid losing a job. In short, learning happens when it is relevant to the immediate needs of the learner and learning tends to be stronger if the perceived need is stronger. That is unless the stress placed upon the learner impedes learning (Lawless & Allen, 2004).

An important aspect of adult learning is that the entire online learning activity needs to evoke positive emotions towards the activity and lower stress and anxiety. Borrowing from language learning theory Stephen Krashen's Affective Filter Hypothesis (Krashen, 1987), which today forms the basis of second language instruction, states that when a person is threatened or the actual learning experience conflicts with a person's way of thinking, the learning experience will not be as fruitful as an experience that complements the person's way of thinking or lowers any possible perceived threat to a person's belief system (Krashen, 1988). It is important to add that affect in leaning is not causal in the sense that persons who have low motivation, anxiety or assign negative attributes to specific learning have greater difficulties learning. Also, positive affect is not causal with respect to learning. Rather, the affective filter hypothesis asserts that positive self-concept and high motivational and low anxiety levels promote leaning. The primary weakness of this theory, however, is that affect is very difficult to identify because it is often very subtle and, thus, very difficult to measure. Also, instrumental learning or learning that is based solely on pragmatic need or convenience, can also be equally, or even more productive, independent of affective concerns. Thus, Krashen hypothesises that the most successful learners learn because they combine both affect and need. Finally, Krashen maintains that learning should be carried out at an *i+1* level, meaning that learning should be at the current learner's level plus an additional input slightly above the level maintained by the learner (Krashen, 1988). Thus, in order to lower stress or negative feelings towards a mobile work-based activity, participants should provide input as to the type of activity and feel they have control over their learning. Furthermore, it is important for adult learners to receive feedback and personally assess the online laboratory experience. Additional self-initiated learning should also be promoted so that adults can learn without any formal evaluation that might be considered part of his/her work record (Rogers & Freiberg, 1994; Combs, 1982).

Andragogy is an adult learning theory that attempts to explain the special needs of adults and how to better help them learn. Since its introduction by Malcolm Knowles, this theory has been extensively used in the 'design of organizational training programs (especially for "soft skill" domains such as management development'). Again, similar to experiential learning theory, according to Zemke (1984), andragogy maintains:

(a)   adults learn best when what they are to learn is of immediate perceived value;
(b)   learners are more satisfied and learn more when they are included in the organization and content of the online activity;
(c)   kinesthetic learning is very important because actually doing things consolidates 'book knowledge' by combining the senses; and
(d)   adults use previous experiences to relate to present experiences, therefore, experiential learning is of vital importance.

It is important to mention, however, that Andragogy has its critics, who basically believe that child and adult learning basically involves the same processes and others who argue that child learning basically teacher-directed learning and adult learning is self-directed. Also, these principles are not exclusive to adults. Children often display the same characteristics. Either way, neurophysiologically, there are significant differences in the way children and adults process information and the way they learn reflects these differences. Recognising that adult learning differs from childhood or adolescent learning can help produce more effective learning.

In order not to create confusion, Rogers (humanistic) and Knowles (andragogy) share many principles, but to better understand the different theories it is important to remember that Rogers is considered a humanist. Thus, recommendations about adult education, although they may sound similar to Knowles, are different in their basic underpinnings.

Important to our discussion on mobile work-based learning and the application of online laboratories, Knowles (1984) provides examples of several andragogy principles that need to be taken into account in the area of computer training:

(a)   There is a need to explain why specific things are being taught (e.g. certain commands, functions, operations etc.).

(b)   Instruction should be task-oriented instead of memorization – learning activities should be in the context of common tasks to be performed.

(c)   Instruction should take into account the wide range of different learner backgrounds; learning materials and activities should allow for different levels/types of previous experience with computers.

(d)   Since adults are self-directed, instruction should allow learners to discover things for themselves, providing guidance and help when mistakes are made.

It is important to note that although these four principals for computer learning were proposed for stand-alone or local-access networks, the same basic suggestions still hold true for online laboratories used as part of work-based learning.

Finally, the Characteristics of Adults as Learners (CAL) model, presented in 1981 by Patricia Cross, combines many of the characteristics of experiential learning proposed by Charles Rogers (Rogers & Freiberg, 1994), David Kolb (Kolb, 1984) and andragogy (Knowles), mentioned previously in this section. The CAL model is based on differences between personal characteristics (physical, stage of life, experiences, general cognitive development etc., as well as psychological, social and cultural variables) and situational characteristics (voluntary vs. obligatory learning program, full-time vs. part-time attendance, etc.) (Cross, 1981).

Adulthood brings many changes and the CAL model considers these changes. Personal characteristics, for instance, include physical changes that can affect learning such as deteriorations in eyesight, hearing and reaction time. As far as intelligence is concerned, independence, decision-making skills, reasoning, conceptualising, abstract thinking and vocabulary skills tend to improve. Finally, situations adults face are quite different and affect learning, attitudes and motivation. Some of these 'life phases' and developmental stages include marriage, job changes and retirement, to name just a few, as well as other variables which may or not be directly related to age (Knowles, 1984).

Situational characteristics consist of part-time versus full-time learning and voluntary versus compulsory learning. These situational variables play a very important part in how, where and when the teaching/learning process can actually take place. This aspect particularly affects schedules, administrative procedures and the potential locations where learning can take place.

According to this model (Zemke, 1984), four basic things characterise adult learners:

(a)   participation is motivated by both positive and negative factors;
(b)   participation is correlated to anticipated learning outcomes;
(c)   a sense of security precedes the need for achievement; and
(d)   expectations of rewards affect motivation.

In sum, there are several important implications for persons developing work-based adult mobile learning environments.

(1)   Work-based mobile learning, in general, and online laboratories in interactive mobile learning environments, in particular, should take advantage of the previous experience and cognitive development of the users. For an online lab experience to function optimally, students should be familiar with similar real-world experiments/experiences where they have physically manipulated the materials in person. The cognitive load placed upon adult learners using mobile or remote systems in the workplace should be minimised to account for aging.
(2)   Because the brain changes, life circumstances change, life experiences differ and expectations evolve. Consequently, mobile learning in the workplace should consider these variables when developing curricula or applications using mobile or remote systems. In the field of engineering, for example, two engineers may be doing the same remote experiment but according to personal and situational variables they may interpret the results differently or apply the knowledge they gained in different manners. Therefore, work-based mobile learning should allow communication among participants and it is indispensable for participants to share perspectives and expand on their knowledge,

based on the extensive experience of peers. This implies post activities subsequent to any mobile online experience, where open-ended discussion and activities permit the students to involve themselves cognitively and use their previous knowledge and experience.

(3) Adults are motivated quite differently than younger learners. Adults tend to be more motivated by intrinsic and instrumental motivation, meaning that they are more self-motivated and the rewards they expect are generally due to the satisfaction of doing things and experiencing success. Increasing or maintaining self-esteem and pleasure are strong secondary motivators for engaging in learning experiences. It must be mentioned, however, that the positive consequence of obtaining a pay raise or the fear of negative consequences such as being transferred or terminated are also important motivators. For work-based mobile learning, this means that the activities should not be threatening to the leaner and should be incentivised with positive consequences. Adult learning is often a means to an end, not an end in itself. Therefore, in the context of mobile learning and online laboratories, the learning and practice offered should be directly related to the one central point that is being covered and that one point should be directly related to the knowledge set, skills, abilities and competencies they require in the workplace.

(4) Adults need to have as much choice as possible in developing and implementing their learning experiences. Consequently, adult learners using online laboratories need to have some input into what the work-based mobile experience should entail. This is also true for online laboratory experiences as the previous experience of adults is often considerable and the insight they provide can make subsequent learning more effective. In other words, when possible, online laboratories need to be open-ended, allowing students to select among several experiments that can produce the same or similar results. If older students, in particular, have a choice regarding the activities and can discuss their results freely with their peers, they will be more satisfied with the learning experience. Furthermore, studies show that self-correction and peer-correction are more effective than teacher-correction. This is, in part, because it is less stressful and threatening for the student.

(5) Adults are more self-directed and prefer more autonomous learning. Adults connect what they need to learn with what they must learn. They are also more selective in keeping and using the information they are presented. This, however, does not mean that they do not need considerable guidance. Work-based mobile learning systems for adult learners need to be more open-ended and permit them to commit errors and then provide them the feedback necessary for them to self-correct.

(6) Although adults have many more life experiences, not all life experiences are positive. Adult learners tend to 'hold on' to previous knowledge, customs and habits they have developed. Therefore, adult learning in the context of work-based mobile learning and online laboratories needs to permit adult learners to affect necessary changes in a non-threatening way. Therefore, affectivity is most important in permitting adult learners to construct changes within themselves, according to constructivist theory (Cross, 1981). This is a particularly important point when introducing technologies in the workplace. Work-based mobile learning has been limited by resistance from adult learners refusing to adopt new technologies. Again, this is often because they have not had previous positive experiences with technologies that they can bring into mobile learning environments.

Undoubtedly, there are many more aspects of theories related to adult learning that have not been covered here. However, the basic points mentioned, when applied successfully to work-based mobile learning and online laboratories, will greatly contribute to developing the educational philosophy, curricula, online materials and tools, online laboratories and practices, and the appropriate socio-emotional and organisational environment needed to successfully apply mobile learning in the workplace.

The following section will specifically discuss learning in online laboratory environments before moving on to discuss the technical specifications of an interactive mobile learning environment that considers many of the aforementioned educational premises.

Considerations about e-learning and mobile learning

E-Learning can be defined as the utilisation of internet, intranet, software and any other e-media to combine the power of all the new technologies to enhance the learning process. E-learning introduces a different way of learning that can help students in many ways. Students can access a large amount of information, study on their own, be more confident, and communicate with fellow classmates, released from traditional classroom stress. However, e-learning is not intended to replace traditional learning. It can be used alone or in conjunction with more than one traditional learning method; in this case, the term blended learning is used (Hassan, 2009).

Usually, e-learning platforms provide several services. Some of these services are common and have grown since computers were first used in education; other services can vary from one platform to another. One of the most important services for any e-learning platform is the learning content and content presentation.

Much effort has been devoted to the reuse of teaching materials and the result was the introduction of the term Learning Objects (LO) (Hassan, 2009). Learning Objects offer a conceptualisation of the learning process. The Institute of Electrical and Electronics Engineers (IEEE) defines learning objects as 'any entity, digital or non-digital, which can be used, re-used or referenced during technology supported learning' (Hassan, 2009).

Assuming that e-learning content has a life cycle which includes a number of phases; the content passes through these phases before the learner can interact with it. Each phase has a specific purpose or objective that enhances the leaning content. E-Learning lifecycle content includes analysis, design, authoring, assembly, transport, storage, delivery, interaction and monitoring (Hassan, 2009).

Mobile learning, or m-learning, has many definitions on how people can learn or stay connected with their learning environments that include their classmates, instructors and instructional resources through mobile devices (Hassan, 2009).

The LabView PDA module for designing mobile applications

The LabView PDA module allows users to create custom, user-defined applications for Palm, Windows Mobile, Pocket PC and Windows CE devices. This can be achieved with a LabView programming environment in the same way it is developed for a PC application and later deploying it to a PDA. It also allows for the development of data acquisition applications with Compact Flash and PCMCIA DAQ cards.

The LabView PDA module also includes some libraries of sub VIs developed to take advantage of some resources available on PDAs and smartphones, such as short message services (SMS) and telephony. Furthermore, it is also possible to use most of the known functions and Application Programming Interfaces (API) available when developing applications for PCs.

It is possible to deploy applications with the LabView PDA module for the most common operating systems found for these devices, like Windows Mobile, Palm OS and it is also possible to deploy it for emulated or real devices via a synchronisation tool like Microsoft Activesync for Windows Mobile. Because of the limited graphical capabilities of these devices, the controls and indicators are sized and scaled and the functions palette is reconfigured.

The READ (Remote ASIC Design and Test)

The READ laboratory is based on an *in-system programmable* analog device which permits the implementation of several analog functions commonly studied in electronics courses. The flexibility of the measured device permits users to change the various characteristics of a circuit without requiring external components or even its removal from the testing platform. The programmability of this device allows the designer to realise thousands of distinct analog circuits and filter characteristics from a given circuit architecture.

By assuming a fixed architecture, the ordinarily complex task of designing a desired analog circuit or filter can be reduced to a simple table-based process, instead of designing the whole circuit from scratch. Circuit programming and uploading are achieved by means of a windows-based application called PAC-Designer. The analog circuit can be designed and simulated at a PC with free available schematic-based software and a built-in simulator (PAC-Designer), or it can be exported to other applications (see Figure 10.2).

Figure 10.2 PCB with the ASIC

For PC-based clients, the PAC-Designer software is also available remotely and is delivered via our Citrix Presentation server, where users can change circuit schematics as required. For mobile clients, however, this feature is not available and we assume that predefined analog functions should be already uploaded to the device.

On PC-based clients, the platform allows for the realisation of a complete cycle that includes programming, simulating and testing a specific configuration. On the other hand, for mobile clients, users are not able to change or design a circuit as this functionality is still not supported.

The process of testing the circuit includes applying an input signal and measuring the output. Signal inputs are generated by the software that controls the hardware and are converted to an analog signal on the output. The system was designed and assembled to offer the same functionalities to remote lab users than if they were executing the experiment locally. Furthermore, this concept can also be applied to perform experiments with other programmable devices, for example with digital circuits.

The ispPAC10 device has 4 analog inputs and 4 analog outputs. Among the functionalities of the system, users can choose an input to apply an analog signal as well as to read. The user is able to choose the waveform shape, amplitude, frequency and signal offset.

This part of the chapter focuses on a practical example, our READ system. It provides remote users with access to real experiments. It relies on a data acquisition card to generate signals and read responses with the aid of the NI DAQmx driver software, which can be called from the LabView to program NI measurement devices. The driver software has an application programming interface (API), which consists of a library of VIs, functions, classes, attributes, and properties for creating applications with data acquisition.

Figure 10.3 shows the network topology of the remote laboratories and clients.

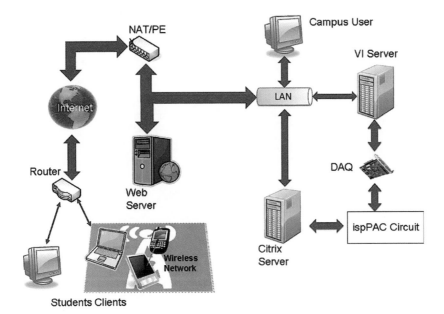

Figure 10.3   Network topology of the online experiments

The communication between the server and client was developed with the Application Programming Interface (API) for TCP/IP communication from LabVIEW.

The server processes the client requests by applying the desired signal to the circuit under test and returning the measurements. Clients were designed for PDAs as well as for Windows PCs and requests from both are treated seamlessly by the server. Due to the resource constraints of PDA devices, not all of the features designed for a client running on a PC are performed when accessing the system via PDAs, for example, the already mentioned possibility of designing circuits is not available with mobile devices (see Figure 10.4).

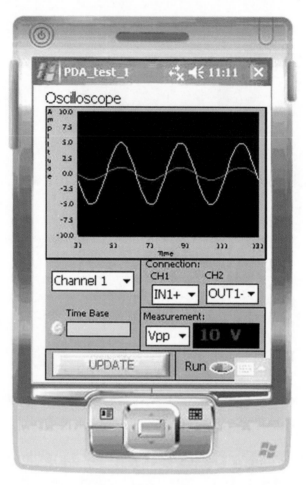

Figure 10.4   Example of a VI deployed to a WM5 emulator

Another approach to implement this communication with LabView is using shared variables to transmit data between multiple computers using simple coding techniques because they are faster and simpler to implement, when compared to similar communication methods. Shared variables use the Publish-Subscribe Protocol (PSP), which is a form of User Datagram Protocol (UDP). Sharing these variables is possible because of the Shared

Variable Engine (SVE). For standalone applications based on shared variables, it is necessary to install the SVE separately. For PDA devices, it is also necessary to install the support for shared variables (NI, 2010). The SVE is where a variable resides on a computer. It manages network communications and bindings, all of which can be configured from within LabView. Shared variables are an easy way to transfer data between targets over a network due to their high level, easy configuration and set up interfaces. Shared variable servers use UDP port 2343 and a range of UDP ports from 6000 to 6010 for incoming and outgoing packets and the clients use a range of UDP ports beginning with port 5000. The number of ports above 6000 that the network-published shared variable servers use depends on the number of servers running on the computer. The NI-PSP protocol also uses TCP ports and it begins looking for available TCP ports at port 59110 and increases upward until it finds an available port (NI, 2010).

Table 10.1 shows a comparison between TCP/IP and shared variables.

	Shared Variables	TCP/IP
Implementation	Fast	Takes more time to develop applications
Implementation complexity	Easy implementation	More complex
Portability to other client platforms	Low. Relies on LabView installed on the client	High. client can be developed in different platforms
Problems with network security policies	Several TCP and UDP ports must be opened	Flexible to choose any port

Table 10.1 Comparison between TCP/IP and shared variables

The latest version of this system is so far only available for PC clients and is delivered as a Java Applet. The user-interface of this laboratory can be seen in Figure 10.5. This new version will be adapted to run also on mobile devices but the functionalities available here are the same, except for the possibility of designing the desired circuit.

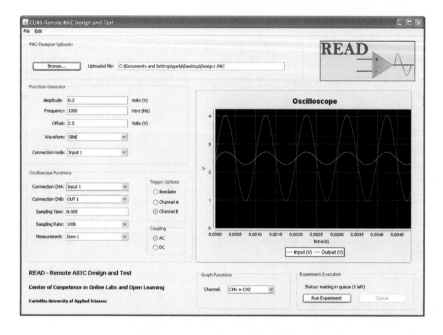

Figure 10.5   User-interface for PC clients

Basically, the system emulates the functionalities of an oscilloscope and a function generator by allowing the user to control some parameters that govern the data acquisition.

The parameters (seen on Figure 10.5) *amplitude, frequency, offset* and *connection node* are used by the function generator while *connection CHA, connection CHB, sampling time* and *sampling rate* specify govern the data acquisition of performed by the oscilloscope. The graphical representation of the measurements can be seen on the graph displayed.

For mobile clients, it is necessary to consider the limitations regarding screen size; therefore, some of these parameters might be suppressed, as seen in Figure 10.4.

Conclusions

A new wireless remote lab system was developed to enable university students and practicing engineers to access experiments via the internet from their mobile devices. The types of experiments under consideration were mainly electronic circuits at the junior undergraduate level for electrical engineering students. However, adult learners can also benefit from this online lab experience in actual workplace settings.

The most important consideration when designing a remote laboratory client to be accessed by devices like PDAs and Smartphones is their limited resources compared to PCs. Therefore, it is necessary to optimise the clients to compensate for these limitations, which leads to a reduction of features available for such labs.

Remote mobile solutions are attractive tools because they have many potential applications in industries and e-learning. Wireless mobile experimenters have a great advantage because they are not subject to limitations of locomotion, although they do require good network (wireless) infrastructure to perform experiments and still are limited with regard to some aspects, as pointed out by some authors. These limitations can be summarised by: limited processing capabilities and resources, screen size and display resolution and variety of operating systems available (Khaddage, 2009). The last point must be highly considered if a mobile learning application is intended to be broadly delivered. In that case, different operating systems must be supported. For this reason, we understand that each specific situation must be studied within a given scenario prior to implementation.

Moreover, remote systems can be very useful when applied to solutions involving the often substantial costs of transporting people or equipment. Different institutes and schools could share experiments and knowledge in a collaborative manner that parallels real-life working conditions. Also, by using remote solutions, it is possible for institutions with more limited financial resources to take advantages of expensive equipment installed at other institutions by means of a cooperative network of remote systems.

Importantly, online labs can be also used in workplace settings where there is a pressing need to apply these systems to continually provide learning opportunities for workers who must adapt to rapidly changing conditions.

The work presented with this chapter shows one possibility for providing remote control over one specific device (ispPAC10) to clients running on mobile devices.

Finally, we would like to point out that the solutions shown are also applicable to other labs or experiments by an easy to adapt standard solution.

References

Aktan, B., Bohus, C., Crowl L., & Shor, M. (1996) 'Distance learning applied to control engineering laboratories'. *IEEE Transaction on Education 39*(3), pp. 320–326

Billett, S. (2004) 'Workplace participatory practices: conceptualizing workplaces as learning environments'. *Journal of Workplace Learning 16*(6), pp. 312–324

Bloom, B., et al. (1956) *Taxonomy of educational objectives: Handbook I. The cognitive domain*. New York: David McKay & Co

Bruner, J. (1996) *The culture of education*. Cambridge, MA: Harvard University Press

Combs, A. (1982) 'Affective education or none at all'. *Educational Leadership 39*(7), pp. 494–497

Cross, K. (1981) *Adults as learners*. San Francisco, CA: Jossey-Bass

Enloe, C., Pakula W., Finney, G., & Haaland, R. (1999) 'Teleoperation in the undergraduate Physics laboratory – Teaching an old dog new tricks'. *IEEE Transaction on Education 42*(3), pp. 174–179

Euan, D., Good, L., & Good, M. (2005) 'Effects of laboratory access modes upon learning outcomes'. *IEEE Transaction on Education 48*(4), pp. 619–631

Harris, R., Simons, M., & Moore, J. (2005) *A huge learning curve: TAFE practitioners' ways of working with private enterprise*. Adelaide: NCVER

Hassan, M. & Al-Sadi, J. (2009) 'A new mobile learning adaption model'. Paper presented at *4th ICML – International Conference on Interactive Mobile and Computer Aided Learning*, 22–24 April, Amman, Jordan

Hofstein, A., & Lunetta, V. (2004) 'The laboratory in science education: Foundations for the twenty-first century.' *Science Education 8*(1), pp. 28–54

Khaddage, F., Lanham, E. & Zhou, W. (2009) 'A proposed blended mobile learning model for application in Higher Education.' Paper presented at *4th IMCL – International Conference on Interactive Mobile and Computer Aided Learning*, 22–24 April, Amman, Jordan

Knowles, M. (1984) *The adult learner: a neglected species.* 3rd edn. Houston, TX: Gulf Publishing

Kolb, D. (1984) *Experiential learning: Experience as the source of learning and development.* Prentice-Hall

Krashen, S. (1987) *Principles and practice in second language acquisition.* London: Prentice-Hall

Krashen, S. (1988) *Second language acquisition and second language learning.* London: Prentice-Hall

Laird, D. (1985) *Approaches to training and development reading.* MA: Addison-Wesley

Lavín-Mera, P., Torrente, J., Moreno-Ger, P., & Fernández-Manjón, B. (2009) 'Mobile Game Development for Multiple Devices in Education.' Paper presented at *4th IMCL – International Conference on Interactive Mobile and Computer Aided Learning*, 22–24 April, Amman, Jordan

Lawless, N., & Allen, J. (2004) 'Understanding and Reducing Stress in Collaborative e-learning.' *Electronic Journal of e-learning 2*

Maughan, P. (2008) 'From theory to practice: insights into faculty learning from the Mellon Library/Faculty Fellowship for undergraduate research.' In Kohl-Frey, O., & Schmid-Ruhe, B. (eds) *Advanced users: information literacy and customized services. Proceedings of the Konstanz workshop on information literacy (KWIL)*, pp. 9–23. Available online at <http://kops.ub.uni-konstanz.de/volltexte/2008/5905/pdf/tagungsband1.pdf> (accessed 26/04/10)

Pohl, M. (2000) *Learning to think, thinking to learn: Models and strategies to develop a classroom culture of thinking.* Cheltenham, Vic.: Hawker Browntow

Revans, R. (1982) *Origins and growth of action learning.* Bratt-Institute fur Neues Lernen

Rogers, C. & Freiberg, H. (1994) *Freedom to learn.* 3rd edn. Columbus, OH: Merrill/Macmillan

Rogers, C. (1969) *Freedom to learn.* Columbus, OH: Merrill

Shen, H., Xu, Z., Dalager, B., Kristiansen V., Strøm, Ø., Shur, M., Fjeldly, T., Lu, J. & Ytterdal, T. (1999) 'Conducting laboratory experiments over the internet.' *IEEE Transaction on Education 42*(3), pp. 180–185

Tuttas, J., & Wagner, B. (2001) 'Distributed online laboratories.' *Proceedings of the International Conference on Engineering Education*. Available online at <http://www.ni.com> (accessed 14/01/10)

Wankat, P. (2004) 'Analysis of the first ten years of the Journal of Engineering Education'. *Journal of Engineering Education 93*(1), pp. 13–21

Zemke, R., & Zemke, S. (1984) '30 things we know for sure about adult learning.' *Innovation Abstracts VI (8)*

SARAH CORNELIUS AND PHIL MARSTON

11 Work-based simulations: Using text messaging and the role of the virtual context[1]

Abstract

Simulations provide learning experiences which help to prepare learners for work-related tasks and real-world experiences and allow the application of theoretical knowledge to practical situations. This chapter outlines the design of alternate reality simulations that make use of SMS text messaging to provide authentic learning experiences. The design of the first SMS simulation to be developed – a flood disaster scenario for an undergraduate course in applied geomorphology – is discussed. Details are also provided of a contrasting simulation for a mentoring experience developed for work-based learners. Findings from mixed methods studies informed by activity theory, which aimed to evaluate learners' experiences of both simulations, are presented. These findings raise issues which may influence successful implementation of SMS simulations, in particular the need for careful consideration of contextual issues and sensitive implementation of real-time mobile learning with work-based learners. The chapter also introduces the 'virtual context' – a persistent, consistent, realistic and engaging physical and social scenario which is distinct from the physical and social context in which the learner is located. Finally, the chapter proposes guidelines for the successful implementation of similar alternate reality simulations using SMS.

---

1   A number of colleagues from the University of Aberdeen have contributed significantly to the design and development of the SMS simulations, in particular Alastair Gemmell, Ian Finlayson and Chris Aldred. Thanks are also due to Steve Sidaway at <http://txttools.co.uk> for assistance with technical aspects of the messaging system used.

Introduction

Simulations are an accepted and widely adopted approach used to prepare learners and workers for situations where real-world experiences would be too costly, sensitive, dangerous or logistically impossible. They permit the application of theoretical ideas to practical situations without risk, allow learning from mistakes and develop confidence in learners' decision-making abilities. Successful simulations are authentic and relevant, and provide re-playable experiences that tap into learners' emotions (Aldrich, 2004). They are an opportunity to experiment and gain experience to help learners' challenge their preconceptions and reconstruct meaning in a way which is in line with models of work-based and experiential learning (Raelin, 1997; Schön, 1983).

This chapter introduces the design of alternate reality simulations using text messaging (SMS) which have potential as effective and authentic mobile learning activities. Implementations in formal and work-based learning contexts (with undergraduate geography and work-based adult literacies practitioners) are described and evaluated and it is argued that work-based learning implementations require consideration of a complex set of issues associated with the virtual context of the simulation scenario and the work context of the learners themselves.

The chapter also discusses the notion of the 'virtual context', a context which supplements the physical and social contexts identified in recent definitions of mobile learning (for example Wali et al., 2008). Consideration of the virtual context aids conceptualisation of the simulations and will help with the description and implementation of similar activities.

Background: The development of a flood simulation

In early 2004 the requirements for a real-time simulation of a natural hazard scenario were formulated. A role-play scenario was required for final year geography undergraduates which would run across a university network, provide a variety of scenarios and need minimal staff intervention. The simulation should give learners an opportunity to deploy their theoretical knowledge about the nature of specific natural hazards to practical ends; allow them to develop an appreciation of the dynamics of hazard situations; and enable investigation of the problems of reconciling competing viewpoints about disaster management strategies in the face of a hazardous event.

Two desktop simulations that specifically dealt with natural hazard management scenarios were considered for inspiration, ideas and possible 'off-the-shelf' solutions. One was the Collaborative Forest Fire Fighting Simulation Tool (CFFFST) (<http://geovrml.com/eng/CIFSC/>) developed for the French Civilian Defense training schools. The other was a tool called FloodRanger (<http://www.discoverysoftware.co.uk/Flood-Ranger.htm>) that had been developed with funding from the Office of Science and Technology in the UK as part of the Foresight programme (BBC, 2004). Both applications met the majority of the requirements set out above, however, while they both offered a certain degree of role-play, neither provided a simulated work placement experience. In addition, developing a similar application to meet the needs of the geography course would have had very high resource implications, requiring 3D skills, game engine programming experience, time and personnel which were not available to the development team.

Having identified role-play as a significant requirement for the simulation, three other potential solutions were considered. During 2004 a pilot TV series from the BBC, called Crisis Command, was being broadcast. In each episode of the series 'players' were given the task of advising government while the UK experienced a crisis such as flooding in London (see <http://www.ukgameshows.com/page/index.php?title=Crisis_Command>). Second, Alternate Reality Games (ARGs) such as 'I Love Bees' (<http://www.argn.com/2004/12/halo_2s_i_love_bees_alternate_reality_game/>) were becoming popular as marketing tools for products such as Halo2 (a video game for Microsoft's X-Box console). ARGs provide a fictional narrative delivered through every-day media (such as web-pages, print, SMS and phone-calls). Third, the JISC funded e-MapScholar Virtual Placement (Cornelius et al., 2005) also employed a role-play approach. This involved learners in the role of a placement student undertaking research for a (fictional) virtual company and interacting via email with fictional company employees (played by academic staff). Significant features of these three examples are that they offer the possibility of realistic simulations with familiar modes of interaction and they focus on role and narrative without the need for a dedicated software interface. However, the more open-ended the possibilities in the role-play, the greater the need for expensive human intervention and orchestration. Any simulation developed along these lines would need a systematised activity to avoid significant human intervention (i.e. academic staff time).

The solution developed drew on ideas from the real-time role-play simulation model provided by the e-MapScholar Virtual Placement and used a scenario based on the well-documented flooding which occurred in the French town of Vaison-la-Romaine in 1992. Development initially centred on the development of (real) websites that would provide useful (fictional) media streams on which learners could draw during the simulation. Web pages would provide weather data, news reports and other information and these would be supplemented by opportunities for email correspondence with relevant organisations such as local authorities.

To develop the content a clear 'event narrative' and mapping of the scenario was required. The history of the real events that took place in Vaison-la-Romaine and knowledge of the geomorphology of the area were used to create a series of manageable events on a 72-hour time line. Key events in the course of the flood, those that should influence mitigation decisions, were identified and termed 'event horizons'. This mapping exercise indicated that the Vaison-la-Romaine scenario lent it self to a branching tree framework (Aldrich, 2005). Possible courses of action were plotted at each of the event horizons together with key pieces of information that would be needed for appropriate decisions to be made in advance of the event (see Figure 11.1).

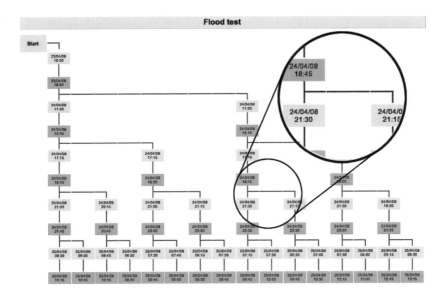

Figure 11.1 The branching tree framework for the SMS flood scenario. Darker rows represent event horizons from the scenario mapping exercise.

It quickly became clear that the simulation could be developed with only a limited amount of key information delivered at critical points on the time-line and the use of simple binary decisions. With this insight the need for supporting web-sites and associated development overheads was brought into question. Software was required to cater for two primary activities: encoding the branching tree and communicating with the participants. The tree structure was stored in a database with the information for nodes (event horizons) entered via a web-based form (see Figure 11.2). Communication with participants needed to be available in real-time over the 72 hour period that the events took place. A number of options were considered, including regularly updated web-pages, email and SMS. Web-pages and email were easy and would incur negligible running costs but would not provide a compelling level of realism and immediacy since this would require 24/7 access to a desktop PC and regular checking by participants. Although incurring a cost to both participants and the sender, SMS (with email backup) was selected as this offered the potential to provide a more realistic experience.

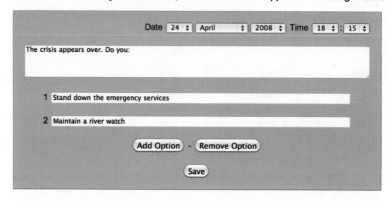

There has been a heavy thunderstorm, but river levels still appear to be falling in Laval

Date [24 ‡] [April   ‡] [2008 ‡] Time [18 ‡]:[15 ‡]

The crisis appears over. Do you:

1   Stand down the emergency services

2   Maintain a river watch

(Add Option) - (Remove Option)

(Save)

Figure 11.2   Web-based form for entering and editing information for the nodes

The simulation for the flood scenario as outlined above has been implemented and evaluated with two cohorts of geography undergraduates and the model has been extended to a contrasting example in which the learner plays the role of a work-based mentor for new students on a teaching qualification. These two implementations have provided opportunities to explore both the theoretical and technical design of work-based simulations and learners' experiences of such activities. The next section presents the key principles behind the design of these simulations, then the two case studies are explained. Some of the findings of the evaluation of the two scenarios are discussed since these reveal differences in undergraduate and work-based learners' responses to the simulations and have helped to provide evidence of issues that require consideration for successful implementation of SMS based activities in work-based situations.

The design of SMS simulations

SMS simulations exploit the opportunity offered by text messaging to take learning beyond the classroom and provide an authentic experience to augment course content. A number of general principles lie behind their design. These include the need for replication of an authentic situation; the use of realistic methods of communication; the inclusion of a real-time element; personalised decision-making and flexible implementation.

An SMS simulation should replicate an authentic situation. The replication of a real-world, work-related experience has been an important principle behind the simulations. Already mentioned are scenarios which address disaster management following a natural disaster and the development of a mentoring relationship with a distant mentee. Other scenarios under discussion ranged from the management of maternity patients to issues of classroom inclusion. All these scenarios draw on real experiences and provide authentic learning to increase motivation through engagement with relevant real-world problems and learning by doing (Lombardi, 2007).

SMS is increasingly being used in work-related situations, therefore, use for replicating authentic scenarios has grounding in reality. In a recent example, the BBC web-site (BBC, 2008) reported a case where a surgeon in Africa was assisted in the performance of a life saving amputation on a boy by text messages sent to him from colleagues in the UK. Anecdotal evidence from some of our own learners, who are also tutors in community education settings, suggests increasing use of SMS in their work setting for communication with younger clients. SMS has other uses in real world scenarios where work takes place in distributed locations and in emergency incident response and information distribution. The service developed after the Haiti earthquake (ReutersLink, 2010) and the UK Floodline Warnings Direct service (Environment Agency, 2010) are examples of authentic applications where the use of SMS is embedded in practice. Replicating such authentic practices with technology allows the creation of distinctive contexts that support learning (Thorpe, 2010).

To improve authenticity and exploit the anytime, anywhere opportunities offered by using SMS the simulations replicate scenarios that take place in real-time. A volcanic eruption, medical emergency or even distraught mentee would not restrict their activities to office hours; instead, events may happen and decisions be required when it is inconvenient for those involved. Ad-hoc tasks, which are set at unknown and unpredictable times and which interfere with everyday routines, have been shown to motivate learners (Frohberg & Schwabe, 2006), and the scenarios all make some use of the opportunity to go beyond normal hours and disrupt learners' lives outside their 'normal' study times to promote engagement with the situations. The disruptive element of the simulations is one of their key characteristics and is explored further later in the chapter.

During each scenario the learner receives a series of text messages. Some messages provide information about the scenario (see examples in Table 11.1). In between each information message, at an appropriate time interval, come other messages which require the learner to make a decision and return a response (see Table 11.1). Another information message follows which tells the learner what the result of their decision has been; and so the cycle continues. The model is in line with that used in decision-making games and books (such as Jackson & Livingston, 1982) and has been implemented using the branching-tree model outlined above (Figure 11.1). Although all learners engaging with a particular simulation start with the same message, the decisions they make will generate an individual pathway through the branching-tree. Careful design allows distinct end points to be developed which indicate the route taken by individuals. Reviewing the path taken provides an opportunity for learners to reflect on their decision-making and consider alternatives. For adult and work-based learners experiences outside of normal practice facilitate reflection (Boud et al., 1985) and reflection is widely acknowledged as an important component of professional learning and development (Moon, 1999; Schön, 1983).

The role of the simulation within a course or programme of study should be flexible. SMS simulations have been used to allow application of theoretical knowledge to practical situations, and to encourage reflection on professional skills following engagement in an authentic experience. The integration of the use of mobile devices with reflection has been advocated in work-based learning contexts including teacher education (Aubussen et al., 2009) and for junior doctors (Pimmer, 2009). The simulations can also be deployed with or without a link to assessment, depending on the preferences of the tutor and the needs of the learner. This flexibility enhances reusability of the model and effective implementation by individual tutors.

Case studies of SMS simulations

SMS simulations have been developed for two contrasting scenarios: the flood disaster simulation and a mentoring scenario. In the flood simulation, introduced earlier, the learner plays the role of a utilities manager making decisions to try to prevent disaster. In the mentoring simulation the learner plays the role of a mentor (an experienced literacies tutor) developing a new relationship with a distant mentee (a student on an adult literacies course). The key features of both simulations are summarised in Table 11.1.

	Flood simulation	Mentoring simulation
Who were the learners?	Final year undergraduates studying Applied Geomorphology	Work-based learners on a course for 'Practice Tutors' supporting the Teaching Qualification in Adult Literacies (TQAL)
What were the aims of the simulation?	To provide an opportunity to apply theory learnt to a practical situation; to encourage rapid decision-making in an authentic context	To promote thinking about the mentoring relationship prior to meeting new mentees.
What was the 'Virtual context'?	Based on the real town in which the flooding occurred. The learner plays the role of a utilities manager.	Based on the model of mentoring used in the TQAL programme. This involves one mentor working with one mentee at a distance to provide support during their studies.

What is the role of the tutor?	Design of scenario, population of events database, briefing, supporting simulation by playing the role of a manager at HQ who provides additional information on request, assessment.	Design of scenario, population of events database, briefing, support, facilitation of reflective discussion following the simulation.
Why was this approach appropriate?	SMS provides real-time access anywhere to learners allowing an authentic experience to be provided.	SMS provides an opportunity for dispersed work-based participants to engage in an authentic activity.
What did the design look like?	Simple decision tree structure with 5 levels leading to 32 possible outcomes. The scenario unfolded in real-time over 3 days matching the real events which took place in South East France in 1992.	Complex decision tree with some 'switch backs' leading to distinct good/bad outcomes, and simplified 'middle-way' outcomes. The scenario unfolded over differing time periods (from 1 day to several days) depending on learners' responses.
How was the simulation implemented in the course?	Towards the end of the course. Assessment involved submission of a log of decisions made and justifications for these. Implemented 2006, 2008	At the start of the course. Not assessed, used as an opportunity to promote discussion. Reflection on the activity could be integrated into later assessments by individual learners if desired. Implemented 2009
What did the messages look like?	Example information message: *A period of intense rain is forecast for the river basin. This rain, which is frontal in nature, is likely to last for up to 8 hours in the lower basin.* Example decision message: *Thunderstorms are forecast for the late afternoon. Do you 1) Take no action; 2) Initiate flood watch procedures* If a decision was not returned by a deadline (normally 2 hours) option 1) would be taken by default.	Example information message: *Unexpectedly a TQAL student leaves induction event early.* Example decision message: *Do you: 1) Wait for them to contact you; 2) Send them a text message confirming your contact details.* If a decision is not returned by a deadline (normally 2 hours) option 1) would be taken by default.

Table 11.1   Features of the flood and mentoring SMS simulations

Evaluations of learners' and tutors' experiences of the SMS simulations were undertaken following implementation in 2008 and 2009. Informed by an Activity Theory perspective on mobile learning (Sharples et al., 2007), a mixed methods study aimed to investigate issues related to control, context and communication. Sixteen undergraduates (70 per cent of the cohort) responded to a questionnaire and two were interviewed. From the cohort of work-based learners fifteen (75 per cent) responded to a questionnaire and three were interviewed. In both cases the tutor and educational technologist were also interviewed. Participation throughout was voluntary and it is recognised that comments from the small number of interviewees may be unrepresentative of the groups as a whole. However, they are still considered valuable in providing an insight into the experiences of learners.

The key themes which emerged from the empirical evidence are discussed further below: the real-time element and disruption caused by the activity; evidence of engagement and emotional involvement; and issues of control and communication. The effectiveness of the simulations for learning is also explored. The findings indicate the two groups had different experiences of the simulation and these reflect the characteristics of the learners, the nature of the simulations and the approach taken by the tutors. Whilst it is readily acknowledged that they are drawn from two small-scale cases, the issues discussed may have wider significance for the implementation of mobile learning with work-based learners.

Real-time and disruption

The simulations both adopted a model that involved messages arriving outside normal office hours to intentionally disrupt the local physical and social context of the learner and require them to return at irregular intervals to the context of their scenario (the virtual context). Undergraduates engaging with the flood simulation were most often at their place of residence or at the university when they received messages. In general the disruptive aspect of the activity was regarded favourably. One interview respondent commented that she thought 'a wee bit of integration of our life, student life and university life was quite good [...] it was with us all the time'. Many learners responded to the messages swiftly but some took time to consider their responses before replying – they engaged in a period of reflection and in some cases research and preparation before submitting an answer. Even where learners were in work situations which required phones to be switched off, they dealt with this by responding when they could or accepting that a decision would be made on their behalf. One indicated that the default answer was what they would have chosen anyway. Overall this group enjoyed the real-time element of the simulation. They seemed to acknowledge that, as the tutor put it 'natural disasters don't work business hours'.

For participants in the mentoring simulation issues of disruption were more pronounced. Over 85 per cent of respondents received messages whilst they were at work and in some cases this created significant problems. Several respondents outlined the need to have phones switched off for lengthy periods and this led to messages backing up and default replies being recorded on their behalf. Respondents reported responding quickly to most messages, suggesting perhaps that they wanted to deal with them promptly to allow them to return to their real context. For some participants it may be that finding time to engage with the simulation was an issue and this echoes the experiences of learners engaged in other 'non-timetabled' learning, for example informal professional development (Cornelius & Macdonald, 2008) and mobile ad-hoc-collaboration (Frohberg & Schwabe, 2006). However, for others this pattern of quick responses reflected their 'normal' pattern of communication by text message. One respondent, for example, commented that they replied quickly 'out of habit'.

The inability to reply immediately due to work or other commitments created confusion for some mentoring participants and led to operator errors as they tried to sort out the backlog of messages and work out which ones had arrived first. In some instances the arrival of messages was reported as being intrusive or even 'inappropriate', for example when they arrived whilst driving or visiting relatives in care settings, and this contributed in some cases to dis-engagement with the simulation.

In summary, findings suggest that for some of the work-based learners the simulation disrupted other aspects of their lives, with specific examples of intrusion into private lives. However, others regarded the use of SMS as no more intrusive than normal texting. Practices for mobile phone use at work included having phones switched off or inaccessible for lengthy periods and messages were generally dealt with quickly when the opportunity arose. This is a different pattern of experience than for the undergraduates, where real-time activity and the integration of university and 'other' lives was welcomed and the opportunity to reflect before replying was sometimes taken up.

Engagement and emotional involvement

The flood simulation participants generally enjoyed the simulation – 60 per cent of respondents looked forward to messages arriving. Evidence of engagement and enjoyment emerged right from the beginning of the activity. One interviewee commented that

> waiting for the first message I was quite excited because obviously you didn't know what it was going to say. I was a bit nervous because I wasn't sure how much research we would have to do ...

She had been sitting with peers waiting for the first message: 'we were all pretty excited I think. We were all like "who is going to get the first one?"' Aside from fun and enjoyment there was also evidence of empathy for the characters in the virtual context. The tutor reported students suffering a 'mild case of trauma' when mix-ups with messages led to them wiping out most of the population they were supposed to be defending. He reported that 'they would come here saying "I just feel frustrated, I thought I'd done my best, but I've killed 50 people"'.

Learners particularly liked the flood simulation activity because the assessment was not an essay and this may have encouraged further involvement. One interview respondent summed up the value of involvement and the feeling of control over the activity that this led to: 'you did feel involved and you did feel that you were doing something a bit different. [...] you actually had some sort of say in the way it went, what happened, what we could do'. Another respondent suggested that 'a higher level of involvement encouraged us to do more work'.

The mentoring simulation was less successful in terms of generating emotional engagement and involvement. There are several possible explanations for this. First, the simulation was integrated into the course at the last minute once it was clear that technical problems had been ironed out. This prevented the tutor from contextualising it within earlier learning and led to a rushed and possibly incomplete briefing. Second, a lack of familiarity with some of the functions of their mobile phones (such as finding the symbol for an equals sign required in the answers) may also have tripped up some learners. These issues, together with the backlog of messages due to phones being switched of for lengthy periods, meant that some learners followed a path through their simulation which largely consisted of default decisions taken for them. As a result, they often became confused or disengaged or they may have tried to engage not realising that they had lost control over the path of the scenario. Thus, beyond initial enthusiasm for the simulation, emotions expressed tended to be frustration or anxieties. One interviewee started off 'really excited' but ended up 'disengaged'. Another got 'irritated' and 'quite grumpy because I wanted it to work'. The third commented on her surprise at the emotions expressed in online post activity discussions which suggested a level of engagement and empathy with the scenario clearly beyond her own:

> I was quite fascinated, because they were saying they didn't like it, that it left them really frustrated, and they were really emotional about it, whereas I was in no doubt ...it wasn't real.

Thus it seems that where a simulation is carefully designed and implemented emotional engagement is possible and beneficial. Emotional engagement is of particular value since research suggests that this may have a bigger influence on participants' sense of presence than 3D realism of the kind that might be found in virtual worlds such as Second Life (e.g. Banos et al., 2004). Westera (submitted) suggests that credibility is more important than realism or authenticity in computer games and that 'fictitious, non-existing, non-authentic realities may provide valuable learning experiences' (p. 4). He cites research (Reeves & Ness, 1996) which indicates that true interpersonal responses can be provoked by experiences that draw on limited representational or technological efforts – a category into which the SMS simulations might be placed.

Evidence from the use of ad-hoc activities (Frohberg & Schwabe, 2006) highlights the motivational potential of unpredictable tasks, but the role of assessment in promoting engagement also warrants consideration. Whilst authentic learning may improve motivation for adult learners where there is the potential to solve professional problems (Westera, submitted), there is evidence from the mentoring participants that loss of patience and disengagement may be the result when the way in which scenario operates is not completely clear or the narrative not sufficiently compelling.

Control and communication

For the undergraduate participants the use of mobile phones and text messaging was clearly an intriguing and effective approach. It made use of readily available and familiar resources. For this group of learners their mobile phones could be viewed as an 'extension of the self' (Gibson, 1979; cited by Rettie, 2005) which allowed access to the scenario at any time. Although designed as an independent activity, there was evidence of communication taking place between learners to support their engagement. This appears to have supported community building – one interviewee commented that 'it was a good bonding exercise'. Texting between friends also occurred in a supportive and exploratory role. One respondent revealed 'I did text a friend […] it was nice to see how everyone else was doing'. There were also reports of jokes about saving the town posted on Facebook.

For the work-based learners, however, issues of control and communication were more likely to present barriers. These learners have a more complex relationship with their mobile phones – maybe owning more than one, paid for in different ways and used for different purposes. There may be tensions about 'who pays?' when a phone is used for learning and whether this is regarded as a personal or work-related activity. Attwell (2009) suggests that there may be resistance to user-owned mobile devices being used for work unless they are funded by the employer and Aubusson et al. (2009) report tensions created for teaching professionals required to engage with separate mobile devices for personal and work use. Traxler (2009) also hints at the complexity and ethics of acceptable use in educational contexts and these issues may be particularly acute for work-based learners.

There are also issues about the mode of communication. Most of the work-based learners use mobile phones for voice calls more often than texts and employ text messaging for communication with teenage children, younger learners or for the administration of outside activities. In relation to the mentoring simulation several respondents expressed a wish to pick up the phone and speak to their mentee rather than text. The tutor also expressed the view that the time lag between information messages arriving and the request for a response was 'disconcerting' and unrealistic. No evidence emerged of communication between learners during the activity.

For some of the work-based learners issues of control over personal time were significant. One expressed a desire to be able to negotiate when the activity took place to ensure that it would be convenient to participate. This would have prevented messages intruding on other aspects of her life. Mentoring interviewees also spoke about feeling 'out of control' when messages backed up and default responses were returned. They couldn't navigate the 'story' successfully and became disengaged as a result. One respondent was not clear whether she was dealing with one mentee or several. In this case these issues may have been the result of the design of the activity and the limitations of the briefing provided, however, it is also clear that integrating real-time authentic activities using mobile phones into a work context is not straightforward. Attwell (2009) comments on the need to understand what kind of digital practices are acceptable in a work context – here evidence of phones needing to be switched off whilst in situations such as meetings or hospital visits were identified and had to be accommodated.

Learning effectiveness

Westera (submitted) suggests that authentic real-world problems 'trigger higher order thinking processes and active learning strategies' (p. 4) and may help motivate learners to solve problems related to their professional lives. Authentic learning should also provide for 'multiple interpretations and outcomes' (Lombardi, 2007, p. 4). The personalised nature of the SMS simulations offered diverse outcomes and engagement with the

flood simulation appears to have encouraged learning for some participants. Some learners did more work than normal (see earlier comments on
engagement) and considered the application of theory from their studies
to practice, or at least acknowledged that more than common sense was
needed: 'you think it's just common sense sometimes – a flood's going to
come, put out some sandbags – you don't really think of is it going to cost
money, about time, is it going to affect people, what's going to happen
downstream'. Looking at a real life situation may also have encouraged
learners to take a wider perspective on course content. One respondent
stated that 'having to prevent death by text message' had made her 'look
at the situation differently'.

However, responses which indicate a deep level of engagement do
not reflect the experiences of the whole cohort of undergraduate learners. One interviewee reported that 'I know a lot of people did think it was
common sense' and one questionnaire respondent indicated that they had
felt that '"2" was always the correct answer'. However, the tutor reported
being generally pleased with assignment submissions and saw some good
examples of work in which decisions were justified effectively.

The challenges posed by the mentoring simulation, both with learners'
understanding of the context and the process, may have hindered effective
learning in this instance. The learning that occurred here was less about
mentoring, rather more about some of the challenges and potential for
using mobile phones in learning. Several respondents expressed the view
that they were glad they had undertaken the activity and that it had given
them ideas for their own practice. The activity also provoked some reflection
about what actions individuals might have taken in a mentoring context –
in many instances they wanted to do something that was not allowed by
the two options provided, or to be able to qualify their decisions. Online
discussion of the scenario did take place following the simulation, but some
of the cohort merely 'lurked' and others did not engage at all.

Context and SMS simulations in work-based learning

Sharples et al. (2007) suggest that learning occurs in a context, but also creates context, and that mobile learning creates contexts that are constantly being reframed and re-constructed. They revisit Engeström's Activity Theory (Engeström, 1987) to include the notion of 'context' to help define, theorise and categorise mobile learning, whilst recognising that the term has different meanings to different theorists. Having considered learners' and tutors' experiences of the simulation, it is useful to consider the SMS simulations within emerging classifications and theories of mobile learning. The idea of a 'virtual context' has been raised (e.g. Table 11.1) and this has been identified as an important distinguishing feature of the simulations (Cornelius & Marston, 2009).

A simplified version of an activity system (based on Engeström's work and with context as an important element) allows effective analysis of mobile learning activities (Wali et al., 2008; Frohberg et al., 2009). Wali et al. (2008) define context as 'a combination of the properties of the physical location where the learning activity takes place and the rules and division of labour within the community that the learner belongs to' (p. 56). They suggest that 'context crossing' or changes in the physical context (the 'environment' surrounding the learner) and social context (which arises from interactions between people and technology) distinguishes mobile learning. In the SMS simulations this context crossing goes beyond the physical and social contexts of the learner and includes crossing into the virtual context of the scenario. This is a context which cannot be created by conventional learning devices but which has physical properties (physical features and perhaps a real or conceptual geography so that it can be regarded as a place or a space) and within which the learner belongs to a virtual community (associated with their role in the scenario) with associated rules and division of labour.

Frohberg et al. (2009) use the term context to describe the environment of the learner and suggest that there are four contexts which can be used to characterise mobile learning projects:

1) independent: where there is no relationship between the environment of the learner and the learning;
2) formalised: as in a classroom context;
3) physical: where the location of the learner is relevant to the learning; and
4) socialising: where relationships with other learners are important.

In the SMS simulations the environment of the learner is not relevant but still important, as the learner is required to interact with the simulation at whatever location they are in when a message arrives. Our experiences have led us to propose the virtual context as a potential fifth category which may characterise applications such as the SMS simulations (Marston and Cornelius, 2010). The virtual context may appear to be independent but it has a physical and/or social context that exists in a virtual or remote setting. An SMS simulation also requires a persistent and realistic scenario which may or may not be related to a real or imaginary location.

An alternative view is provided by Edwards & Miller (2007), who suggest that learning is a practice of contextualisation rather than something that emerges within a context. Being in the workplace provides a context for learning that is quite distinct from that of formal learning. External as well as internal contexts influence work-based learners (Unwin et al., 2009) and may help explain some of the experiences of mentoring simulation participants. In addition, a greater diversity of social contexts exists in work places than in formal learning relationships found in institutional settings. For instance, there may not be an explicit learner/teacher relationship or even an explicit curriculum. The social context of learning becomes bound up in relationships between employees, their co-workers, their employer, career progression and even how the employee feels about the work they perform. Motivations for learning in the work place are also bound up in these notions of the social context of learning – does the learner wish to progress in his or her career, does the employer wish the employee to progress, or even, does the colleague wish to be out-performed?

The workplace can be an opportunity for authentic, situated and contextualised learning (Lombardi, 2007; Lave & Wenger, 1991; Seely Brown et al., 1989) and a place for learning 'through' work where theory learned in the classroom can be put into practice and tested against reality (Sea-greaves et al., 1996). Access to new contexts (including, we suggest, virtual contexts) may provide opportunities which can overcome constraints on thinking imposed by specific contexts and allow learners to develop alternative ideas and visions (Van Oers, 1998; cited in Guile & Young, 2003). In all cases the workplace brings many contextual dimensions, more than may be apparent if the workplace is considered from a purely pedagogical perspective.

The effective use of SMS simulations in work-based learning

Drawing on ideas presented by Aldrich (2004), our own evaluation of SMS simulations and consideration of relevant theoretical issues we propose a series of guidelines for potential users of SMS simulations in work-based learning. These address issues of context, the preparation of learners and implementation.

1) Most importantly a simulation needs to draw on a persistent, consistent, realistic and engaging physical and social scenario (virtual context). Within this scenario SMS text messaging should be an appropriate tool for communications. The scenario needs to be designed with sensitivity to learners' real work contexts to prevent difficulties in distinguishing reality from the virtual context.

2) Learners should be thoroughly briefed to ensure they have a clear understanding of the virtual context, their role within this and issues such as the timing of the activity. For work-based learners timings may need to be negotiated to successfully accommodate other aspects of their lives and existing work commitments. They may also need to take into consideration socio-cultural, technological and ethical issues (Attwell, 2009; Aubusson et al. 2009) such as 'Which phone?', 'Who pays?' and whether the simulation can be successfully accommodated within acceptable mobile phone practices at work.

3) A pilot 'familiarisation' run is essential to ensure technical competence and to permit discussion of options (such as message receipts or forwarding) which may be used to personalise the simulation and make it operational within organisational constraints. A pilot will also help learners prepare for the disruptive element of the simulation.

4) The simulation itself needs to be authentic and engaging to provide motivation and promote cognitive engagement. Although none of the work-based learners reported high levels of engagement with their scenario, it is clear from the flood simulation that a well-designed simulation can be enjoyable and engaging and promote deep learning. The scenario should also be designed with the expectation that learners may communicate 'behind the scenes'. Whilst no evidence of such communication emerged from our cohort of work-based learners, where learners are part of a more established community of practice this may occur.

5) Even where things don't go as planned due to technical or operator issues, the opportunity to reflect on both content and process either through discussion or preparation of assessment will be valuable. In a work-based learning context it may well be that the most significant learning will not be about the simulation scenario itself but engagement with the process may have relevance to other work functions and requirements. It is unlikely that there will be a simple or single path from learning objectives to learning outcomes for all learners.

Concluding remarks

Mobile technologies are changing the way we work, the jobs we do and the organisations that we work for. Educators face significant challenges in adapting current structures and approaches to support the development of work-based learners in a mobile age. Within this rapidly changing environment mobile phones offer opportunities, particularly as they support anywhere, anytime access to learners.

This chapter has presented two case studies of the use of SMS alternate reality simulations for learning. The first was a successful implementation with campus-based undergraduates. The second was a less successful experience for work-based learners. Whilst there are differences in the contexts of the two scenarios, the role-played by the tutor, the briefing provided to learners and associated assessment, some important findings emerge which have relevance for the implementation of similar mobile learning with work-based learners. In particular careful consideration of the work context of learners is necessary and any activity must be implemented with sensitivity to contextual issues. In addition learners' understanding of the virtual context of the simulation is important and opportunities for briefing and preparation prior to any simulation activity should be provided.

Further research is currently underway to help develop a robust framework for the development of additional simulations, to explore the experiences of learners in other contexts, and to investigate the application of the framework in other virtual contexts. In the view of some authors authentic learning is not provided without community participation (Lombardi, 2007), and there is value in collaborative reflection for work-based learning (Boud et al., 1985). Thus, one area of particular interest is the development of collaborative role-play activities using SMS such as an emergency response situation in which individuals take on different roles within a team.

References

Aldrich, C. (2004) *Simulations and the future of learning.* San Francisco, CA: Wiley

Aldrich, C. (2005) *Learning by doing: The essential guide to simulations, computer games, and pedagogy in e-learning and other educational experiences.* San Francisco, CA: Wiley

Attwell, G. (2009) *Implementing a socio-cultural ecology for learning at work – Ideas and issues.* Position paper prepared for Technology enhanced learning in the context of technological, societal and cultural transformation, WLE/LMLG workshop at the Alpine Rendex-Vous in Gramisch-Partenkirchen, December 2009. Available online at <http://www.pontydysgu.org/wp-content/uploads/2009/11/Graham+Attwell.pdf> (accessed 01/12/09)

Aubusson, P., Schuck, S., and Burden, K. (2009) Mobile learning for teacher professional learning: benefits, obstacles and issues. *ALT-J* 17(3), pp. 233–247

Banos, R., Botella, C., Alcaniz, M., Liano, V., Guerrero, B., and Rey, B. (2004) 'Immersion and Emotion: Their Impact on the Sense of Presence.' In *CyberPsychology & Behavior* 7(6), pp. 734–741

Boud, D., Keogh, R., and Walker, D. (1985) *Reflection: Turning experience into learning.* London: Kogan Page

British Broadcasting Corporation (BBC) (2004) FloodRanger. Available online at <http://newsvote.bbc.co.uk/1/hi/technology/3500747.stm> (accessed 22/12/09)

British Broadcasting Corporation (BBC) (2008) 'Surgeon saves boy's life by text.' *BBC News Website.* Available online at <http://news.bbc.co.uk/1/hi/health/7761994.stm> (accessed 01/12/09)

Cornelius, S., & Macdonald, J. (2008) 'Online informal professional development for distance tutors: experiences from the Open University in Scotland.' In *Open Learning* 23(1), pp. 43–55

Cornelius, S. & Marston, P. (2009) 'Towards an understanding of the virtual context in mobile learning.' *ALT-J 17(3)*, pp. 161–172

Cornelius, S., Medyckyj-Scott, D., Forrest, D. and Elcock, A. (2005) 'The e-MapScholar Virtual Placement.' *Planet* 15, pp. 26–28. Plymouth: GEES Subject Centre. Available online at <http://www.gees.ac.uk/planet/p15/sc.pdf> (accessed 04/01/10)

Edwards, R. & Miller, K. (2007) 'Putting the context into learning.' *Pedagogy, Culture & Society 15*(3), pp. 263–274

Engestrom, Y. (1987) *Learning by expanding: an activity-theoretical approach to developmental research.* Helsinki: Orienta-Konsultit

Environment Agency (2010) 'Sign up to our free flood warning service.' Available online at <http://www.environment-agency.gov.uk/homeandleisure/floods/38289.aspx> (accessed 26/01/10)

Frohberg, D., Göth, C., and Schwabe, G. (2009) 'Mobile learning projects – A critical analysis of the state of the art.' *Journal of Computer Assisted Learning 25*(4), pp. 307–331

Frohberg, D. & Schwabe, G. (2006) 'Skills and motivation in ad-hoc learning.' *CollECTeR: Conference Proceedings Collaborative Electronic Commerce Technology and Research.* Available online at <http://www.collecter.org/archives/2006_June/17.pdf> (accessed 10/02/10)

Guile, D., & Young, M. (2003) 'Transfer and transition in vocational education: Some theoretical considerations.' In Tuomi-Gröhn, T., & Engeström, Y. (eds), *Between school and work: new perspectives on transfer and boundary-crossing* (pp. 63–84). Oxford: Elsevier Science

Jackson, S., & Livingston, I. (1982) *The warlock of firetop mountain*. London: Puffin Books

Lave, J. & Wenger, E. (1991) *Situated learning: Legitimate peripheral participation*. Cambridge: University of Cambridge Press

Lombardi, M. (2007) *Authentic learning for the 21st Century: An overview*. In Oblinger, D. (ed.) *Educause ELI Paper 1*. Available online at <http://net.educause.edu/ir/library/pdf/ELI3009.pdf> (accessed 04/01/10)

Marston, P., & Cornelius, S. (2010) Further development of the context categories of a mobile learning framework. *Journal of the Research Centre for Educational Technology 6*(1), pp. 70–75. Available online at <http://rcetj.org/index.php/rcetj/article/view/86> (accessed 15/04/10)

Moon, J. (1999) *Reflection in learning and professional development: Theory and practice*. Abingdon: RoutledgeFalmer

Pimmer, C. (2009) 'Mobile Work-based learning and context'. Position paper for Technology enhanced learning in the context of technological, societal and cultural transformation, WLE/LMLG workshop at the Alpine Rendex-Vous in Gramisch-Partenkirchen, December 2009. Available online at <http://www.pontydysgu.org/wp-content/uploads/2009/11/Christoph+Pimmer.pdf> (accessed 01/12/09)

Reeves, B. & Nass, C. (1996) *The media equation: How people treat computers, television, and new media like real people and places*. Cambridge: Cambridge University Press

Rettie, R. (2005). Presence and embodiment in mobile phone communication. *PsychNology Journal 3*(1), pp. 16–34

ReutersLink (2010) *Foundation launches unique SMS service for Haiti 'quake survivors*. Available online at <http://reuterslink.org/news/HaitiEIS.htm> (accessed 26/01/10)

Schön, D. (1983) *The reflective practitioner: How professional think in action*. New York: Basic Books

Seagraves, L., Osbourne, M., Neal, P. Dockrell, R., Hartshorn C., and Boyd, A. (1996) *Learning in smaller companies (LISC) Final report*. University of Stirling, Educational Policy and Development

Seely Brown, J., Collins, A., and Duguid, P. (1989) 'Situated cognition and the culture of learning.' *Educational Researcher 18*(1), pp. 32–42

Sharples, M., Taylor, J., and Vavoula, G. (2007) 'A theory of learning for the mobile age.' In Andrews, R., and Haythornthwaite, C. (eds), *The SAGE handbook of e-learning research* (pp. 221–247). London, Sage

Thorpe, M. (2009) 'Technology-mediated learning contexts.' In Edwards, R., Biesta, G., and Thorpe, M. (eds), *Rethinking contexts for teaching and learning* (pp. 119–132). London: Routledge

Traxler, J. (2009) 'Students and mobile devices: choosing which dream.' *ALT-C 2009 'In dreams begins responsibility' – Choice, evidence and change*, 8–10 September 2009, Manchester. Available online at <http://repository.alt.ac.uk/643/> (accessed 03/01/10)

Unwin, L., Fuller, A., Felstead, A., and Jewson, N. (2009) 'Worlds within worlds: the relational dance between context and learning in the workplace.' In Edwards, R., Biesta, G. and Thorpe, M. (eds), *Rethinking contexts for teaching and learning* (pp. 106–118). London: Routledge

Wali, E., Winters, N., and Oliver, M. (2008) 'Maintaining, changing and crossing contexts: an activity theoretic reinterpretation of mobile learning.' *ALT-J 16*(1), pp. 41–57

Westera, W. (submitted) 'Reframing contextual learning: Anticipating the virtual extensions of context.' *Educational Technology and Society*. Available online at <http://hdl.handle.net/1820/2112> (accessed 24/02/10)

Ethical issues relevant for (researching) mobile learning

KEVIN BURDEN, SANDY SCHUCK AND PETER AUBUSSON

12 Ethical professional mobile learning for teaching and nursing workplaces

Abstract

The ubiquity, accessibility and flexibility of mobile technologies suggests they will be valuable for professional learning, particularly in professions where most of the work does not occur at a set workstation. This chapter focuses on two such professions: teaching and nursing. But their use by these professions is not unproblematic (Aubusson, Schuck and Burden, 2009; Fisher, Higgins and Loveless, 2006; Wishart, 2009). While mobile activities are likely to contribute to these professionals' learning in the workplace, a tension arises regarding the ethical nature of such activities. This chapter explores the complexities and confusion faced by teachers and nurses in their use of work-based mobile learning. The chapter considers the ethical issues involved in the use of mobile technologies to capture, reflect upon and share moments of professional learning in these work-based contexts. It suggests a number of ethical principles which might provide a useful guide for professional practice for teaching and nursing and beyond.

Introduction

One of the chapter's authors attended a conference of professionals working in multi-disciplinary teams to design new schools in the UK as part of the Building Schools of the Future (BSF) initiative (<http://www.

number10.gov.uk/Page5801>). During the conference dinner the author was engaged in conversation by a senior architect working on the project who described how he had used the video camera on his personal mobile phone to spontaneously capture evidence of poor workmanship in the construction of a local school. The evidence was immediately used to discipline the worker who was responsible for this work and the architect could see no problems or ethical issues arising from the use of his mobile device in this manner. This stands in contrast with similar incidents where employees and employers have used their mobile devices to capture video evidence in the workplace, often illicitly. In the case of one well documented example, a nurse who filmed examples of malpractice on National Health Services (NHS) hospital wards[1] was subsequently disciplined and struck off the nursing register for undertaking activity which was deemed unethical. These two contrasting examples serve to highlight the complexity and lack of consistency apparent in work-based contexts where mobile technologies have been used to capture practice for various purposes.

This chapter investigates the ethical issues that may arise in work-based use of mobile technologies for professional learning. A small-scale empirical study underpinned the need for the development and articulation of principles for ethical mobile learning in the workplace. Our initial focus was on teachers and schools as ethical issues in the school context are more starkly apparent than in other workplaces. The focus is timely as teachers are beginning to explore the potential of their personal mobile devices for purposes of professional learning. Our investigation of ethical issues in school settings brought to the fore comparisons with nursing and the health industry. These two professions operate in workplaces where personal data are particularly sensitive and stakeholders can be vulnerable. Our awareness of the similarity of these two professions with regard to ethical issues of mobile learning led to interviews with nurses to explore their views and experiences of using mobile technologies in their workplace. This chapter sets out to examine and clarify these various ethical issues and concerns by comparing the teaching and nursing profession across an international

---

1   'Secret filming nurse struck off.' BBC News. Available at <http://news.bbc.co.uk/2/ hi/uk_news/england/sussex/8002559.stm> (accessed 16/08/10).

dimension. We start by investigating the use of such devices in a teaching context as this was the stimulus for exploring the ethical issues across both professions.

The case for mobile devices in teachers' workplaces as tools for professional learning

Mobile learning is still relatively ill-defined (Eteokleous & Laouris, 2005) and the authors adopt O'Malley's defintion: '... learning that happens when the learner takes advantage of learning opportunities offered by mobile technologies' (O'Malley, et al., 2003, cited in Sharples, 2006, p. 7). Mobile technologies have now developed sufficiently to become powerful recording devices for the capture of spontaneous data. They are ideally suited to work-based learning in professions such as teaching and nursing where there is an imperative to develop professional learning which happens immediately and without prior warning. Compared to traditional camcorder and camera technologies, mobile technologies are infinitely more portable and unobtrusive. They also enable professionals to capture audio notes or recordings which might include their own reflective thoughts, discussions with pupils or patients and to be able to do so discretely with no obvious indication that recording is taking place.

Mobile devices enable professionals to capture instances of their practice for reflection and dissemination in ways that normal recording devices would prohibit. At the cost of some loss in picture and audio quality they provide 'always connected' availability furnishing professionals with tools to deepen their own understanding of their work. But their use in this way is not unproblematic and the ethical issues associated with workplace use of mobile technologies have not been widely studied or documented (Traxler, 2009; Wishart, 2009). In particular, use of these technologies in the workplaces of teachers and nurses give rise to a particular set of ethical issues which have not been sufficiently studied or discussed.

Workplace learning for teachers

Mobile learning of teachers can be a type of workplace learning. Continuing professional development takes place largely within schools ('the workplace') as do many crucial parts of initial teacher education. Yet, though
there is a wealth of literature on initial teacher education, teacher induction, teacher professionalism and the continuing professional development
of teachers, it seldom connects with literature on the nature of workplace
learning; exceptions confirm the rule (see e.g. Eraut, 1994). Hodkinson
& Hodkinson (2005) argue that the teacher professional development
literature does not yet appear to fully appreciate the value of workplace
learning. While workplace learning is essential to the success of teachers, it
is often not recognised as professional development and so gets little legitimation (Retallick, 1999). Conversely, workplace literature often highlights
the distinctiveness of workplace learning and its differences from formal
learning. However, Billett (2002) argues that focusing on these differences is not helpful. He suggests that both types of learning derive from
the community's social, historical and cultural practices and both have a
concern for the continuity of practice. It is perhaps more useful to look
at learning in broader terms as participation in social practices. From this
conception of learning it is then possible to derive an understanding of
the significant features of workplace learning. These include the interde-
pendence of working and learning with the nature and structure of work
determining the learning activities and guidance to learning (Billett, 2001).
As well, the learning is strongly shaped by contextual factors such as the
norms and goals of the particular work setting and the attitudes and values
of the learner towards this setting. Retallick (1999, p. 34) suggests that
workplace learning is characterised by being 'task-focused, ...collaborative
and it often grows out of an experience or a problem for which there is
no known knowledge base'. Also of importance in workplace learning is
learning though reflection. Workplace learning can usefully be conceptualised as a growing capacity to make contextually sensitive, situationally
appropriate judgements in challenging circumstances (Beckett & Hager,
2002; Korthagen & Kessells, 1999). Mobile learning would appear to fit
well with this conceptualisation of workplace learning for teachers. This
is discussed further in the next section.

Why mobile technologies for teacher workplace learning

A key aspect of teacher workplace learning is its social nature. Research indicates that collaboration is critical for effective teacher professional learning (Aubusson, Steele, Brady and Dinham, 2007; Burbank & Kauchak, 2003; Clement & Vandenberghe, 2000). These authors note that the process of collaborative learning promotes critical reflection on practice; acknowledges teachers as active learners and producers of knowledge; and supports teacher decision-making.

As a result of this emphasis on collaboration for professional learning, harnessing the power of mobile technologies to provide collaborative communities for teachers' professional learning would seem to be of value. The benefits of mobile technologies are that they enable interactions with people both beyond and within one's own school; offer support even if geographically isolated; provide access to expertise over a range of areas readily available in an online learning environment; and build personal and professional support networks.

Teachers exist in a 'professional landscape' (Connelly & Clandinin, 1997) and teachers' practical wisdom is an important feature of this landscape. Practical wisdom originates in experience. It tells teachers what will not work but it is not simply a set of recalled successes and failures. It is built on a capacity to analyse and synthesise which allows the production of a coherent set of principles and beliefs that inform practice (Aubusson et al., 2009). We have long known (Noddings & Witherell, 1991) that teachers exchange practical wisdom and test its veracity in discussions with others, often sharing their knowledge in the form of stories and anecdotes. These stories are frequently limited to small groups in school departments. Mobile technologies provide a vehicle for the rapid exchange of anecdotes and stories with a wide, diverse community. This, at least implicitly, invites scrutiny of the practical wisdom embedded within them. It is noteworthy that making such wisdom public and inviting scrutiny are central elements of teacher professional scholarship (Shulman, 2000).

The table below indicates how mobile technologies facilitate workplace learning for teachers:

Characteristics of workplace learning	Appropriateness of mobile technologies
Collaboration	Facilities to share and participate in communities of practice
Task-focused	Productivity tools for work (e.g. production, editing, sharing) all available in one device
Originates in authentic problems	Support genuine problem solving in authentic contexts (e.g. internet enabled searching, working with others online)
Context specific	Facility to match context with appropriate content or information (e.g. GPS)
Reflective	Facility to record reflections spontaneously and without mediation (e.g. audio recordings to a blog)

Table 12.1   Alignment of teacher workplace learning with mobile devices

Table 12.1 illustrates that mobile learning devices offer a significant number of features which correspond with characteristics of workplace learning. This suggests that mobile devices have a powerful role to play in mediating the learning process for professionals. They facilitate collaborative working practices both within and across an institution. This might include the sharing of resources but also the co-production of new knowledge as in the case of a wiki. By definition, most of a teacher's professional learning will be located in the workplace and mobile devices facilitate task-focused learning in real or authentic contexts. Given their size and ubiquity, they are unobtrusive and can be used to capture the moment spontaneously. The use of a mobile device to capture examples of practice on camera or video may not significantly change the existing dynamics of a classroom. This contrasts with the footprint and physical presence of a normal full size video recording device such as a film camera which is likely to significantly change the dynamics of the classroom. Mobile devices also combine features which enable specific context data to be located and matched to other predetermined data in ways which faciliate workplace learning. Through the use of GPS data, for example, it is possible for a teacher to use a context aware diary which is aware of which part of the building she/he is working within and can match specific data relevant to that part of the building and the individual (e.g. details of homework which needs to be collected from a specific class or group).

However, with these benefits of mobile learning come certain ethical concerns and dilemmas, and these are the focus of this chapter. Before discussing these dilemmas we outline some of the uses for mobile technologies in professional learning of teachers and consider their relationship to uses by health educators.

The use of mobile technologies for professional learning by teachers and students

Mobile technologies, such as the latest generation of video-phones, increasingly offer the potential for teacher creativity as producers, rather than simply consumers of knowledge. These devices are now capable of video and audio capture at a quality that is sufficiently professional for their use as learning objects in a variety of different environments, including both face-to-face and online. Whilst the ubiquitous and ever growing presence of services such as YouTube provide teachers with an unparalleled selection of video resources to download, the advent of next generation mobile technologies now presents a real opportunity for teachers to undertake authorship of these materials in addition to being consumers (Kearney & Schuck, 2006). These activities are already starting to occur as teachers become aware of the simplicity behind the production and sharing of meaningful authentic resources. It is only a small step to replicate this process with the immediacy afforded by mobile recording devices rather than static devices.

Mobile technologies can be used to produce artefacts that provide varied perspectives of activities and starting points for extended discourse between students and teachers. Teachers can learn from students' perspectives and students gain from deconstructing teaching moments with their teachers so that they can see the rationale for their teacher's actions. Mobile devices can, therefore, help to forge a genuine partnership between students and teachers in the capturing of learning moments and a triangulation of learning experiences from these different viewpoints. Thomson & Gunter

(2006, p. 839) discuss processes they used to work with school students to develop a 'student's eye' set of evaluative categories' and suggest that the process of viewing students as researchers can be both transformative and disruptive. Given that genuine reframing of practice often benefits from disruption, this process is likely to be valuable for teacher learning. As well, Cook-Sather (2006) suggests that acknowledging and listening to student voice indicates a position in which students are seen as active participants in their own learning. While this partnership might well be challenging for teachers, it would be likely to encourage students to work with, rather than subversively against the teacher and the school.

In a recent study (Aubusson, Schuck and Burden, 2009), the authors found that teachers used mobile devices for professional learning in a number of ways. These included videoing, audio recording and photographing student role plays, reflecting on classes and celebrating students' work. As well, advisory teachers and consultants used the technologies for sharing and dissemination of good practice. Teachers discussed use of the mobile technology for staff development in which student activities were shown to other teachers, in particular, early career teachers. Such technologies have also been noted as being used for staff development in remote communities in Australia.

To extend our understanding of teachers' workplace usage of mobile device for learning and the ethical issues that arise, we investigated how nurses and nurse educators, a profession with similar ethical constraints, use mobile technologies for their learning. We were eager to ascertain if the ethical issues in such use were in any way similar to those that were found in schools.

The use of mobile technologies for professional learning by nurses and nurse educators

Like teaching, nursing aims to become an evidence-based profession and mobile technologies offer many opportunities to support this aspiration. But perhaps even more than for teaching, the use of mobile technologies for workplace learning in nursing is in its infancy. However, the potential for mobile learning is clear. Some possible uses are to support evidence-based practice, where student nurses could collate data at the point of care and write memoranda on the care as well as reflections on their practice and own learning. Nurses can also access webpages to gain information about medication, which would add to their learning about care. Sharing information with other nurses to evaluate the care being provided would also be useful. As well, using images taken of a patient (for example, a wound) in the ward would help to make the case much more authentic when discussed in classes. Nurses already use some mobile devices, such as PDAs, to record daily transactions and there is tremendous scope for extending these uses to encompass aspects of workplace professional learning. Nurses noted that texting was already used in some aspect of health-care such as providing a reminder for patients to take prescribed medication. The opportunity to video-record vignettes, such as the process of administering an injection, was seen as an ideal application of the technology, although the dissemination and sharing of these recordings for professional purposes was seen as rather more problematic.

However, all these uses, and those of the teachers, discussed above, have ethical implications and in both cases the stakeholders (teachers, students, nurses and patients) involved are vulnerable to a certain degree. Also, there is a duty of care involved in interactions. For this reason, we decided to find out educators' and nurses' views on the ethical aspects of such use. Our research questions were the following:

- What is the nature of mobile learning in teaching and nursing workplaces?
- Are there any ethical issues arising which are particular to these workplaces?

Methodology: Investigating the issues

A qualitative interpretive approach was used in this small-scale study to ascertain educators' and nurses' views. This approach acknowledges the personal and social nature of learning and the importance of teacher agency. The study aimed to obtain a deep understanding of the way that teachers use mobile devices to learn both within and outside their workplaces. While the findings related to the use of mobile devices in this study are discussed in more detail in a separate paper (Aubusson, Schuck & Burden, 2009) this chapter focuses on the ethical aspects of such use as a stimulus to a broader discussion about ethical use of mobile technologies for workplace learning of teachers and nurses.

Participants

The authors interviewed eight educators in the UK and Australia, comprising teachers, teacher advisors and teacher developers. The eight research participants were selected because they are stakeholders in influencing professional learning and/or engagement with information and communication technology among teachers in schools. Pseudonyms have been used to ensure confidentiality. Five nurse educators in these two countries were also interviewed to gain a complementary impression of the issues of using mobile technologies in similar, if different workplaces. We wished to gain a sense of how their practices aligned with teacher practices and to ascertain if any ethical issues were common.

Data collection

A semi–structured interview schedule focused on participant views of, or experiences with mobile technologies; the ways in which they are used in professional learning; and current policies, ethical issues and influences that promote or hinder mobile professional learning. The questions acted as a guide to target the research aims but the interview progressed as conversation where both interviewer and interviewee engaged in a dialogue about ideas, comments, stories and episodes recounted. Interviews ranged in length from forty to ninety minutes. The original interview schedule was developed for teacher respondents. This was subsequently modified so that it was appropriate for the interviews with nurses and nursing educators. Sample questions are provided in the Appendix.

Analysis

The analysis sought to explicate and interpret participants' views, perceptions and understanding of this phenomenon. The research team collaboratively analysed the data obtained from interviews by coding, memoing and using the constant comparative method (Bogdan & Biklen, 1992). The analysis was guided by 'a ladder of analytical abstraction' to establish an interpretive framework for the phenomenon under study (Miles & Huberman, 1994, p. 92). This process is particularly appropriate in early explorations of emerging practices. This system of analysis constructs a map formalising key elements of the phenomenon and indicates how they are connected and may influence each other (Miles & Huberman, 1994). Coding proceeded in stages through discussion of instances among researchers until the agreed elements could survive re-testing against the data set. The coding generated the following themes pertaining to ethical issues:

- sharing of digital materials for professional purposes and issues around spontaneity;
- archiving and potential public access to events and materials intended for a limited audience;
- issues of power, authority and vulnerability; and
- informed consent.

Findings: Ethical issues

Issues around the spontaneous creation of digital data/materials
for professional purposes

The major ethical issue that was discussed by both teachers and nurses was related to spontaneity. All agreed that incidents that could provide valuable and authentic learning opportunities could not be predicted or scripted and, accordingly, recording of such incidents needed to be spontaneous. This raised the issue of how to get informed consent at the time of recording. For teachers, students are unable to give consent without parental consent and this is impossible to get at the instance that the incident occurs. For nurses, it may well be that the patient is unable to give consent at the moment that it is required. Further, stopping to gain consent removes the spontaneity of the moment and is likely to reduce the authenticity of the material.

Although there has been little research into how schools handle and deal with permissions of this nature, it appears that this level of consent is interpreted very broadly by schools both in the UK and Australia, enabling them to capture and disseminate video recordings, images and audio data from a broad range of activities with an unspecified range of purposes. Unlike a typical research ethics consent proposal for a research undertaking, school permissions policies tend to be vague and non-specific, certainly in terms of capturing and using such data. In all of the cases where such permission was sought, teachers reported that their institutions utilised an annual permissions form which parents signed at the start of the academic year. This precluded the need for teachers to apply for specific permission to capture images or video during the academic year itself and appears to facilitate a very spontanous and unrestricted use of such technologies.

However, this issue and lack of restriction on such use was of concern to the teachers and they referred to it often:

> It has to be a pre-arranged and agreed activity. So for example, you wouldn't get a teacher filming through a window a teacher doing an experiment ...It's all agreed in advance ...there is the fear factor – the YouTube fear factor as we call it here – where is it going to go [the video] once it has been done? (Dean)

The same issue appeared to be handled differently by nurses, in both the UK and Australian context. None of the nurse educators who were interviewed believed it would be possible, at the present moment, for nurses to capture video or images of their practice without prior consent and permission: 'in terms of making a record of anything I think you would have to get written consent'. This was a result of stringent regional policies, protocols and guidelines which explicitly prohibit the spontaneous use of devices such as cameras, mobile phones and laptops. It was suggested that the profession should look at ways of gaining consent that would allow spontaneous use of data for professional learning. One suggestion was that patients be asked to sign a generic consent form on booking into hospital.

Whilst capture of authentic experiences and practices was seen by teachers as an important feature of mobile technologies (albeit one fraught with difficulties in practice), the use of these devices to capture reflection in authentic contexts was also seen as a real value. But this again raised issues of an ethical and professional nature as expressed by one of the nurses:

> ...it would be better quality evidence, better quality information to reflect on. It would be more immediate, more real..more authentic ...but I think there are lots of things in the culture and the anxiety about the ethics which would inhibit that. The culture is risk averse ...you are very cautious about how you record things. It's this idea about recording things that is the problem.

This issue of risk aversion and fear of litigation was a prevalent theme in the nurse educator interviews. Although the rationale is officially couched in the language of ethical consent and patient confidentiality, there is a sense in which practitioners suggest this is sometimes used to mask a deeper underlying fear by hospital administrators and managers around litigation and the management of risk. Similar concerns also played a part in the mindsets of teachers.

Archiving and potential public access to events and materials intended for a limited audience

A key issue in both the teaching and nursing data concerned the security of data archives. Both professions expressed their beliefs that security of data was paramount. This, above all other issues, appears to dictate how mobile devices might be used both in teaching and nursing. At its extreme, the protection of patient data and confidentiality can mean teachers and nurses are not even allowed to take potential recording devices, such as mobile phones, into their workplaces.

It is interesting to note that there were a range of views about the storage and archiving of material. One of the key differences among those interviewed related to the risk of information intended for a *limited audience* becoming *publicly distributed*. For some, this had to be managed upfront because the view was that the distribution was almost impossible to control with certainty. In contrast, those who were more relaxed about digital recording considered that the distribution could be controlled and managed.

However, there was broad consensus that dissemination to a wider audience without permission is unethical. One interviewee suggested that there was some similarity between what might occur in a class and what might occur in a doctor's practice. For example, a doctor might share a patient's records with a specialist to assist in diagnosis. Similarly a

> teacher might use records ...(captured) on a mobile device to use in consultation with trusted colleagues about how to deal with something. But the material would have to be destroyed immediately after. Provided the use is clearly understood and agreed to, it's useful to have diagnosis done by second trusted people. If students objected then that would have to be respected.

Thus critical elements involved in determining what is ethical depend on the level of confidence one has in the professionalism of others.

It was clear that the concern here was not so much about the use of the material for learning but centred around perceptions about the potential use of the material. What *could* happen was the limiting factor. The nurse educators suggested that guidelines were needed for ethical use and these guidelines should suggest that data is destroyed after use. However, they noted the dilemma arising in that the data in the form of photographs and notes would provide others with an opportunity to learn 'so it would be a pity to lose them'. All were in agreement that the danger of having such material in digital form was that it could find its way to placement on the web and thus to access by a much larger audience than was originally intended.

Issues of power, accountability and vulnerability

The adoption of mobile technologies in the workplace by professionals such as teachers and nurses raises complex issues around accountability and power. They also bring into play the vexed issue of vulnerability, both for the professional involved and for the students and patients.

In our interviews with teachers it was evident that some are beginning to experiment with pupil-teacher as well as the more established teacher-pupil assessments of performance, using the mobile device as a recording tool. A few teachers reported how their students were allowed to record pre-arranged aspects of their lesson which were used to provide feedback to the teachers from the students themselves. This was seen as tremendously powerful in terms of authentic learner-centred feedback for teachers, although it does not appear to be common judging from the data we collected (Aubusson, Schuck and Burden, 2009). More often teachers reported using their own mobile devices to record pupil performance, such as in a PE or dance lesson or when pupils made presentations to the class.

This raises the issues of power and vulnerability when mobile technologies are used in the workplace. Whilst it might be assumed that pupils and patients are the only vulnerable parties in this power relationship, evidence suggests it is not always the case.

The two Australian nurse educators felt that the power-relationship was very much one way with the nurse being the person in control. They reminded the interviewer of the vulnerability of the patient and, therefore, of the nurse-patient relationship. They felt that the ethical issue of respect was one that needed consideration before mobile devices were used to share information about a patient. In contrast, their UK counterparts raised an alternative perspective in which the patient might be empowered in the relationship through the use of such technology. One nurse educator described an incident where a patient asked for permission to use a mobile phone to record her consultation. Upon reflection the nurse educator recognised how this type of activity might give greater power to the patient and expose the nurse to intrusive scrutiny.

> [T]here is a bit of a danger in authentically recording something ...there is too much exposure for people ...it would be too shocking for people to see the real authenticity of it ...Maybe more for other professionals than patients.

In this case, the nurse in question suggested it might affect the power relationship between patients and staff in a positive manner for the patient but not necessarily for the practitioner: 'The power could shift in the relationship with patients because patients could be involved in that reflection on what happened.' Hence it has potential to enhance and widen the nature of the nurse/patient relationship because patients are able to become more active in negotiating their own health care.

Teachers have also been vulnerable in cases where students have surreptitiously used their mobile phones to video the lesson before uploading it to YouTube or some other social networking site. We question whether this use of the technology – quite aside from the ethical and legal considerations – makes teachers and nurses more accountable for their actions as well as more vulnerable. How does the potential use of technology in these ways alter the power-relationship which exists in these professions and are these issues given sufficient considerations before the technology is introduced and used?

This discussion raises some interesting questions around practitioner accountability which we might reasonably extrapolate back to the original focus of the chapter, that of teaching. Will teachers become more directly accountable for their practice if pupils are able to make authentic recordings in the classroom, in the same way suggested by the nurse educators?

Informed consent

The requirement to gain informed consent from participants is a universal aspect of ethical procedures and protocols in higher education research. In both the teaching and nursing professions practioners have a duty of care towards their students and patients which also requires informed consent to be gained before data can be collected and used for any purpose. However the issues of ethical consent, duty of care and informed consent or permissions are not unproblematic. In the UK context the need to gain informed consent – from parents or guardians – to capture pupil data such as video or images, is widely recognised and practiced. Guidelines from Becta, the UK 'government agency leading the national drive to ensure the effective and innovative use of technology throughout learning', set out what is considered to be good practice in this respect and schools generally interpret these by asking parents or guardians to sign a 'blanket' consent form which covers the entire academic year (Becta, 2005).

The contrast with healthcare and nursing in the UK is particularly stark. Where schools and teachers are guided by a set of recommendations and guidelines, practitioners in the NHS are subject to a multiplicity of rules and procedures which appear to be mandatory and strictly enforced. The notion of gaining a 'blanket' permission to capture patient video or images seems both impractical and unworkable. Patients are not, on the whole, admitted to hospital on a long term basis and there is a well established set of protocols which require patients to give individual informed consent (unless this is impossible) for any instance where recording (e.g. video, audio and images) is required. This requirement is formal and exists at many levels within the NHS including the individual NHS Trusts and the various regulatory bodies for nurses and other practitioners. The contrast between schools and hospitals in this respect was noted by several of the nurse educators who talked about the labyrinthian complexity required to undertake any kind of research in hospitals, including the capture of images, video and other data:

...whereas in the NHS you would have to go to the local trust, go through trust ethics, trust governance, before you could even start to run a mobile project ...(UK nurse educator)

Guidelines for, and school policies on mobile phone use in Australia and the UK[2] often are more about student than professional use. They appear to be broadly of two types. One takes a more educative stance that tends not to outline specific use but rather promotes consideration of others, avoiding harm and mutual respect. Others specify specific permissible and banned uses. Some school policies require mobiles to be turned off during school while others permit use on silent modes outside the classroom. Most specify sanctions for misuse, at least while at school. The policies for teachers often derive from broader guidelines of permissible uses of technology in the workplace, much of which is applicable to mobile technologies. Broader policies regarding the use and capture of video, photos and audio have been in place long before the arrival of cheap digital devices. There is insufficient space for any detailed analysis of policy here but, given the changing capabilities, it would be useful to review current guidelines.

Spontaneity and ethics

The capacity for spontaneity lies at the heart of mobile professional learning. The ubiquity and growing acceptance of small mobile devices in many parts of life as well as their routine use for digital capture makes them relatively unobtrusive – even in the workplace. However, this usage does not fit well with current protocols and practices in both teaching and nursing. In these professions, if something is to be video-recorded, for example, then it is expected (and usually required) to make arrangements in advance. This misses the key advantage of mobile technologies. Much of the credibility of a digitally captured workplace experience lies in its authenticity. If we

---

2   See, for example, <http://www.aeutas.org.au/fileadmin/user_upload/Publications/ Mobile_phones.pdf> (accessed 16/12/09).

are to learn vicariously from workplace episodes then the quality of the professional learning is derived from their perceived realness. Often, in both nursing and teaching, the outcomes for the 'client' require an appropriate, spontaneous response tailored to the individual in the situation as it arises – not something prepared in advance like a 'here's one I prepared earlier' cooking show. In traditional models of research, such trustworthiness, credibility and authenticity have been universally valued and much sought after. However, these could only be achieved through prolonged engagement in the workplace with endless hours of video-recording until participants became oblivious to persistent hum of the tape. An almost endless record, with its significant cost, was needed to capture the occasional point of interest. By contrast the mobile device is becoming ever present and habitually used as required to capture salient events. This is not without its disadvantages. It means that there is nothing that might go unrecorded in the workplace. Also, by choosing what and when to capture, much of the 'editing' process occurs in advance of the recording. This is essential as the records are very short but it may lead to events, potentially productive for professional learning, going unnoticed and unscrutinised. On the plus side, it may also focus the professional's attention on what is important as well as make the process of reviewing events less time-consuming and more manageable in a busy professional's life.

While the potential of mobile professional learning is promising, its realisation remains vexed and ethically challenging. Many of the issues raised could be addressed by a code of practice with a set of procedures to follow. In particular, ensuring informed consent for collection of specific artefacts and strict controls over the management of information including encryption and password protection would go a long way towards ensuring the probity of the process (see e.g. Aubusson, Schuck and Burden, 2009). However, while such a guide may be useful, it remains a mechanistic response to a human problem related to trust and treating each other fairly and avoiding offence, upset or hurt. It is axiomatic in ethical matters that there is a need to balance risks and benefits. The question remains how to exploit the potential of mobile devices in professional workplace learning while at the same time minimising threats to others. At this early stage of this phenomenon it is useful to consider some general principles of ethical professional learning that may guide our thinking.

Ethical professional learning: General principles

The findings above indicate there are particular ethical challenges for teachers and nurses, in mobile learning in the workplace. Groundwater-Smith & Mockler (2007) constructed ethical guidelines derived from their experiences in teacher practitioner research. These were adopted and adapted by Aubusson, Ewing and Hoban (2009), who proposed a set of interrelated key elements for ethical action learning which is a form of professional learning. We argue these have relevance for professional mobile learning in both teaching and health workplaces. We elaborate on them below to provide guidance for ethical use of mobile devices in professional learning in these workplaces:

Trust and confidentiality

Ethical professional learning with others is underpinned by mutual trust. It also requires that those associated with the professional learning ensure that discussions and information remain confidential within the workplace. In research the perceived danger often arises from risks related to broad publication of potentially harmful information. In professional learning the potential harm within the workplace is often great because those involved are typically easily recognised even when normal practices are employed, such as the use of pseudonyms and de-identification of site of data collection. Trust and confidentiality cannot be imposed but they grow as organic features of the professional learning process. This trust may come gradually and might best be developed though gradually increasing depth and extent of information exchange and sharing. Whilst this type of trust is unlikely to develop in the context of a short nurse/patient exchange which might only take place over a period of thirty minutes, for example, it has more relevance for teachers and students where the relationship develops over an extended period of time. In these circumstances we would suggest mobile devices are not used until the students and teachers have developed a relationship of mutual trust. For example, teachers need to be assured that they can trust their students to provide constructive feedback when acting as co-researchers with mobile devices.

Genuine collaboration

Notions of genuine collaboration include mutual respect, acknowledgement of the contribution of others as well as embracing the needs and interests of others. These notions also stress that professional learning in the workplace typically involves the time and commitment of others. Consequently, professional learning process and its outcomes need to yield (or at least have potential to yield) direct benefits to all participants. In teaching, we have discussed use of mobile technologies in collaboration amongst teachers and also in teacher-student collaborations. A genuine collaboration is of mutual benefit to the parties concerned. Hence, teachers using mobile technologies for their learning need to ensure that the outcomes of that learning will ultimately enhance their teaching and be of value to their students. Typically, sharing events with other teachers needs to be purposeful and of benefit to both collaborating parties. However, teachers, students, nurses and patients may choose to engage in the process for altruistic reasons, for example, without expecting personal gain and only anticipating gain for others. The notion of mutual respect is also of importance in collaboration. Hence, nurses who are engaged in professional learning through capturing discussions with patients need to be mindful that the patients' privacy and dignity are not challenged in any way.

There seems little doubt that benefits would arise from teacher-student and nurse-patient collaboration where patient or student either collect artefacts and/or contribute in significant ways to the analysis or the artefacts. The benefits would acrue to the individual student or patient in their learning or treatment in that these may be made more effective as a consequence of feedback. At the very least, there could be adapation to serve specific needs and preferences. Such a collaborative process could add a significant dimension to the professional learning as well as provide insights from significant stakeholders (patients and students) in health and education settings. The potential of such collaboration faclitated by mobile technologies appears significant. The actual implementation and application of the process remains under-researched and ripe for investigation.

Transparency

This does not merely require that there is agreement about what 'information' is to be obtained and what will be done with it. It implies that all participants will have a say in the purposes for which it is obtained and what will be done with it. As well, there is a need for consultation about how the professional learning is initiated and issues arising as it proceeds. There is also a need to ensure that the teachers and nurses in the workplace have an opportunity to check and confirm information, evidence and ideas that arise from the professional learning processes in which they engage. For example, if a teacher is video-recorded in class for the purposes of professional development or performance management, it is important that the teacher has the opportunity to view this artefact in the context in which it is used. In the case of a video which is produced as evidence of performance management, a teacher might understandably wish to veto certain aspects of the final record. Similarly, if a nurse's performance is captured on a mobile device, the nurse needs to be aware of what has been captured and how it will be used. Specifically, the nature and content of any standard commentary that is provided with the recording ought to be agreed to by the professional who has been recorded.

Consequences

Here the central argument is that there is a responsibility to assess the risks arising from action taken in professional learning. Some consequences of mobile learning may have greater risks associated with them than others. Risks may derive from a variety of actions including sharing and publishing, gathering evidence and practical (even well-intentioned) interventions. For example, the action might comprise the capturing of images or video to support an early career teacher who is having difficulty in maintaining discipline. While there is little risk associated with the sharing of those images with a mentor to get feedback on the lesson, if the images find their way onto the internet and are accessible by others, the risk increases greatly. An example in the nursing context is one concerning care and diligence of patients. A nurse who is distracted by their use of the mobile device, albeit for purposes of professional learning, might not be devoting sufficient attention to their patient. The greater the risk, the more important it is to ensure careful surveillance, monitoring and feedback systems to prevent potential harm.

Accountability

In their workplace, teachers have accountabilities to many stakeholders: their society, their students, their employers, parents and peers to name some. In professional learning there is a need to balance these accountabilties and consider in particular such matters as the right of each to know what is being learnt and what evidence has been gathered. In the simplest terms this may require a professional at times to withhold information and at other times release it; to gather evidence and keep it to a local few, with reasonable prospects of making decisions that improve the lot of others or to make it widely available to expose weaknesses or reveal paths to success. One characteristic of professions is that its members seek ongoing improvement for the profession as a whole. Recorded data may provide authentic experiences opening up practices for scrutiny, thus contributing to professional ethics.

Each of these elements increases in complexity, or indeed may require modification, when school children, adolescents or patients become willing or *de facto* partners in the process. If evidence is gathered in the classroom it raises questions about who owns it and who determines what can be done with it? If the professional learning takes place, at least in part, in the workplace then how are trust, collaboration and transparency to be managed with one's students, patients and colleagues? And, how does the relative position of power between teacher and student or nurse and patient influence the negotiation that takes place? Furthermore, if engagement in professional learning supported by mobile technologies changes the relationship between nurse and patient or teacher and student, as we would predict, then is the application of these professional guidelines sufficient to ensure that the relationship is positive without any sense of exploitation of one party by the other?

Conclusion

The literature and findings from our small study both indicate there is significant value in using mobile devices for workplace learning of teachers and nurses. Such use leads to a need for clear ethical guidelines to ensure appropriate and beneficial outcomes. Consequently, the study of ethical issues in both teaching and nursing workplaces has been a useful exercise. It appears that many of the issues discussed above are common to these two professions. This suggests that the development of ethical guidelines for one will inform the development of guidelines for the other. We argue for further investigation of these two workplaces to provide a basis for future protocols for mobile professional learning in the two areas.

It seems one ethical response to the inherent dangers of digital capture with mobile technologies in the workplace would be to ban such use. However, workplaces for education and healthcare have a responsibility to society. There is a moral imperative to avoid harm. So too it is incumbent on us to enable professional learning and to exploit the full potential of technologies to achieve this end. This requires the development of practical, defensible guidelines to facilitate the professional use of mobile technologies for learning in the workplace. This chapter has both sought to explore the risks and to consider the potential benefits to inform this facilitation. It recommends that ethical practice with workplace participants be based on trust and confidentiality, genuine collaboration, transparency, risk assessment of actions and accountability.

Appendix

Guiding questions for teachers and education professionals in this study relating to ethical issues included:

We are particularly interested in mobile teacher learning which involves teachers in digitally capturing classroom events to share with other teachers to stimulate professional conversations.

- What ethical issues does it raise?
- How might these issues be addressed?
- What advice would you give to teacher leaders in the field about mobile professional learning?
- Are you aware of any policies that might prevent or promote this type of activity by teachers?
- What is your view of these policies?

The guiding questions for the nurse educators and health professionals included:

- In what ways have you seen/or are you aware of mobile devices being used by nurses as part of their professional practice (give examples)?
- Do the use of such devices offer opportunities for professional learning (e.g. reflection; recording and analyzing practice etc)?
- Are there any guidelines or protocols for the use of this type of device (i.e. for professional learning rather than research)?
- Do you see any ethical issues arising from the use of these devices in the workplace (elaborate on this)?
- Are there any policy documents that govern use in health care?

References

Aubusson, P., Ewing, R., & Hoban, G. (2009) *Action Learning in Schools: Reframing teachers' professional learning and development*. London: Routledge

Aubusson, P., Schuck, S., & Burden, K. (2009) 'Mobile learning for teacher professional learning: benefits, obstacles and issues.' *ALT-J 17*(3), pp. 233–247

Aubusson, P., Steele, F., Brady, L., & Dinham, S. (2007) 'Action learning in teacher learning community formation: informative or transformative?' *Teacher Development 11*(2), pp. 133–148

Beckett, D., & Hager, P. (2002) 'Life, work and learning: Practice in postmodernity.' *Routledge International Studies in the Philosophy of Education 14*. London: Routledge

Becta (2005) *E-Safety: Developing whole-school policies to support effective practice.* Coventry: Becta

Billett, S. (2001) *Learning in the workplace: Strategies for effective practice.* Sydney: Allen & Unwin

Billet, S. (2002) 'Critiquing workplace learning discourses: Participation and continuity at work.' *Studies in the Education of Adults 34*(1), pp. 56–67

Bogdan, R., & Biklen, S. (1992) *Qualitative research for education.* 2nd edn. Boston, MA: Allyn & Bacon

Burbank, M., & Kauchak, D. (2003) 'An alternative model for professional development: investigations into effective collaboration.' *Teaching and Teacher Education 19*(5), pp. 499–514

Clement, M., & Vandenberghe, R. (2000) 'Teachers' professional development: a solitary or collegial (ad)venture?' *Teaching and Teacher Education 16*, pp. 81–101

Connelly, M., & Clandinin, J. (1997) 'Teachers' personal practical knowledge on the professional knowledge landscape.' *Teaching and Teacher Education 7*(13), pp. 665–674

Cook-Sather, A. (2006) 'Sound, presence and power: "Student Voice" in educational research and reform.' *Curriculum Inquiry 36*(4), pp. 359–390

Eraut, M. (1994) *Developing professional knowledge and competence.* London: Falmer Press

Eteokleous, N., & Laouris, Y. (2005) 'We need an educationally relevant definition of mobile learning.' In *4th World conference on mLearning Mobile technology. The future of learning in your hands.* Presented at the mLearning, Cape Town, South Africa

Fisher, T., Higgins, C. and Loveless, A. (2006) *Teachers learning with digital technologies: a review of research and projects. Futurelab Report no.14.* Available online at <http://www.futurelab.org.uk/research/lit_reviews.htm#lr14> (accessed 15/04/10)

Groundwater-Smith, S. & Mockler, N. (2007) 'Ethics in practitioner research: An issue of quality.' *Research Papers in Education 22*(2), pp. 199–211

Hodkinson, H. & Hodkinson, P. (2005) 'Improving schoolteachers' workplace learning.' In *Research Papers in Education 20*(2), pp. 109–131

Kearney, M. & Schuck, S. (2006) 'Spotlight on authentic learning: student developed digital video projects.' *Australasian Journal of Educational Technology 22*(2), pp. 189–208

Kelchtermans, G. & Ballet, K. (2002) 'The micropolitics of teacher induction. A narrative-biographical study on teacher socialisation.' *Teaching and Teacher Education 18*(1), pp. 105–120

Korthagen, F. & Kessells, J. (1999) 'Linking theory and practice: changing the pedagogy of teacher education.' *Educational Researcher 28*(4), pp. 4–17

Miles, M. & Huberman, M. (1994) *Qualitative data analysis.* 2nd edn. Beverley Hills, CA: Sage

Noddings, N. & Witherell, C. (1991) 'Epilogue: themes remembered and forseen.' In Witherell, C., & Noddings, N. (eds), *Stories lives tell: Narrative and dialogue in education* (pp. 279–280). New York: Teachers College Press

Retallick, J. (1999) 'Teachers' workplace learning: towards legitimation and accreditation.' *Teachers and Teaching: Theory and Practice 5*(1), pp. 33–50

Sharples, M. (2006) *Big Issues in Mobile Learning. Report of a workshop by the Kaleidoscope Network of Excellence Mobile Learning Initiative.* Nottingham: Learning Science Research Institute

Shulman, L. (2000) 'From Minsk to Pinsk: why a Scholarship of Teaching and Learning.' *The Journal of Scholarship of Teaching and Learning 1*(1), pp. 48–53

Traxler, J. (2009) 'Students and mobile devices: choosing which dream.' *ALT-C Proceedings*

Thomson, P. & Gunther, H. (2006) 'From "consulting pupils" to "pupils as researchers": a situated case narrative.' *British Educational Research Journal 32*(6), pp. 839–856

Wishart, J. (2009) 'Ethical considerations in implementing mobile learning in the workplace.' *International Journal of Mobile and Blended Learning 1*(2), pp. 76–92

JOCELYN WISHART

13 Ethical concerns relevant to researching work-based mobile learning[1]

Abstract

This chapter addresses the current challenges of planning for research into work-based mobile learning where questions arise over how to implement current ethical guidance when investigating, what has proved to be not only a moving target, but also one that can capture and store a wealth of often personal information, including images. The handheld mobile device is well matched to work placement-based learning for it has potential to support just-in-time, location- and context-based learning as well as communication between workplace and study base. However, it is also carried between personal and work contexts, is used spontaneously and raises questions of ownership not least because information captured on it is so easily shared via the internet. The discussions reported in this chapter originally arose from a discussion workshop held out at the University of Bristol in 2008 and funded by its Institute of Advanced Studies.

1   The framework and some of the material in this chapter were first published in an article in the second issue of the *International Journal of Mobile Learning* and responses are invited from the mobile learning community as to the viability, feasibility, possibilities, practical and ethical challenges involved in the use of such a framework. The author wishes to acknowledge the contributions made by participants and presenters at the IAS Workshop held in Bristol in June 2008.

Introduction

This chapter raises questions for consideration by all those researching or planning to research the use of mobile devices for teaching and learning or training in workplaces such as hospitals, offices, factories, design centres and schools. Such workplace-based personal and professional development is viewed as essential for students of many professions including medicine, law, education, catering, social care and nursing. Many trainees are known to benefit from time spent on an industrial placement such as those offered in engineering, plumbing, computing and business degree programmes. Recording, reflecting on and reviewing of student progress during their placement off-campus is easily provided for through handheld mobile devices such as smartphones and personal digital assistants (PDAs). However, researching such use requires careful planning with respect to a range of ethical issues.

Researchers and the trainees in work-based settings being studied continue to find using personal, mobile technologies a challenge; though now it is much less a technical challenge than one requiring institutional and cultural innovation in permissions and behaviours within these settings. In addition, we should note that the nature of research into the use of mobile learning in the workplace involves investigating the use of personal, private devices by people of a range of ages and abilities. This will immediately raise questions in researchers' minds, as well as in those of the students' tutors' over how best to approach a potential minefield of ethical issues. These range from privacy with personal data wittingly or unwittingly stored by the student users on their phones, through informed consent (especially over the use of images), ownership of and secure storage for the information they have captured and confidentiality to concerns over safety. Use of mobile devices is also associated with Web 2.0 software and user-generated content leading to students personally familiar with social networking applying similar standards and expectations in their professional roles.

These issues will be discussed in this chapter and ways forward suggested in order to ensure that research into the integration of mobile learning into work-based education for professions such as health care, catering, engineering and teaching proceeds sensitively and responsibly. Also, the chapter presents a framework for consideration by the mobile learning community that can be used to highlight or prioritise ethical considerations before conducting research into the use of mobile devices by students in workplaces, schools and hospitals.

Why do researchers consider ethics?

Questions over ethics in research arose as a result of a number of dubious, unpleasant and, in some cases illegal, medical and psychological experiments carried out with human participants during the first half of the twentieth century. The worst cases are attributed to Nazi doctors working in concentration camps during World War II. The first code of research ethics, the Nuremberg Code, was a major outcome of the Nuremberg Trials set up to prosecute war criminals post-World War II. Since then all professions publish a code of ethical behaviours or standards that are expected of their members. The ethical codes of practice of both the American Psychological Association and the British Psychological Society have their origins in the Nuremberg code which highlighted participants' rights to informed consent and freedom from harm. Other, more recently developed professional associations relevant to mobile learning research, such as the American and the British Educational Research Associations, have also developed similar codes that focus on ensuring that no detriment occurs to participants as a result of their participation in research. However, ethical concerns relevant to investigating mobile learning in the workplace also include those arising from the field of computing research. The Association for Computing Machinery, the world's largest educational and scientific computing society has a Code of Ethics and Professional Conduct that centres on general moral imperatives such as honesty, fairness, well-being of others and respect for property including intellectual property as well as avoiding harm.

Mason (1986) proposed four ethical concerns as being specific to the Information Age:

- privacy – which information can be withheld and which cannot, under what conditions and with what safeguards;
- accuracy – the authenticity, and fidelity of stored information;
- ownership – both of the information and the channels through which it is transmitted;
- accessibility – what information does a person or an organization have a right or a privilege to obtain, under what conditions and with what safeguards?

This led to an early emphasis on issues of ownership and accuracy which was maintained by Anderson and Blackwood (2004) who were the first researchers to publish on the debate on ethics of the use of mobile technologies in education. Their interests focused on legal and privacy issues relevant to college and higher education (HE) such as ownership and copyright of material stored on mobile devices. However, this is also a particular issue for workplace mobile learning research where learners or trainees have access to sensitive material that companies do not allow to go 'beyond their gates'. Anderson's (2005) second paper on privacy issues further develops the implications of researchers tracking participants' personal use of mobile devices enabling access to their personal information, but neither paper considers the use of mobile phone cameras. Nor do they address issues associated with the need to capture evidence of learning during a college or HE student's work based learning placement for later assessment.

Why is researching workplace-based mobile learning a special case?

Sharples (2007) helpfully identified a number of issues in identifying the most appropriate research methods to consider when developing investigations into workplace-based mobile learning. The first and most obvious is that the learners are mobile. The researcher aiming to study how they learn in different locations will be tracking them across a range of locations that vary: from home or recreation to work and including travelling between these and from real to virtual environments. Each location will have an associated socio-cultural context that includes the formal and informal social and professional codes that govern the way learners use (and feel comfortable about using) mobile devices. Other challenges for the researcher are: that learning may well be distributed and mobile devices are communication tools leading to the probability of having multiple participants in several different locations. Also it may involve a variety of personal and institutional technologies giving researchers opportunities to access informal and personal learning activities as well as formal, work-based tasks. Burden et al. (see Chapter 11, this volume) add spontaneity to this list, pointing out that it is important to professional mobile learning for it brings authenticity to mobile learning episodes. How is a researcher to capture this?

Nor is it easy researching at the 'leading edge' of a technological innovation. Researchers investigating the use of PDAs in workplace settings such as those in the ALPS (Assessment & Learning in Practice Settings) project with trainee midwives (Dearnley, Haigh and Fairhall, 2008) or with trainee teachers (Wishart, McFarlane and Ramsden, 2007) have found trainees reluctant to even bring the mobile device to work for fear that it would be socially unacceptable or cause disruption. In a study of trainee teaching assistants loaned PDAs, concerns over possible loss of the expensive devices or even becoming a possible target for thieves were reported by Nikoi and Edirisingha (2008).

Ethical questions pertinent to the special nature of mobile learning were first presented to the mobile learning research community by Traxler and Bridges (2004). They offered an outline for ethical mobile learning research that highlights three areas: informed consent, confidentiality and differentials in power between researcher and researched associated with age and class. The issue of informed consent was highlighted in the UK when the Cityware project at the University of Bath (O'Neill et al., 2006) hit the news under the headline: 'Bluetooth Big Brother uses mobiles and laptops to track thousands of Britons'. It is difficult for researchers asking for consent to be clear about how much participants really understand about the capabilities of their mobile devices. Traxler and Bridges (2004) also highlight privacy with reference to researchers' access to system data logs that record learners' activity and location. Confidentiality, linked by Traxler and Bridges to how difficult it is to ensure in cyberspace as technical systems are complex and leaky, has also become big news in the UK today as portable, media storage devices, such as mobile phones and USB memory sticks, containing data from the workplace are regularly being reported lost or stolen. Privacy and confidentiality are also at the forefront of workplace managers' concerns as will be discussed later with respect to students using mobile devices to support their training. Vavoula (2009) highlights the personal, private nature of mobile learning alongside the elusivity of mobile learning outcomes as particular issues for researchers aiming to establish ethical procedures. She notes that researchers are likely to be uncertain of what will constitute the mobile learning experience and then asks (p. 345) 'how accurately can they inform the participants of what data is sought and why?'

Current ethical guidance on researching learning

In his contribution to the report on the 'big issues' of mobile learning, Winters (2006) concludes that the ethical dimension is critically important to researching mobile learning and is becoming even more relevant as society moves towards a world where ubiquitous technology is ever present.

All academic researchers in training and education are made aware of the importance of this ethical dimension as part of their own professional training. Professional associations, too, regularly review their codes of ethical conduct. The British Educational Research Association (BERA) revised their guidelines for educational research most recently in 2004 (BERA, 2004) in order to recognise the diversity of the association members' research and their ethical concerns. This resulted in a 13-page document centred on the principle that all educational research should be conducted with an ethic of respect for the person, knowledge, democratic values, the quality of educational research and academic freedom. The guidelines are laid out by considering issues of responsibility; firstly to participants and subsequently to sponsors of research and the community of educational researchers. Responsibilities to the participant include ensuring researchers are given informed consent voluntarily, that they consider the pros and cons of deception carefully, offer participants the right to withdraw, taking particular care with children and vulnerable young people or adults, incentives and possible detriment arising from participation in research and issues of privacy and disclosure of the results. It is intended that the Council of the British Educational Research Association will continuously update the guidelines to ensure that, as circumstances change, the Association provides the most up to date support for its members. With similar intentions the published ethical standards of the American Educational Research association (AERA, 2000) currently forming a 12-page document were revised in 1996 and in 2000.

Wali (2007) exemplifies this guidance in her study of where and how students used portable laptops. She described how addressing these ethical challenges and concerns can become a lengthy process when she presented her research in a workshop run by the Centre for Excellence in Work-Based Learning for Education Professionals (WLE Centre) at the Institute of Education, London, UK. First, it was necessary to gain students' informed consent to install system-monitoring software in their laptops to gather data about their use of the laptops before actually installing the software. Students also had to be notified of the reason for such recording, the range of uses to be made of its outcomes and their agreement sought on releasing the outcome into different kinds of public domain. Second, students' informed consent to be observed in formal and informal settings had to be obtained. Third, students' anonymity and privacy had to be ensured by removing students' identification from the data, especially the log files, once collected and ensuring that the collected data is not accessible to anyone other than the researcher. The students' main concern was their privacy and anonymity. Further ethical and practical challenges included: getting the different universities involved to agree permission to observe students in informal settings and to installing system-monitoring software on students' laptops. The universities were also concerned about confidentiality and students' privacy. Also some technical problems were encountered as a result of conflicts between the security software installed on students' laptops and the system monitoring software.

The challenge of employing current guidance

However, a different perspective arises when we consider mobile learning in the workplace, what about the employing company's rights to privacy and confidentiality? Where the workplace involves vulnerable people, such as patients in hospital and young children, they too have rights to privacy and confidentiality and to be fully informed before they give consent to being involved in research. Yet it is in those very same workplaces that mobile devices are proving useful in supporting trainees with both learning and assessment. Recent examples include teacher trainees working with children and young people (Wishart, 2006), apprentice bakers (Chan, 2006; see also Chapter 4, this volume), plumbers (Savill-Smith & Douch, 2009), nursing students (Treadwell, 2005) other trainees within healthcare settings (Taylor et al., 2007) and students in leisure and tourism (Oliver, 2005). All of these needed to be able to capture images and sometimes video of competences and skills whilst on placement. Many teachers and lecturers are also mobile learning researchers.

For example, the Personal Inquiry project (Sharples, 2007, 2009) illustrates well the range of ethical issues that need to be addressed before researching in schools. This project was set up to investigate the use of mobile devices, in this case netbooks, that can easily be carried between formal and informal settings to support inquiry science learning. Semi-structured investigations to be carried out by 11- to 14-year-old pupils were introduced and planned in school but were conducted outside school, in the home and in Science Centres. General ethical principles considered by the research team included the following:

- employing a participatory design where participants (pupils and teachers) were active in the design and evaluation of the project;
- all participants were willing volunteers and kept fully informed of the purpose of the project;
- permissions were to be obtained from all the children, their teachers and parents;
- studies in the home will be with the signed informed consent of all target children and their parents;
- other children in the family will be asked for their assent;
- project staff subject to enhanced Criminal Records Bureau (CRB) checks;
- researchers will not go unaccompanied into homes;
- all data will be anonymised and kept confidential; and
- participants and their schools will not be identified in publications or presentations (unless they wish to be).

Though, in the event, the way the data was collected had to be modified due to communication difficulties in obtaining consent from some disengaged families. Other issues specific to the mobile learning nature of the project included those related to monitoring opportunities and to ownership of data, privacy and copyright. Those relevant to monitoring opportunities included:

- Children will be using the technology as part of their curriculum work, so teachers should be able to monitor the online activities as they occur and to inspect all the collected data;

- Children will be fully informed about how their learning activities out-side the classroom may be monitored by teachers and researchers; and
- Children will be able to decide where and when to collect data.

It was decided that the system would not continuously monitor movement and activity but would be set up to only log actions and data explicitly entered by the children. Those relevant to ownership of data, privacy and copyright included the following:

- All data collected will be subject to the provisions of the UK Data Protection Act 1998, in particular Section 33 of the Act relating to data collected for the purposes of research;
- Material captured or created by the children will be subject to normal standards of copyright and fair use, and inappropriate material will be deleted;
- Authors of teaching materials and field data will retain copyright and moral rights of authorship over their material; and
- A condition of participation will be that the project has rights to publish the material for academic and educational purposes (either crediting the authors or anonymising the material where appropriate and by agreement).

Obtaining permission for research on using mobile devices to support learning in health care workplaces has also been particularly difficult in England. Projects need to be cleared by the research ethics committees of both the researchers' home institution and the primary care trust(s) where the mobile learners will be working. Most individual trusts, exemplified here by the West Sussex Hospitals Trust, maintain concerns especially with respect to the ability to take photographs with mobile phones.

> The patients' confidentiality, dignity, privacy and protection of data is paramount. Only officially authorised Trust equipment, for a direct legitimate clinical reason, will be used to record, store and communicate electronic images. The use of any other mobile technology, for the purpose of taking photographs is prohibited throughout the Hospital. (West Sussex Hospitals Trust, 2006)

Yet, once permissions are arranged, as in the ALPS Centre for Excellence in Teaching and Learning pilot run at Leeds Metropolitan University (Taylor et al., 2007), the use of mobile phones to photograph patient care to evidence dietetics and physiotherapy students' learning proved successful. Benefits of using a mobile device to send images and text to Mediaboard (a web-based multimedia message board) in order to create a learning log included better access to and recording of information, greater tutor and peer support and ICT skills development.

The ALPS projects also highlight the importance of researcher sensitivity to the workplace culture. Sandars & Dearnley (2009) noted several incidents in which students were reprimanded by clinical staff, including assessors, whilst legitimately using their devices for data entry in clinical settings. Patients, too, apparently reported their nurses for 'texting' whilst on duty. This was related to the perception that using mobile technology was 'play not work'. However, Savill-Smith & Douch (2009) report acceptability and even interest in video resources on trainees' iPods in a study of trainee plumbers from experienced plumbers who would have laughed at a trainee bringing a book to their workplace.

What are the key ethical issues for researchers in mobile learning?

The aforementioned studies researching the potential of mobile learning to support trainees and students in colleges, schools and hospitals are testing the current guidance especially with respect to the use of images and informed consent. In order to ease the path to researching the use of mobile devices to support learning and training in a wider range of workplaces we need ready answers to researchers' questions such as the following that have already arisen in discussion with the author and colleagues:

- What if I see inappropriate images on a students' mobile phone?
- How do I set up a study on handhelds in a college where the use of mobile devices is banned?
- Can I keep photos of a patient's cuts and bruises taken on a trainee nurse's PDA for their wound care project?
- A teacher trainee has sent in video of his pupils as evidence of teaching through role-play – can I show it to others?
- Am I sure that the use of mobile phones with young people is actually safe?

It was decided to consult more widely over these concerns and a discussion workshop on ethical issues affecting mobile learning was set up to invite the members of the international research network 'Adding a Mobile Dimension to Teaching & Learning'[2] to debate these issues and recommend ways forward. A discussion workshop is a recognised method of collaborative knowledge construction through discussion and debate amongst peers or experts. The 'Adding a Mobile Dimension to Teaching & Learning' research network focuses on handheld technologies such as PDAs, smartphones, mobile phones, play stations and MP3 Players and how they can support teaching and learning. Its members include internationally respected researchers and practitioners in mobile learning. The network has run interdisciplinary workshops funded by the Institute of Advanced Studies at the University of Bristol since April 2006. The network itself has grown to over 100 individuals and each workshop has been attended by 12 to 24 members. Whilst the number of members of a particular discussion workshop is not large enough to be a representative sample of the entire population; the findings from the group debates are agreed amongst the workshop participants whose expertise and experience ensure conclusions are reliable and valid.

The workshop on ethical issues affecting mobile learning took place in June 2008 and participants recruited through advertisement to the IAS 'Adding a Mobile Dimension to Teaching and Learning' research

---

2   <http://www.bris.ac.uk/education/research/networks/mobile/> (accessed 16/08/10).

network. Therefore, participation was voluntary and participants were fully informed as to the purposes of the workshop. In order to facilitate knowledge construction the workshop was designed to promote discussion and engage both participants and presenters in active debate. Its aims were for the participants to identify the range of ethical considerations linked to mobile learning in professional workplaces through discussion and to debate whether or where current ethical codes of practice need updating. The workshop comprised a series of presentations and small group discussions followed by a plenary discussion where conclusions from the small group discussions were debated with the whole group. Outcomes included an agreed set of key ethical issues to be drawn to the attention of the mobile learning research community.

Participants concluded that there were six key issues that underpinned the ethical considerations currently arising in research into mobile learning and that those issues are particularly prevalent when researching trainees' use of mobile devices to support learning on placement. These are shown in Figure 13.1.

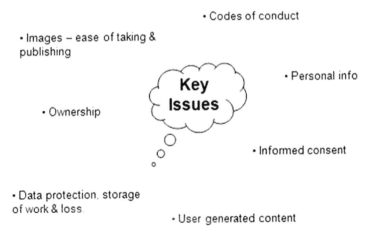

Figure 13.1 Key ethical issues in workplace-based mobile learning

Codes of conduct

The first key issue was the presence of a multiplicity of published professional codes of conduct. Both researchers and practitioners look to their relevant professional code of ethical conduct for guidance. A number of these codes were known to the group. Some examples are the following:

- BERA (2004) *Revised Ethical Guidelines for Educational Research* – just over 4,000 words
- AERA (2000) *Ethical Standards of the American Educational Research Association* – 3,400 words
- ACM (1992) *Code of Ethics and Professional Conduct* – 3,000 words
- BCS (2006) *Code of Conduct for British Computer Society Members* – 1,400 words.

In addition, where the workplace involves children, young people or vulnerable adults, as is the case for schools and healthcare settings, anyone researching learning or training must learn about the relevant practitioner's duty of care. For example, a teacher's duty of care to underage pupils is to meet the standard of care that can be expected of a competent professional, acting within the constraints of the circumstances (NUT, n.d.). This duty of care does not derive from legislation, but it is has been upheld in the English courts as a duty which has derived from laws established through common use and case law precedents and is sometimes referred to as 'in loco parentis', i.e. a teacher should act as a prudent parent would. Researchers investigating mobile learning in schools and healthcare settings will need to plan how this duty of care may be included in their investigations. For instance, Jonker and Wijers (2009) reported how they had programmed the route back to school into their location-based game Mobile Math played by secondary school children on the streets of Amsterdam.

Researchers and practitioners do their best to comply with the standards mentioned above and codes as exemplified earlier in the discussion of ethical issues considered by Wali (2007) and Sharples (2007). However, even though the professions strive to keep them up-to-date as mentioned earlier in this chapter, new mobile technologies that seamlessly mix personal and work-based information are not directly addressed by these codes. Additionally a researcher needs not only to be mindful of their own code but also that for the workplace where research is planned to take place.

Informed consent

The issue of informed consent, the second key issue arising from the workshop and one mentioned in most professional ethical codes, is a particular example. Researchers in mobile learning are finding that their participants are often unaware of the entire range of functions of their mobile devices and/or the details of the information that their mobile device records and which can be unintentionally shared with a researcher. These include information as to their location as well as personal notes and images.

Functions that are not understood well by many mobile device users include browsers that store internet histories and Bluetooth. Dr Vassilis Kostakos, research associate on the Cityware project at the University of Bath, said: 'The really nice thing about Bluetooth is that when you are walking down the street, although you are not talking to anyone, your Bluetooth device can be talking to other devices' (Kostakos, 2007). Not everyone in the locality being observed agreed with him that being recorded for the research project as a result of leaving Bluetooth set to 'discoverable' was 'really nice'. In another project, also based in Bath, researchers working with young teenagers investigating the use of mobile devices with GPS to record traffic pollution had not anticipated the level of detail they would obtain about where children lived (Woodgate, 2008).

Personal information

Greater sharing of personal information between home and school is reported to be a positive feature of the use of mobile devices in schools (McFarlane et al., 2008). However, a few teachers have been surprised by items left on the children's PDAs by their parents. New social codes that have arrived with social networking sites such as Facebook, MySpace, Bebo and Flickr and the popularity of blogging indicate that considerable numbers of people are becoming less concerned about sharing personal information than in previous years. However, Traxler (2005) reminds us of the need for employers (and consequently researchers in the workplace) to take care with off-the-shelf synchronisation software which may automatically copy personal information inappropriate to the workplace from a mobile device onto an office PC. Another example of the automatic provision of personal information is that of repairmen and delivery van drivers who now carry GPS enabled handhelds running applications specific to their work. Their routes to and from jobs including any breaks can now be both timed and tracked.

Ownership, user-generated content and images

The fourth key issue was device ownership with particular reference to trainees or students using mobile devices on long-term loan or acquired through schemes that part-fund purchase over time such as those being deployed in some UK schools and further education colleges. If the device user does not fully own the device questions arise over who is responsible for the data stored on that device. Also who owns the rights to the images taken by a trainee with a mobile device in the workplace, the employer, the training institution or the trainee themselves? The ease of taking and publishing images with mobile devices was highlighted as another key issue and is clearly one of the most important concerns with respect to training in the workplace. Many employing institutions have actually banned camera phones from the workplace because of concerns over possible breaches of confidentiality whether accidental or deliberate. This is a particular challenge in healthcare and school-based settings (West Sussex Hospitals Trust, 2006, Wishart, 2005) where trainees could use mobile devices to record notes and images to support later revision and reflective practice but the current socio-cultural climate and concerns over storage and protection of images leaving the workplace prevail. It is interesting to note that searching the image sharing website Flickr in January 2010 with the phrase 'my teacher' returned 12,962 images. Not all of these are taken in school but many are. This upswing in user-generated content (another key issue) for the wide range of social networking sites provides a ready publishing outlet, not only for images, but also for personal data.

Data protection

The final key issue noted was data protection. Small mobile devices often containing important personal data and/or records of activity on behalf of an employer are regularly lost or stolen. Though there are ways to protect lost information, such as those used by the ALPS projects (Campbell, 2009) which include encrypting data on the device and memory card. Also if a trainee's device is not in use for a short while it will lock and any lost devices can be locked remotely. However, such data may well also be uploaded by a diligent trainee, employee or researcher onto a home computer – we need to consider who is responsible for keeping it safe? Where data acquired by means of a mobile device is to be assessed for a trainee's qualification or a child's progress in school it needs to be held safely. But by whom and for how long? What happens when the storage system becomes full? The UK Data Protection Act (Great Britain, 1998) clarifies a number of terms, makes provision for data subjects and data users but doesn't really address these issues, only suggesting in Section 33 that exemptions on storing data for research only apply if the data are not processed in such a way that substantial distress is, or is likely to be, caused to any data subject.

New tensions

As a result of the various debates and discussions during the workshop on ethical issues affecting mobile learning, the participants concluded that there is currently a tension developing between our current legal and professional codes and new multi-cultural, multi-generational social codes. This led them to question whether professionals engaged in mobile learning should continue to closely and unquestioningly follow current ethical guidance for researchers and for the workplace being researched that results in comprehensive but complex detailed consent forms and guidelines. It may be better, and less time-consuming, to address ethical concerns by working from the original ethical principles rather than from formal codes such as BERA, AERA and BCS which will have to be updated now and regularly for the foreseeable future to take into account issues such as those discussed earlier in this chapter. This would also enable researchers to deal more confidently with the changing contexts and situations that following mobile learners brings about.

Established ethical principles

Others though have shared similar concerns. Working in the then developing field of information and communication technologies in the 1940s and 50s led Norbert Wiener, now known as the founding father of Cybernetics, to consider the social and ethical impact of the coming 'automatic age' (Bynum, 2005). He proposed three 'great principles' of justice (Wiener, 1954) which are the following:

- Justice requires freedom i.e. the liberty of each human being to develop freely the full measure of the human possibilities embodied in him.

- Justice requires 'the equality by which what is just for A and B remains just when the positions of A and B are interchanged.'
- Justice requires benevolence that is 'a good will between man and man that knows no limits short of those of humanity itself.'

These resonate well with three of the four basic principles that are widely accepted by the biomedical community and commonly used to guide moral deliberations today (Mallia, 2003). These four principles were originally described by Beauchamp and Childress (1983) in their discussion of principles of biomedical ethics. The fourth principle is non-maleficience, which gives us the following:

- beneficience (doing good);
- non-maleficience (avoiding harm);
- autonomy (respecting choice); and
- justice (equality of access to resource).

In addition, where their workplace involves those less able to look out for themselves such as in medical or educational contexts, responsible adults such as doctors, nurses and teachers have a duty of care.

Introducing a framework for considering ethics associated with researching work-based mobile learning

It is clear that researchers are currently facing challenges in applying the current ethical guidance from multiple codes of conduct designed for particular, mostly static contexts in their investigations of mobile participants at work in a range of locations. The focus on key ethical issues for researching work-based mobile learning combined with a return to the fundamental principles underpinning ethical behaviour resulting from the 'Adding a Mobile Dimension to Teaching and Learning' network's discussion workshop may be a more helpful way forward for the mobile learning research community. Therefore, the following framework, see Table 13.1, was drawn up to aid researchers in planning for ethical considerations. Each cell in the table where a key ethical issue intersects with an underpinning ethical principle becomes an opportunity for reflection as to what is current practice and what is good practice. Codes of conduct have been omitted from the original list of key ethical issues as it is suggested that the framework is used to generate discussion amongst researchers before checking the appropriate code in order to more freely suggest the range of issues to be addressed. In this way, the relationship between acting in an ethical manner and the codes of conduct could be strengthened as the codes seem to be a product that results from discursive communication and negotiation between the participants and the researchers.

	Do good	Avoid harm	Respect user choice	Share resources fairly
Personal information and images				
Informed consent				
Ownership				
Data storage and protection				
User-generated content				

Table 13.1 Framework for prioritising ethical issues for consideration before engaging in research into work-based mobile learning

Not all intersections will give rise to relevant concerns depending on the situation under consideration and in some instances it will be hard to balance principles. For example with using mobile devices to capture and share images 'avoid harm' may conflict with 'respect user choice' however, the act of considering the ethical issues involved will alert the researcher or educator to the need to come to an agreement with participants or students respectively with respect to that key issue. Such negotiation between the learners, their trainers or tutors and researchers in discussion about ethical issues will be ongoing; the initial moment of intrinsic reflection about ethical issues supported by this framework can only be a starting point.

The following scenario is presented in order to exemplify the framework's potential.

> A researcher seeks to evaluate how a web-enabled mobile phone containing a camera and an integral pico-projector that can display video, web pages, contacts etc. on a nearby surface may be used by a trainee hairdresser effectively to support their learning.

The framework can then be used as indicated in Table 13.2 to help suggest the questions over ethical issues that the researchers need to consider how best to manage.

Ethical issue	Do good	Avoid harm	Respect user choice	Share resources fairly
Personal information and images	What personal data would it be useful to the trainee to store on the device? How will being able to capture and share video support their training?	How will the researcher treat any personal information found? Will there be disruption to others in the salon?	On discovering the information being disclosed, the trainee may decide not to continue further with the project at any point	
Informed consent	Is the trainee aware that any personal data/images stored by them may be seen by the researchers? Are the workplace mentors aware of the potential disruption? What will the clients be told? How will their opinion be taken into account?		During the project the salon manager may decide not to continue further with the project at any point	

Ownership	Who will own any images/ video taken in the salon?	Are the animations/ video to be shown licensed for public use?	Has a participatory research design been considered?	How are the devices to be distributed?
Data storage and protection	Will the trainee need to store client information or images on the device? What protection/ permissions need to be in place?			
User-generated content	Are trainees aware of good practice in seeking permission to publish their images/video?		If a trainee chooses not to publish their own videos, will it affect their grades?	Can all trainees on the course access each others' content?

Table 13.2 Ethical issues to be prioritised before researching trainee hairdressers' use of pico-projection and cameras on handheld devices

This framework was piloted with a group of eight mobile learning research-ers during the 'Education in the Wild: Contextual and location-based learning in action' workshop at Stellar's (the EU Network of Excellence) Alpine Rendez-Vous (Wishart, 2009). It became quickly clear that 'shar-ing resources fairly' was less helpful a principle except in consideration of ownership and where user-generated content or resources could be shared with the community. The most frequently considered principle was 'avoiding harm' receiving 16 of the 35 comments made whereas considera-tion amongst the group of key issues was much more evenly spread with each gaining between 6 and 8 comments. The most frequently completed cells, each by four participants were avoid harm:personal information and images, avoid harm:ownership and avoid harm:data storage and protec-tion. Examples given of these were mostly focused on ensuring anonym-ity for participants through cropping images or removing identification from log files. However, one particular example reported, of the researcher deliberately not reporting a personal life blog that identified a participant managing two lovers, brings Sharples' (2007) comment on deleting inap-propriate data found on pupils' netbooks in the 'Personal Inquiry' project to mind. Both incidents raise the question of who decides when something is inappropriate. The framework proved to be usable and useful, especially in forcing researchers to consider potential benefit of being engaged in research for the participants. Examples of this included creating location-based content for others to access and engaging in personally relevant learning activities. However, participants found it difficult at times to distinguish between key issues as images are personal data and often a key part of user generated content.

Conclusions

This chapter has reviewed a wide range of ethical considerations relevant to researching workplace-based mobile learning. There are certain key ethical issues currently arising in researching mobile learning that challenge researchers because of the mobile and personal nature of the devices used and the way they are used across contexts and locations. These are the following:

- the prevalence of personal information and images,
- the need to obtain informed consent,
- ownership of content on the mobile devices and sometimes the devices themselves,
- data storage and protection and
- the emphasis on user-generated content.

It is proposed that a return to the fundamental principles underpinning ethical behaviour may be a more helpful way forward for the mobile learning community facing challenges applying current ethical guidance than attempting to address every item in whichever code of conduct is most applicable. The framework based on fundamental principles, shown in Table 13.1, was developed to assist researchers with this and it has been shown to have potential to support both ethical mobile learning and learning about ethics.

Lastly, one ethical issue of import that has not yet been addressed in this chapter is that of accessibility. Under the Disability Discrimination Act 1995 UK employers are required to ensure that suitable user interfaces are available for all their employees. Sandars and Dearnley (2009) reported this as an ethical concern relevant to the use of mobile technologies for work-based assessment in their review of the ALPS projects. Physical disabilities, such as reduced vision or limited hand mobility, may preclude effective use of a mobile device due to the small size of the screen and keyboard. They recommend that this is explored with institutions and employers before project implementation. However, they found that dyslexic students engaged more effectively with the mobile devices than they had done with paper-based approaches.

References

Association for Computing Machinery (ACM) (1992) *Code of Ethics and Professional Conduct.* Available online at <http://www.acm.org/about/code-of-ethics> (accessed 01/09/08)

British Computer Society (BCS) (2006) *Code of Conduct.* Available online at <http://www.bcs.org/server.php?show=nav.6029> (accessed 01/09/08)

AERA (American Educational Research Association) (2000) *Ethical Standards of the American Educational Research Association.* Available online at <http://www.aera.net/AboutAERA/Default.aspx?menu_id=90&id=222> (accessed 01/09/08)

Anderson, P. & Blackwood, A. (2004) *Mobile and PDA technologies and their future use in education.* Bristol, UK: JISC. Available online at <http://www.jisc.ac.uk/whatwedo/services/techwatch/reports/horizonscanning/hs0403.aspx> (accessed 17/11/08)

Anderson, P. (2005) Mobile technologies and their use in education – New privacy implications. Paper presented at Privacy Technology and the Law, London, UK, April 2005. Available online at <http://www.jisclegal.ac.uk/events/privacy05/Presentations/Anderson_paper_privacy.doc> (accessed 17/11/08)

Beauchamp, T. & Childress, J. (1983) *Principles of biomedical ethics.* Oxford: Oxford University Press

BERA (British Educational Research Association) (2004) *Revised Ethical Guidelines for Educational Research*. Available online at <http://www.bera.ac.uk/publications/guides.php> (accessed 01/10/08)

Bynum, T. (2005) 'Norbert Wiener's vision: the impact of the "automatic age" on Our Moral Lives.' In Cavalier, R. (ed.), *The impact of the internet on Our Moral Lives* (pp. 11–25). New York: State University of New York Press. Available online at <http://web.comlab.ox.ac.uk/oucl/research/areas/ieg/e-library/bynum.pdf> (accessed 16/04/10)

Campbell, R. (2009) 'Towards a competent and confident professional workforce: An interprofessional partnership between ALPS, employer representatives and Professional, Statutory and Regulatory Bodies'. Workshop presentation. University of Leeds, 21 May 2009. Available online at <http://www.alps-cetl.ac.uk/documents/PSRBreport09_001.pdf> (accessed 05/01/10)

Chan, S. (2006) 'm-learning for work based apprentices: a report on trials undertaken to establish learning portfolios.' Paper presented at *mLearn 2006*, Banff, Canada, October 2006

Great Britain (1998) *Data Protection Act*, Chapter 29, London: The Stationery Office

Jonker, V. & Wijers. M. (2009) 'Living points of interest.' Paper presented at *Education in the Wild: Contextual and location based learning in action*. Stellar Alpine Rendez-Vous, 2–3 December 2009

Kostakos, V. (2007) *Bluetooth helps Facebook friends*. BBC News Interview, Thursday, 16 August 2007. Available online at <http://news.bbc.co.uk/1/hi/technology/6949473.stm> (accessed 16/11/08)

Mason, R. (1986) 'Four ethical issues of the information age.' In *MIS Quarterly 10*, pp. 5–12

McFarlane, A., Triggs, P. and Yee, W. (2008) *1:1 access to mobile learning devices. Researching mobile learning – Interim report to Becta*. Available online at <http://partners.becta.org.uk/upload-dir/downloads/page_documents/research/mobile_learning.pdf> (accessed 06/11/08)

Mallia, P. (2003) 'Biomedical ethics: the basic principles.' *studentBMJ 11*, pp. 131–174. Available online at <http://student.bmj.com/issues/03/05/education/142.php> (accessed 15/11/08)

National Union of Teachers (NUT) (undated) *Key aspects of law for NUT representatives*. Available online at <http://www.teachers.org.uk/test/keyaspects_law.php> (accessed 15/11/08)

Nikoi, S. & Edirisingha, P. (2008) 'Accounted learning: A WoLF-oriented approach to mobile learning.' Paper presented at mLearn 2008, Ironbridge, UK, October

Oliver, C. (2005) 'The road to mobile learning.' *Fine Print – Victorian Adult Literacy and Basic Education Council Journal 28*(3), pp. 10–14

O'Neill, E., Kostakos, V., Kindberg, T., Fatah gen. Schiek, A., Penn, A., Stanton Fraser, D., and Jones, T. (2006) *Instrumenting the city: Developing methods for observing and understanding the digital cityscape.* Paper presented at UbiComp 2006, Orange County, CA. Available online at <http://www.cs.bath.ac.uk/pervasive/publications/ubicomp06.pdf> (accessed 15/11/08)

Sandars, J. & Dearnley, C. (2009) 'Twelve tips for the use of mobile technologies for work based assessment.' *Medical Teacher 31*, pp. 18–21

Savill-Smith, C. & Douch, R. (2009) 'The use of mobile learning to break down barriers between education and Further Education.' Paper presented at the 3rd WLE Mobile Learning Symposium: Mobile learning across cultures, education, work and leisure, London, 27 March

Sharples, M. (2007) Evaluation methods for mobile learning. Paper presented at Research Methods in Mobile and Informal Learning. How to get the data we really want, WLE Centre of Excellence, Institute of Education, London, 14 Dec

Sharples, M. (2009) 'Methods for evaluating mobile learning.' In Vavoula, G., Pachler, N., and Kukulska-Hulme (eds), *Researching mobile learning: frameworks, tools and research designs.* Oxford: Peter Lang, pp. 17–39

Taylor, J., Coates, C., Eastburn, S., and Ellis, I. (2007) 'Interactive learning using mobile devices to enhance Healthcare practice education.' Paper presented at EFODL International Conference: Demonstrating Transformation: Pr@ctice, Process and Product, Belfast, Northern Ireland, May. Available online at <http://www.lmu.ac.uk/health/alps/documents/EFODL%20presentation.ppt> (accessed 17/11/08)

Traxler, J. (2005) 'Institutional issues: embedding and supporting.' In Kukulska-Hulme, A., & Traxler, J. (eds) *Mobile learning: A handbook for educators and trainers.* London: Routledge, pp. 173–187

Traxler, J. (2007) 'Change with flux.' Paper presented at *mLearn2007*, Melbourne, Australia, October

Traxler, J., & Bridges, N. (2004) 'Mobile learning – the ethical and legal challenges.' Paper presented at mLearn 2004. Mobile Learning Anytime Everywhere, Bracciano, Italy, June

Treadwell, I., (2005) 'Using portable technology for assessment of practical performance.' Paper presented at *mLearn 2005*, Cape Town, South Africa. Available online at: http://www.mlearn.org.za/CD/papers/Treadwell%20removed.pdf (accessed 17/11/08)

Vavoula, G. (2009) 'Issues and requirements for mobile learning research.' In Vavoula, G., Pachler, N., and Kukulska-Hulme (eds), *Researching mobile learning: frameworks, tools and research designs* (pp. 339–349). Oxford: Peter Lang

Wali, E. (2007) 'Are they doing what they think they're doing? Tracking and triangulating students' learning activities and self reports.' In Vavoula, G., Kukulska-Hulme, A., and Pachler, N. (eds), *Proceedings of the WLE Workshop on Research Methods in Informal and Mobile Learning: How to get the data we really want* (pp. 35–40). London: WLE Centre of Excellence, Institute of Education

West Sussex Hospitals NHS Trust (2006) *Mobile phones and communication devices.* Trust Policy and Procedure Document ref. no: PP(06)189. Available online at <http://www.wsh.nhs.uk/documents/TrustPolicies/PDFs/PP(06)189%20-%20 MobilePhonesAndCommunicationDevices-348410.pdf> (accessed 15/11/08)

Wiener, N. (1954) *The human use of human beings: cybernetics and society.* 2nd rev. edition. New York: Doubleday Anchor

Winters, N. (2006) 'What is mobile learning?' In Sharples, M. (ed.), *Big Issues in Mobile Learning: Report of a workshop by the Kaleidoscope Network of Excellence Mobile Learning Initiative* (pp. 7–11). Nottingham: LSRI, University of Nottingham. Available online at <http://www.lsri.nottingham.ac.uk/msh/Papers/ BIG_ISSUES_REPORT_PUBLISHED.pdf> (accessed 05/01/10)

Wishart, J., McFarlane, A., and Ramsden, A. (2005) 'Using personal digital assistants (PDAs) with internet access to support initial teacher training in the UK.' Paper presented at *mLearn 2005*, Cape Town, South Africa, October

Wishart, J., Ramsden, A., and McFarlane, A. (2007) 'PDAs and handhelds: ICT at your side and not in your face.' In *Technology, Pedagogy and Education 16*(1), pp. 95–110

Woodgate, D. (2008) 'Ethical issues involved in students' and young people's use of mobile devices.' Paper presented at IAS Workshop, Seven ethical issues affecting mobile learning, Bristol, UK, June

SECTION 5

Near-future scenarios for work-based mobile learning

CHRISTOPH PIMMER AND URS GRÖHBIEL

14 Mobile learning in corporate settings: Results from an expert survey[1]

Abstract

Against the background of the rising mobility of employees, technological innovations and the increasing importance of work-based learning, a central question is whether and how mobile devices can be used to support employees' learning processes in the near future. This question was addressed to fifty-six international experts in a two round survey, combining Delphi and scenario-based methods. They evaluated four mobile learning scenarios, described the scenarios they expected in the immediate future and identified benefits as well as barriers and conditions of implementation. In addition, the interviewed experts evaluated inherent tensions and proposed ways of addressing these.

The findings of the survey show that social interaction and reflection on learning processes received the most positive evaluation as did content-based scenarios with examples focusing on contextualised learning. The integration of learning at work was described as the most important area of inherent tension which has to be addressed. In the near future mobile learning in companies is anticipated mainly in the form of learning 'just-in-case', based on human-computer interactivity.

1   This chapter was presented as a paper at mLearn 2008 in Telford.

Theoretical background and research question

Definition of corporate mobile learning

Although mobile learning may blur the lines between work and learning, research requires a clear definition and demarcation of the subject addressed: corporate mobile learning takes place 'when mobile employees are supported in their learning activities with portable computational devices'. An activity is defined as learning when it leads to a deeper understanding and takes place within a didactical framework. The framework is defined by the curriculum, teachers or by the learners themselves (compare Göth et al., 2007, p. 2). Pure information retrieval which does not to lead to more in-depth knowledge or skills acquisition will not be considered as learning (Frohberg, 2008). Distinctive to mobile learning is the mobility of the learner, rather than the portability of the technology (Sharples, Vavoula and Taylor, 2005). Mobile learning 'happens when the learner is not at a fixed, predetermined location' (O'Malley et al., 2003, p. 6). Employees may learn either while they are locally mobile (wandering), moving around within an area such as a hospital or a construction site or when they are moving between different work locations (visiting, travelling), as is the case for field staff or sales representatives (compare Kristoffersen & Ljungberg, 1999, p. 31). However, the use of portable, computational devices[2] such as smartphones, PDAs, tablet PCs or notebooks for learning purposes is also a prerequisite.

Mobile learning in companies – Literature review

Mobile learning has mainly been implemented and examined in schools and institutions of Higher Education. Companies seem to be more hesitant to deploy mobile technologies for learning (Härtel et al., 2007). The existing body of literature clearly reflects this finding. 'Corporate mobile

---

2   In the following shortened to 'mobile devices'.

learning' was addressed by Pasanen (2003) in a chapter of the book 'Mobile Learning'. The author describes mobile learning as using the flexibility of mobile devices for the access to, and the production of learning material, for learning communication and for the management of learning. He stressed the importance of an integration of mobile learning into the corporate information infrastructure and the strategic importance of mobile solutions: mobile learning encourages innovation and offers new business opportunities. Moreover, Pasanen identifies further benefits from the different perspectives, for example, effective learning material collection (student's viewpoint) or improved customer service (customer's viewpoint) (Pasanen, 2003). His arguments are based on a review of the literature and his own conclusions without collecting primary data.

Non-scientific contributions from the field of commercial and industrial training indicate that companies might benefit from this barely established form of technology-enhanced learning. For example, according to a 'case study' from a bank – which distributed audio messages to employees – the feedback from the involved managers was '100% positive' (Weekes, 2008). Another large financial institution delivered compliance training courses to their employees using the Blackberry. The results included a more timely completion and a 12 per cent higher completion rate compared to the control group within a two-month testing period (Swanson, 2008).

Mobile learning has also been deployed in the ICT sector. An international telecommunications provider delivered mandatory compliance training sequences to nearly 30,000 engineers on-the-road. Another complex engineering scenario was depicted by a French research institution (David et al., 2007, p. 3): a mobile learning platform provides engineers with the opportunity to study small contextualised and personalised learning sequences while repairing manufacturing plants. The contents are displayed via WiFi and RFID technology on see-through goggles with an integrated screen. If the engineer has a problem s/he can contact an expert by chat or contextualised e-mail which automatically includes machine references. The purpose of the activity, beside the plant repair, is the internalisation of important functions and repair principles. However, the scenario has not been tested in companies so far. In a third example, a huge multinational computer technology and consulting company provided small, personalised information for a group of employees. The profile was based on Human Resource data and completed by the employees according to their qualifications, expertise and interests. If relevant content was available the learners were instantly notified via mail or SMS. Due to high technology requirements only a small percentage of the employees had the capability to download the contents on their mobile devices (von Koschembahr & Sagrott, 2005, p. 165).

In an on-the-job learning project a mobile feedback and diary application was developed for apprentices who work temporarily in companies. The students answered daily questions about events and feelings on their mobile phones. In addition, they could document their experiences and enrich their feedback with pictures, videos and sound taken with a camera phone. The evaluation with 23 students concentrated mainly on the usability of the product. The impact of using the tool has not been evaluated so far (Pirttiaho et al., 2007, p. 221). Another project illustrated how learning materials can be created and shared by learners: staff at an Intensive Care Unit video-recorded how they handled technical equipment with a video camera. The sequences were provided to colleagues who viewed them on handheld mobile computers immediately on site via RFID technology. The scientific evaluation showed that these practices augmented informal peer-to-peer learning (Brandt et al., 2005). However, in spite of widespread camera phones and mushrooming online video platforms the practice of producing and sharing videos has not entered mainstream use in businesses so far.

In conclusion, no systematic research on mobile learning in companies has been conducted as yet. There are some papers on the use of mobile learning in companies. Most of them are non-scientific, without serious evaluation, conducted by internal evaluators. Consequently, they are of little scientific significance. However, they might provide ideas of upcoming mobile learning trends.

Generally speaking, corporate training is more content-oriented than based on social interaction (Kukulska-Hulme & Traxler, 2005, p. 39). It remains to be seen whether this focus will be shifted by mobile devices, whose communication capabilities have been considered amongst the most useful features in mobile learning projects (compare for example Sharples et al., 2005).

Catalysts for mobile learning in enterprises

In 2003 – in a Delphi study on the development of mobile learning – broadband technologies and 3G portable devices were considered important and wireless internet access was described as the 'backbone of mLearning' (Dye et al., 2003, p. 49). Today mobile broadband coverage has remarkably improved and mobile technologies such as cell phones are widespread (compare for example Bakom, 2007) and multifunctional: smartphones are combining more and more capabilities – ranging from telecommunication and video capturing to personal information management (Livingston, 2004). At the same time costs for telecommunication have been decreasing (compare Eurostat, 2008). This is a key factor in the spread of mobile learning (Dye et al., 2003, p. 49). The Horizon Report seeks to identify emerging technologies likely to have a significant impact on teaching, learning, or creative expression within learning-focused organisations. It also emphasised the importance of mobile technologies: 'grassroot videos' and 'mobile broadband' are two out of six technologies that are likely to enter mainstream use (New Media Consortium and EDUCAUSE, 2008, p. 3). Both are closely related to mobile learning.

Mobile employees with poor access to stationary IT infrastructure are also considered as important drivers for mobile learning in companies: fewer and fewer jobs are performed at fixed locations, project teams are formed temporarily (Bergmann, 1999, p. 14) and, consequently, the number of mobile employees is on the rise (Lesser, 2005, p. 3). If mobile workers are supported with mobile devices, the existing technology is likely to be used for learning purposes as shown in the health sector: analysing the use of PDAs in medical and nursing professions, Luanrattana et al. (2007) reported that PDAs are widely used for work routines and increasingly for educational purposes. In a more general analysis of the potential of mobile learning in the health sector the author claimed that: 'Mobile learning is being embraced because mobile computing is being embraced in this sector' (Burger, 2006).

The corporate learning landscape is also changing: work-based and informal learning are gaining in importance (Lundin & Magnusson, 2003; Hardwig, 2006, p. 191). Recent empirical studies show that the majority of professional competences and skills are acquired through informal learning (compare for example Dehnbostel, 2006, p. 165; Livingstone & Scholtz, 2006, p. 45) such as self-directed efforts or the mentoring of more experienced co-workers. Only few employees regard formal training courses as the most important source of job-specific knowledge (Livingstone & Scholtz, 2006, p. 45).

It is claimed that skills such as problem-solving abilities and autonomy cannot be adequately taught from the outside. They have to be developed by self-direction in appropriate learning conditions (Hardwig, 2006, p. 191). Employees should not learn 'just-in-case', but in their work setting, through ongoing changes in their companies (Loroff et al., 2006, p. 7). The main route of learning is to be found by engaging in tasks (Bergmann, 1999, p. 108).

'Learning can no longer be dichotomised into a place and a time to acquire knowledge (school) and a place and a time to apply knowledge (the workplace)' (Fisher, 2000). It is therefore becoming increasingly difficult and ineffective to train employees only in a classroom setting (Hardwig, 2006, p. 7; Loroff et al., 2006, p. 9). However, classroom training should not be played off against other forms of learning. Combined they can lead to new ways of learning (Hardwig, 2006, p. 199) with the potential to improve the learning transfer from traditional classroom training into work routines (Bigalk, 2006, p. 184).

Mobile learning could also address these demands of the changing corporate learning landscape: employees can access information autonomously in informal settings without access to stationary IT-infrastructure. Mobile devices might encourage work process-oriented learning: it is theoretically possible to bring training and practice together and 'to access theory and knowledge in the context in which it is to be applied – in the work process' (Attwell, 2007, p. 3). Due to a focus on 'efficiency gains and cost savings in short timescales' (Kukulska-Hulme & Traxler, 2005, p. 39), some companies might try to enhance productivity through 'just-in-time' learning with mobile devices (compare von Koschembahr & Sagrott, 2005, p. 165). Learning sequences can be accessed exactly when needed (Kukulska-Hulme & Traxler, 2005, p. 39). Sharing images and videos to solve immediate problems might lead to improved mentoring. Mobile devices could also encourage learning processes and reflection, as was the aim of an on-the-job learning project (Pirttiaho et al., 2007, pp. 218 ff). In addition, they may aim to improve the learning transfer from face-to-face training into work routines as in the case of a project carried out by an international airline (Lison, 2004).

Guiding question

Against the background of the increasing mobility of employees, technological innovations and a changing learning landscape, the central question is whether and how mobile devices can be used to support employees' learning processes in the near future.

Research method

Due to the limited number of corporate mobile learning applications and the dearth of scientific literature on the subject the authors primarily used an explorative research strategy. The study was conducted as an expert survey consisting of two rounds. The research design combined Delphi and scenario-based methods. The Delphi method is particularly well suited to new research areas and exploratory studies (Okoli & Pawlowski, 2004, p. 15). It can be characterised as a tool for highly structured group discussions to create solutions for complex problems (Bortz & Döring, 2002, p. 261) and to obtain a reliable consensus among a group of experts. Delphi methods have not only proven to be a popular tool in the general field of research on information systems (Okoli & Pawlowski, 2004) but have also been used in the field of mobile and work-based learning or for the evaluation of evolving learning technologies (compare Dye et al., 2003, Pehkonen & Turunen, 2004, New Media Consortium and EDUCAUSE, 2008). Finally, the Delphi method does not require the experts to meet physically. This would have been impossible for such a huge number of international participants from various fields.

The experts evaluated short, manifold scenarios that might be broadly implemented in the future. Scenarios typically illustrate significant user activities and support reasoning about situations of use (Carroll, 2000, p. 42). The rough scenario descriptions comprised the target group (*Who is learning?*), the framework (*In which business context does the learning take place?*), learning methods and social forms (*How the participants learn?*) as well as technology (*Which mobile and network technologies are used?*). The scenarios should illustrate manifold applications and, therefore, do justice to the variety of mobile learning forms.

Due to the complexity and interpretative scope of the rough scenario descriptions the goal is much better achieved by qualitative data collection techniques. Quantitative methods have primarily been used to triangulate qualitative results. Through this triangulation more credible and dependable information should have been achieved (compare Decrop, 1999, p. 157).

The international group of study participants consisted of 56 experts in the first round: academics in the disciplines of pedagogy, psychology and information technology and managers in charge of in-company training and mobile and e-learning vendors. 39 of them participated in the second round.[3] As differences between university education and corporate training should not be overstated (Kukulska-Hulme & Traxler, 2005, p. 39) experiences in the field of mobile learning can be extrapolated – with care – to business contexts. Therefore, the involvement of academic scientists with experience in mobile learning was considered to be very important. A majority of the interviewed persons were from German and English speaking regions. The research design and results of the surveys were discussed in a sounding board, consisting of experienced scientists and managers in charge of in-company training. Pre-tests served to validate the instruments of data collection.

---

3   Participants/professional background:

	Academics	Managers	Vendors	Not stated	Total
1st round	28	23	5	-	56
2nd round	17	17	3	2	39

In the first round the participants evaluated the potential benefits of four mobile learning scenarios. They carried out quantitative evaluations of potential benefits on a five point Likert scale (ranging from very high benefit to no benefit at all). They were asked to give reasons for their choices. They also described potential future forms of mobile learning in companies and their benefits as well as barriers and conditions. In the second round they were asked to re-evaluate the potential of the four scenarios, taking into consideration contradictory arguments from the first round. In addition, the importance of the mastery of various inherent tensions was evaluated on a four point Likert scale (ranging from very high relevance to no relevance) and approaches to solutions to these tensions were identified.

Limitations

The generalisation of the results corresponding to individual scenarios has to be made with caution, due to the interpretative scope of the given examples. However, the goal of this research was a rich discussion of manifold scenarios and influencing factors in order indicate the direction of mobile learning in companies.

Results

Evaluation results of the four scenarios

Qualitative results

1) The first scenario describes a sales representative who learns with personalised learning objects on his mobile device in quiet moments. The study participants positively highlighted[4] the flexibility in terms of

---

4   All the arguments of this chapter were named at least seven times in the two rounds.

time and space and the personalised, self-directed approach. At the same time they questioned the use of quiet moments for learning purposes. These moments would be frequently used to fulfil working tasks, to relax or to reflect. Critical to success is the learning atmosphere which should be free of distractions and noise.

2) In a further example – where engineers access learning materials on display goggles during repair activities – the situational and problem-based approach was seen as positive. Criticism referred mainly to the difficulty in implementing this scenario caused by the automatic contextualisation of learning materials. An increased error probability through learning while working will also affect the scenario negatively. Lack of time for reflection at work should be compensated by additional phases of reflection after finishing the repair process. This may lead to better internalisation of acquired competences.

3) When nurses document how they handle important work tasks in short video clips, learning and reflection processes are already taking place during the production phase. These videos can be accessed context-sensitively on site by other colleagues on their PDAs. The interviewees criticised that nurses rarely have quiet moments to produce and consume the videos. The experts also questioned whether the nurses had the necessary didactic and technical skills to produce learning materials of high enough quality.

4) In the fourth scenario apprentices in companies answer daily questions from their classroom teacher to reflect on their learning progress and document their learning experiences in an electronic learning diary. They are said to have a particular affinity to mobile phones. The interviewees commented on the consistency of the learning processes through daily incentives. This should positively stimulate motivation and acceptance. Learning transfer between school and work-based learning was considered to be beneficial. The huge effort required by teachers and the high level of self-discipline of apprentices may affect the scenario adversely. In order to realise the scenario successfully many participants recommend the pedagogical use of the feedback in the next classroom training session.

Quantitative results

The scenarios were evaluated similarly and deemed to have *some benefit* or *high benefit* (with arithmetical means between 3.2 and 3.8 on a five point Likert scale).[5] The discussion, however, was controversial: while the scenarios based on human-computer interactivity (*engineer* and *sales representative*) were judged to more similarly across respondents in the second round,[6] the variation in the scenarios with social interaction (*nurse and apprentice*) remained equally high.[7]

For three of the scenarios changes from the first to the second round were not significant. Only the *apprentice scenario* was evaluated significantly higher in the second round:[8] as shown in the matrix in Table 14.1, 13 respondents increased their rating, whereas only nine experts reduced their rating. Overall, this scenario was rated highest in the second round. However, there was some disagreement in the evaluation of the scenario, as shown in Table 14.1. The boxes marked in grey highlight the changes in opinion that contributed to a relatively high standard deviation.

2nd round ⟍ 1st round	☺☺	☺	😐	☹	☹☹
☺☺	1	2	1		
☺	1	9	3		
😐	1	8	2	2	1
☹		1	1	1	
☹☹	1				

Table 14.1 Evaluation of potential benefits between the first and second round

5   Numerical values: 1= No benefit at all, 2= Little benefit, 3= Some benefit, 4= High benefit 5= Very high benefit
6   Standard deviaton of 0.6
7   Standard deviaton of 0.9
8   T-Test, n=35, arithmetical means in 1st /2nd rnd: 3.46/3.66 standard deviation: 1/2 rnd:.919/.906, statistical significance at test with paired samples: .324, numerical values: 1=No benefit at all, 2= Little benefit, 3= Some benefit, 4= High benefit 5= Very high benefit

Considering the means of both rounds, the potential benefit of the scenario *engineer* was – in comparison to the other scenarios – rated highest.[9]
However, also the requirements for realising this scenario were – with little
deviation – rated highest compared to the other scenarios.[10] This reflects
the qualitative evaluation results.

A framework for classifying mobile learning scenarios

The question describing future scenarios – considering target group(s),
learning framework and methods, social forms and technology – has led
to a comprehensive range of more than 30 examples in various thematic
and working contexts. These are classified in the framework below according to their value to work process and their media function (compare also
Gröhbiel & Pimmer, 2008; see Figure 14.1).

	Learning based on Human-computer interactivity	Social interaction
Immediate value to work process: 'just-in-time'	Individual 'just-in-time' learning	Interpersonal 'just-in-time' learning
Potential value to work process: 'just-in-case'	Individual 'just-in-case' learning	Interpersonal 'just-in-case' learning

(left label spanning the two data rows: **Learning has**)

Figure 14.1 A framework for classifying corporate mobile learning scenarios

The framework helps to make the distinction between different degrees of
integration of learning in the work process on the one hand and between
human-computer interactivity and social interaction on the other hand:

---

9   arithmetical means in 1st /2nd rnd: 3.84/3.59
10 Numerical values: 1= Very low, 2= Low, 3= Medium, 4= High 5= Very high.
    Arithmetical mean of scenario engineer: 4.47; The other scenarios were all evalu-
    ated similarly as having between medium and high requirements (3.2–3.5).

Vertical axis

Just-in-time learning has an immediate value to the work process. It comprehends the acquisition of knowledge and skills on-the-job due to immediacy and relevance (Harris et al., 2001, p. 276). Just-in-time learning is job-embedded and, therefore, might consist of learning by doing, reflecting on the experience and generating and sharing new insights and learning with others (compare Wood & McQuarrie, 1999).

Just-in-case learning has a potential value to work process. It is learning for potential future application (compare Harris et al., 2001, p. 276). The emphasis is on knowledge and skills that might be useful later. It is hardly possible to predict whether and when it will be needed (Kirsh, 2000, p. 30).

Horizontal axis

Individual learning is primarily based on Human-Computer Interactivity. It describes the possible courses of action of the individual learner with a learning object (Schulmeister, 2004, p. 12). Feedback is given implicitly or explicitly by the learning object or by the (electronic) learning environment (Schulmeister, 2004, p. 15) depending on the learner's previous actions.

Interpersonal learning refers to the social interactions between humans. It comprises collaborative learning, tutoring, teaching or coaching mediated by portable computational devices; consequently, feedback is provided primarily by peers, mentors, teachers etc.

Both the degree of interactivity and the social interaction are considered by many authors as very important for the success of virtual learning (Schulmeister, 2004, p. 12). The following figure illustrates the classification of beneficial scenarios expected by the experts in the next 2–5 years. The size of the boxes represents the approximate number of scenarios (see Figure 14.2).

348 CHRISTOPH PIMMER AND URS GRÖHBIEL

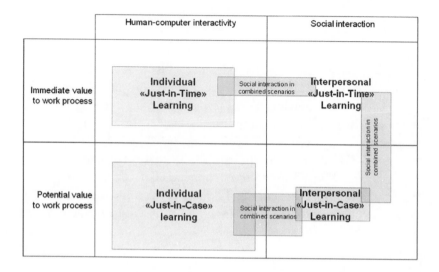

Figure 14.2 Expected mobile learning scenarios in companies in the near future

1) Scenarios situated solely in the area of just-in-case learning were described considerably more often than scenarios based on learning while working: it was primarily examples based on human-computer interactivity that were depicted in this field. This currently prevailing form of mobile learning (compare Frohberg, 2006) is also expected to predominate the corporate landscape in the near future: examples were described where employees such as investment brokers or bank employees learn in advance and apply their knowledge in later phases: they are texted as soon as new materials are available, work on small learning items and then check their knowledge with quizzes.

2) In the area of just-in-time learning, most of the examples were described in the field of human-computer interactivity. Scenarios based on social interaction were cited only in combination with scenarios from other quadrants as illustrated by the following example: if mechanics, medics or builders, who are working on a certain task for the first time, face a problem they can't solve on their own, they can contact an expert with their mobile devices. Details of the objects are captured with the

integrated camera. The expert explains the procedure while annotating the image. The indications are synchronously visible on the screen of the learner's device. If the session is recorded and available to other learners in similar situations, the scenario is expanded to the field of human-computer interactivity.

Beyond the documentation of coaching processes – as described in the example above – the production and sharing of further learning sequences such as incidents, unusual situations or the usage of products by customers, were described several times.

Dealing with inherent tensions

When analysing answers related to benefits several areas of tension were identified. A majority of the respondents attributed high or very high relevance to the mastery of the following four inherent tensions:

1) It is clear that the integration of learning at work is beneficial; at the same time learning and work processes may interfere with each other.
2) Although technical affinity to mobile devices is high for some (groups of) employees, prerequisites for learning such as motivation and self-discipline are sometimes insufficient.
3) Continuous innovation of mobile technologies will lead to noteworthy improvements. However, in the immediate future the technical requirements for the successful implementation of some mobile learning scenarios will not be met.
4) While the production of learning materials by employees creates additional benefits, privacy issues and poor technical or didactical skills of employees may limit this potential considerably.

In order to overcome these inherent tensions the experts made the following suggestions:

To foster the integration of learning processes at work, employees should have time that is explicitly designated for learning. The time used for learning should of course not be paid for directly by the customer. Mobile technologies should only be deployed if they provide an advantage over other technologies. If possible, employees should learn with devices they are already using for work. Quiet moments, if these exist at all, are rarely appropriate for learning.

Certain prerequisites are critical success factors for mobile learning. The persons interviewed proposed enhancing the learners' motivation by means of concrete incentives (for example, the implementation of ePortfolios) or by making mobile learning a requirement. The advantages of the application should be clearly demonstrated to the learner. Approaches related to the peer-to-peer production of learning material require training courses and quality control conducted by teachers. Learners should be able to delete their contents any time.

Conclusions and further discussion

The findings of the expert survey indicate that the following development options deserve closer attention:

1) Just-in-case learning based on human-computer interactivity was described by most of the experts as the prevailing form in the immediate future. While having moderate benefits, the implementation of this kind of scenario seems to be relatively easy. The use of 'quiet moments' for learning does not seem to be appropriate. The personalisation of learning contents and the learning atmosphere were considered as very important to success.

2) The contextualisation of learning and the integration in work processes is very promising. Nearly all experts pointed out the high relevance of this area, which is at the same time challenging: technical and organisational challenges have to be tackled and learners should be given additional time for reflection.

3) Beyond human-computer based learning forms, scenarios focusing on social interaction also provide high potential benefits. Mobile devices can support coordination, coaching and collaboration. Trainers can send messages to coordinate learners' activities and to encourage learning and reflection processes. This can enhance the continuity of the learning process and increase the motivation of the learner as indicated in the apprentice scenario. With low requirements and predominantly positive feedback it is worthwhile to consider how this scenario can be applied to other fields. Integrated telecommunication and collaboration features can make synchronous annotation of pictures possible. This is a capability which could ideally be used for coaching. In this way problems can be discussed and reflected on among learners and tutors.

4) Reservations were expressed in the evaluation of the production and sharing of learning materials. There are demands on learners in terms of the mastery of technical and didactic skills in order to produce learning materials of high enough quality. The learning and reflection processes taking place during the production were very positively highlighted. Particularly in the context of the increasingly popular Web 2.0 applications these kinds of scenarios should be kept in mind.

References

Attwell, G. (2007) 'Personal learning environments – the future of e-learning?' *E-learning papers 2. Quality in e-learning*, p. 5. Available online at <http://www.elearningpapers.eu/index.php?page=volume_pdf_download&vol=2> (accessed 19/04/10)

Bakom (2007) *Fernmeldestatistik. Entwicklung bis zum 31.12.2006 für bestimmte Indikatoren.* Biel. Available online at <http://www.bakom.admin.ch/dokumentation/zahlen/00744/00746/index.html> (accessed 19/04/10)

Bergmann, B. (1999) *Training für den Arbeitsprozess. Entwicklung aufgaben und zielgruppenspezifischer Trainingsprogramme.* Zürich: Hochschulverlag AG an der ETH Zürich

Bigalk, D. (2006) Lernförderliche Arbeitsplätze: Verständnis und Anforderungen. In Loroff, C., Manski, K., Mattauch, W., & Schmidt, M. (eds), *Arbeitsprozessorientierte Weiterbildung. Lernprozesse gestalten, Kompetenzen entwickeln* (pp. 176–187). Bielefeld: W. Bertelsmann Verlag

Bortz, J., & Döring, N. (2002) *Forschungsmethoden und Evaluation.* Berlin: Springer

Brandt, E., Hillgren, P.-A., & Björgvinsson, E. (2005) 'Self-produced video to augment peer-to-peer learning'. In Attwell, J. & Savill-Smith, C. (eds), *Learning with mobile devices* (pp. 17–34). London

Burger, J. (2006) 'The US Healthcare Market for Mobile Learning Products and Services: 2006–2011 Forecast and Analysis. Who is the Real Customer in this Expanding Market.' Ambient Insight's. Available online at <http://www.ambientinsight.com/Reports/ReportsMain.aspx> (accessed 19/04/10)

Carroll, J. (2000) 'Five reasons for scenario-based design'. *Interacting with Computers* 13, pp. 43–60

David, B., Yin, C., & Chalon, R. (2007) 'Contextual mobile learning for appliance mastery.' In Sánchez, I.-A. (ed.), *IADIS International Mobile Learning Conference 2007* (pp. 218–221). Lisbon

Decrop, A. (1999) 'Triangulation in qualitative tourism research.' *Tourism Management* 20, pp. 157–161

Dehnbostel, P. (2006) 'Das IT-Konzept "Arbeitsprozessorientierte Weiterbildung" – Basis für einen zeitgemässe berufliche betriebliche Weiterbildung?' In Loroff, C., Manski, K., Mattauch, W., & Schmidt, M. (eds), *Arbeitsprozessorientierte Weiterbildung. Lernprozesse gestalten, Kompetenzen entwickeln* (pp. 160–175). Bielefeld: W. Bertelsmann Verlag

Dye, A., Solstad, B.-E. & K'Odingo, J. (2003) *Mobile Education – A Glance at The Future. NITH* Norges Informasjonsteknologiske Høgskole. Available online at <http://www.nettskolen.com/forskning/mobile_education.pdf> (accessed 15/04/10)

Eurostat (2008) 'Science and technology'. *Europe in figures – Eurostat Yearbook,* pp. 493–498

Fisher, G. (2000) 'Lifelong learning – more than training.' *Journal of Interactive Learning Research* 11, pp. 265–294

Frohberg, D. (2006) 'Mobile learning is coming of age: what we have and what we still miss.' *DELFI: 4. e-Learning Fachtagung Informatik der Gesellschaft für Informatik*

Frohberg, D. (2008) *Mobile learning.* Dissertation. Institut für Informatik, Universität Zürich

Göth, C., Frohberg, D., & Schwabe, G. (2007) 'Von passivem zu aktivem mobilen Lernen.' *Zeitschrift für E-Learning 4*, pp. 12–28

Gröhbiel, U. & Pimmer, C. (2008) 'Mobiles Lernen: Personalentwicklung jenseits der Schulbank.' *Personal*, pp. 18–20

Hardwig, T. (2006) 'Worauf kommt es bei der betrieblichen Gestaltung lernförderlicher Rahmenbedingungen eigentlich an?' In Loroff, C., Manski, K., Mattauch, W., & Schmidt, M. (eds), *Arbeitsprozessorientierte Weiterbildung. Lernprozesse gestalten, Kompetenzen entwickeln.* Bielefeld, W. Bertelsmann Verlag, pp. 188–202

Harris, R., Willis, P., Simons, M., & Collins, E. (2001) 'The relative contributions of institutional and workplace learning environments: an analysis of apprenticeship training.' *Journal of Vocational Education & Training 53*, pp. 263–278

Härtel, M., Gerwin, W., & Kupfer, F. (2007) *Der Beitrag arbeitsplatznaher elektronischer Informations- und Lernsysteme für berufliche Qualifizierungsprozesse.* Abschlussbericht zum Forschungsprojekt. Available online at <http://www2.bibb.de/tools/fodb/pdf/at_34109.pdf> (accessed 19/04/10)

Kirsh, D. (2000) 'A few thoughts on cognitive overload.' *Intellectica 1*, pp. 19–51

Kristoffersen, S. & Ljungberg, F. (1999) 'Mobile informatics: innovation of IT use in mobile settings.' *ACM SIGCHI Bulletin IRIS'21*, pp. 29–34

Kukulska-Hulme, A. Traxler, J. (2005) Mobile teaching and learning. In Kukulska-Hulme, A. Traxler, J. (eds) *Mobile learning: a handbook for educators and trainers.* London, Routledge, pp. 25–44

Lesser, E. (2005) *The mobile working experience: a European perspective.* Somers, IBM. See http://www.ibm.com/bcs

Lison (2004) 'Konnten Sie die Aufgabe lösen?' *Lufthanseat Mitarbeiterzeitschrift der Lufthansa* 1038

Livingston, A. (2004) 'Smartphones and other mobile devices: the Swiss army knives of the 21st century.' *EDUCAUSE Quarterly*, pp. 46–57

Livingstone, D. & Scholtz, A. (2006) 'Work and lifelong learning in Canada: basic findings of the 2004 WALL Survey.' Wallnetwork. Available online at: http://wallnetwork.ca/resources/SurveyPage.htm (accessed 19/04/10)

Loroff, C., Manski, K., Mattauch, W. and Schmidt, M. (2006) 'Einleitung.' In Loroff, C., Manski, K., Mattauch, W. and Schmidt, M. (eds) *Arbeitsprozessorientierte Weiterbildung. Lernprozesse gestalten, Kompetenzen entwickeln.* Bielefeld, W. Bertelsmann Verlag

Luanrattana, R., Win, K. and Fulcher, J. (2007) 'Use of Personal Digital Assistants (PDAs) in Medical Education.' *Twentieth IEEE International Symposium on Computer-Based Medical Systems (CBMS>07)*, pp. 307–312

Lundin, J. & Magnusson, M. (2003) Collaborative learning in mobile work. *Journal of Computer Assisted Learning* 19, pp. 273–283

New Media Consortium & EDUCAUSE (2008) *THE HORIZON REPORT 2008.* New Media Consortium EDUCAUSE Learning Initiative. Available online at: http://www.nmc.org/pdf/2008-Horizon-Report.pdf (accessed 19/04/10)

O'Malley, C., Vavoula, G., Glew, J., Taylor, J., Sharples, M. and Lefrere, P. (2003) *MOBIlearn WP4 – Guidelines for Learning/Teaching/Tutoring in a Mobile Environment.* Available online at: http://www.mobilearn.org/download/results/guidelines.pdf (accessed 19/04/10)

Okoli, C. & Pawlowski, S. (2004) 'The Delphi method as a research tool: an example, design considerations and applications.' *Information & Management* 42, pp. 15–29

Pasanen, J. (2003) 'Corporate mobile learning.' In Kynaslahti, H. & Seppala, P. (eds) *Professional mobile learning.* Helsinki, IT Press, pp. 115–123

Pehkonen, M. & Turunen, H. (eds) (2004) *A case study on future views of mobile work and work-based learning.* Hämeenlinna, pp. 177–198

Pirttiaho, P., Holm, J.-M., Paalanen, H. and Thorström, T. (2007) ETAITAVA – mobile tool for on-the-job learning. In Sánchez, I.-A. (ed.) *IADIS International Mobile Learning Conference 2007.* Lisbon, pp. 218–222

Schulmeister, R. (2004) *Didaktisches Design aus hochschuldidaktischer Sicht. Ein Plädoyer für offene Lernsituationen.* Available online at: http://www.zhw.uni-hamburg.de/pdfs/Didaktisches_Design.pdf (accessed 19/04/10)

Sharples, M., Corlett, D., Bull, S., Chan, T. and Rudman, P. (2005) 'The student learning organiser.' In Kukulska-Hulme, A. Traxler, J. (eds) *Mobile learning: a handbook for educators and trainers.* London, Routledge, pp. 25–45

Sharples, M., Taylor, J. and Vavoula, G. (2005) 'Towards a theory of mobile learning.' *mLearn 2005: 4th World conference on mLearning.* Banff, Alberta, Canada

Swanson, K. (2008) Merrill Lynch: Bullish on Mobile Learning (Case Study). Available online at: http://www.clomedia.com/includes/printcontent.php?aid=2135 (accessed on 18/04/10)

von Koschembahr, C. & Sagrott, S. (2005) 'The future of learning at IBM: empowering employees through mobile learning.' In Kukulska-Hulme, A. Traxler, J. (eds) *Mobile learning: a handbook for educators and trainers.* London, Routledge, pp. 165–172

Weekes, S. (2008) 'Mobile learning – is anyone using it?' Available online at: http://www.personneltoday.com/articles/2007/06/19/41273/mobile-learning-is-anyone-using-it.html (accessed 19/04/10)

Wood, F. & McQuarrie, F. (1999) 'On-the-job learning.' *Journal of Staff Development* 20, pp. 10–13

JOCELYN WISHART AND DAVID GREEN

15 Future scenarios for workplace-based mobile learning[1]

Abstract

This chapter details the work-based scenarios developed in a series of discussion workshops exploring visions of how mobile technologies will influence the practice of users in Higher Education (HE) and Further Education (FE) in the five years between 2009 and 2014. Three different tools to support futures thinking were used by volunteers from the international research network 'Adding a Mobile Dimension to Teaching & Learning' to develop future scenarios. These scenarios were then sent to other members of the network who reported on the likelihood of each of the different scenarios arising and made suggestions as to enablers and barriers or challenges to their occurrence. Of the twelve future scenarios produced from the three workshops, six were clearly very much centred on workplace mobile learning opportunities. Common to the six visions were an increasing use of just-in-time and as-and-when-necessary training, an increased amount of peer-to-peer networking and collaboration and an approach to teaching and learning that is more collaborative than didactic. Concerns were reported over the need for always-on affordable connectivity and power, the need to manage a wide range of learners' mobile devices and the merging of

1   The authors wish to gratefully acknowledge the contributions made by members of the *Adding a Mobile Dimension to Teaching & Learning* network who played a major part both in the scenario development activities at the workshops on which this paper is based and to the review of the scenarios generated. We are also grateful for the financial support from JISC via the Emerge community for this project.

personal and vocational information and practice. It was pointed out that there will be a need for design specifications for a secure online all-purpose data repository accessible by different browsers according to the device in the learners' hand. It was also concluded that there is an urgent need for students, employers and academic staff to develop agreed practices to establish how mobile devices are to be used responsibly in the workplace.

Introduction

The workshop series reported here was funded by the UK's Joint Information Systems Committee (JISC) as part of the *Emerge Community* activities within its *Users and Innovation* research programme. JISC itself is funded by the UK HE and FE funding bodies to provide leadership in the innovative use of ICT to support education and research. Workplace-based learning (WBL) forms a significant part of many taught programmes, especially vocational ones, in both HE and FE. The scenario-based exploration reported here focused on identifying emerging issues for work- and placement-based learning in these sectors arising from the increasingly likely large-scale use of smartphones and mobile phones. These devices have become well established throughout the HE student community, a survey of 177 students at the University of Southampton found that 94 per cent were regular users and owners of mobile phones (Davidson & Lutman 2007). This dovetails with data from Ofcom (2008) which shows that mobile phone ownership in the 15–24 age group of the UK population is stabilising at around 95 per cent and students to come will be even more experienced in their use. For example, older students in schools that ostensibly ban mobile phones are now regularly being allowed to use the cameras on their phones to record special events or experiments in science lessons to help them revise.

The field of mobile learning itself has been developing fast as a research topic over the past eight years and accordingly ideas of what exactly mobile learning is have also developed. Winters (2006) noted how various groups researching mobile learning have used definitions that fall into four categories:

1) mobile learning as technocentric, where learning is seen as something that makes use of mobile devices, personal digital assistants (PDAs) and mobile phones;
2) defined by its relationship to e-learning, where mobile learning is seen as an extension of e-learning;
3) as augmenting formal education; and
4) as learner centred, enabling the possibility of lifelong learning.

These do not address the unique selling point of mobile learning which is closely linked to the capability of the mobile learner moving between traditionally separate contexts such as the workplace and any associated teaching base supported by handheld technology that they can work with interactively to capture, access and store quantities of information in different multimedia formats. Thus mobile learning can be best described as 'the processes (both personal and public) of coming to know through exploration and conversation across multiple contexts amongst people and interactive technologies' (Sharples, Arnedillo Sanchez, Milrad and Vavoula, 2007).

Piloting mobile learning in the workplace

Both HE and FE institutions place students training for professions such as medicine, building, teaching or hairdressing in the workplace for a significant proportion of their course. These students, often at considerable distance from their teaching bases, need online access to course materials and other context-specific information, to communicate with their tutors and to produce records of their progress and assignments for assessment.

Mentors in the workplace need to authenticate and support this student learning. A number of pilots have been set up to test how mobile technologies can successfully be used to support students on work placements.

For instance, mobile devices have been used to give instant hands-on access to information that would be difficult to carry around on the job. At the James Cook University Hospital in Middlesborough, 5th year medical students tested the use of PDAs providing access to formulae, clinical guidelines, electronic portfolios and other web-based materials. They found portable access to these facilities useful, as was the ability for supervisors to 'sign-off' log books using their normal signatures on the PDA (Cotterill et al., 2008).

Reynolds et al. (2007) found that a PDA proved to be a convenient and versatile mode of access to online education for dentistry students at King's College, London. The 12 students were most positive about being able to make notes for individual study, to keep a diary of their commitments to teaching sessions and to having on the spot access to online support materials, particularly videos.

Teaching is another profession where students need access to a wealth of information. Wishart et al. (2007) found that when student teachers trialled the use of PDAs in school they deemed the calendar or diary to be particularly supportive. E-mail was also used, primarily to maintain contact with other students and the university tutor and the web-browser was used to access information both in class and for personal reasons. Some students used spreadsheets to record pupils' attendance and grades and most, in this pilot involving fourteen trainees, used the word-processor to make notes from meetings and on lesson observations for essays. However, the prevailing socio-cultural climate where mobile phones are often banned and PDA's a rarity meant that trainees often felt uncomfortable using their device on school premises.

In FE mobile technology has been used in the workplace for just-in-time problem-solving such as through the Hairdressing Training programme developed by the University of Manchester's data centre Mimas and now used by 500 students at Stockport College, which offers step-by step guides that run on phones to hairdressing techniques for styling, colouring and cutting (Smith, 2008). Also PDAs have been found to be useful in connecting work-based learners who may otherwise be isolated from learning opportunities. Such devices have been used to assist apprentices in remote rural locations in Lincolnshire to give flexible learning options and to build achievement and self-esteem (Lambourne, 2008) and to provide learning and social networking opportunities to care workers in schools and nursing establishments in the Bourneville area of Birmingham (Brown, 2008). Other projects, such as *My Podcast* at New College, Swindon, involve podcasting with lecturers creating both audio and video podcasts that students can download and play on handheld PDAs or MP3 players for revision or extra support with a topic wherever they happen to be, in the workplace, at home or in college or moving between the two (Warren, 2008).

Finally, one of the largest trials of mobile technology in the workplace, with around 1000 students in five universities in Yorkshire, is that run by the Assessment of Learning in Practice Settings (ALPS) Centre for Excellence in Teaching and Learning (<http://www.alps-cetl.ac.uk/>). This pilot involving nursing and allied health care practitioner trainees focuses on assessment and learning in practice settings. Initial indications (Dearnley et al., 2008) showed that both students and lecturers were positive about a range of benefits of having a PDA however, introducing mobile technology into the clinical setting will require a significant shift in culture and a significant level of training and support.

Looking to the future

While the above-mentioned projects demonstrate the range of learning activities that have been trialled in UK institutions, recent advances in the abilities of the mobile devices themselves offer the chance to deliver new services to learners. The 2009 Horizon Report notes how the adoption of novel interfaces (like the iPhone), the ability of mobile devices to download applications and to be location aware through GPS signals all offer new opportunities for learning. With the addition of broadband-like data connections, the boundary between what is a mobile phone and a portable computer are being ever more blurred (New Media Consortium, 2009). It is in this technology context that the workshop participants came together to imagine future scenarios for the use of mobile technology in learning, drawing on their wide experiences of previous research projects and contemplating how developing mobile technologies could open up new opportunities for connecting learners and teachers.

Methods for developing future scenarios

In the workshop series being reported three different tools were used by members of the international research network *Adding a Mobile Dimension to Teaching & Learning* to develop futures predictions. The *Adding a Mobile Dimension to Teaching & Learning* research network focuses on handheld technologies such as PDAs, smartphones, mobile phones, play stations and MP3 Players and how they can support teaching and learning. Its members include internationally respected researchers and practitioners in mobile learning. The network has run interdisciplinary workshops funded by the Institute of Advanced Studies at the University of Bristol since April 2006. The network itself has grown to over 100 individuals and hosts two to three discussion workshops per year.

The first scenario development tool, used for the workshop focusing on the future practice of users in Higher Education (HE) five years from today (in 2009), was the *Cognitive Foresight* toolkit available from the UK Government Department for Innovation, Universities and Skills (Office of Science and Technology, 2005). It was developed for strategic futures planning and provides guidance on different techniques that can be used in the different stages of developing future scenarios and the ways they can be combined. This first workshop employed driver analysis to build internally consistent future scenarios from an assessment of the way current trends and drivers are influencing the present use of mobile technologies in HE. First the workshop participants 'brainstorm' a range of drivers for the currently observable trends. Next scenarios are produced by taking the drivers identified as having the highest importance and highest impact as orthogonal pairs of axes and visualising up to four scenarios that match the chosen combinations. This method is illustrated in Figure 15.1.

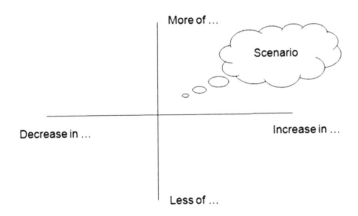

Figure 15.1 Using trends or drivers to generate future scenarios

The second employed the *Futures Technology* workshop method (Vavoula & Sharples, 2007) to look at future scenarios in work-based learning. This is a structured method whereby people, in this case with experience in the specific area of the use of mobile technologies in education, envision and design the interactions between current and future technologies and an activity. Through a series of structured workshop sessions they collaborate to envisage future activities related to technology design, build models of the contexts of use for future technologies, act out scenarios of use for their models, re-conceive their scenarios in relation to present-day technologies, list problems with implementing the scenarios exploring the gap between current and future technology and activity. The workshop method was edited slightly within the time constraints of the day so that the structured sessions comprised:

1) imagineering: brainstorm on desired future learning activities;
2) modelling: in groups, producing models that demonstrate the envisioned activities, complete with related props;
3) retrofit: developing a role-play for another group's scenario using only current technologies;
4) futurefit requirements: listing requirements for the future technologies that have to be in place for the scenario to be realised.

The third discussion workshop on future scenarios in Further Education (FE) followed a method devised by Futurelab (<http://www.futurelab.org.uk>), an educational thinktank aimed at transforming the way people learn that focuses on the potential offered by digital and other technologies. This method for developing scenarios uses non-specific images of people of different ages in different locations printed on cards as a stimulus to thinking. The workshop used cards such as these shown in Figure 15.2 from the *Building Visions for Learning Spaces* sequence of cards.

The workshop participants are asked to envision first a range of learning activities that could be happening within the image and the people involved in them, then the anticipated outcomes and the technological resources that will be needed. One of these activities is then chosen by each of the groups for fuller development into a future scenario.

In each of the above three cases the workshop was set up to start with two initial keynote presentations from recognised experts designed to stimulate thought and discussion. These were followed by a series of discussion activities informed by the futures prediction method being used and facilitated by the research team. A discussion workshop is a recognised method of collaborative knowledge construction through discussion and debate amongst peers or experts. The workshops were run as focus groups taking a phenomenological approach to research with the facilitator encouraging discussion and debate aiming to create an environment where participants felt able to contribute freely.

Each workshop group was audio-recorded with the participants' permission and the transcriptions used to generate scenarios. Participation was voluntary and participants were fully informed as to the purposes of the workshop.

© Futurelab

Figure 15.2 Futurelab's Building Visions for Learning Spaces cards

Finally, the developed scenarios were written up by the project team and sent out to the rest of the *Adding a Mobile Dimension to Teaching & Learning* network for feedback as to the likelihood of each of the different scenarios arising and for suggestions as to enablers and barriers or challenges to its occurrence.

Results: The scenarios created

Three workshops aimed at identifying emerging issues in mobile learning through future scenario development took place, the first was attended by 15 participants, the second was attended by 14 participants and the third was attended by 15 participants. Participants' experiences in mobile learning ranged from PhD students (2–3) studying aspects of deploying mobile technologies in teaching and learning, through learning technology support officers (3–4) and staff developers (1–2) dealing with the changing context of e-learning in HE and FE to a range of academics from lecturers to professors (5–6) teaching about and/or researching mobile technologies in education. Also at each workshop were one or two individuals with specific expertise such as using images in teaching in health care professions at the workshop on future scenarios in HE, using mobile telecommunications in industry at the workshop on work based learning (WBL) and using mobile devices in FE colleges at the workshop on work based learning (WBL).

Of the twelve future scenarios produced from the three workshops, six were clearly very much centred on workplace learning opportunities. These were:

FE 1: Working and learning together on placement in Business Studies

College students on placement for Business Studies are generally set a variety of tasks to be investigated and carried out in their workplace. An example might be 'describe the recruitment and retention process in an organisation'. This programme, in one college, described by the current students as 'boring' and resulting in lots of written work, will be radically revised though students' use of mobile devices, always-on connectivity and multimedia. Mobile devices (handhelds or micro-laptops) will enable students to contact distant peers and college tutors through audio, video, texting and email. This could include multi-way 'question time' video conferencing. Giving or ensuring students have devices with global positioning systems (GPS) would not only allow the teacher to know where all of the students are located but also to let the students know where each other were. By sharing their work, students would know where the gaps were in their knowledge/skills and could identify someone, a peer or a tutor, to fill those needs. GPS would then enable them to find out who was geographically nearest to the person identified and direct him/her to their location. Students could also share their work while 'out in the field' so as to learn how each other is tackling the same problems. They would not have to wait until they get back to their teaching base before comparing notes. Though, once back at the teaching base, the students would be able to store the assets they have created during their time on placement such as video, audio, text inputs and other research notes for assessment and/or sharing with their or future cohorts of students.

Outcomes for this collaborative learning scenario enabled through mobile devices will include not only meeting course assessment requirements but also the development of inter-personal skills such as collaboration skills, learning how to reconcile different information from different sources and communication with people of different ages, social groups and skill sets.

This scenario was thought by others in the network to be likely to come into play before 2015 as the technology is already in place and has considerable potential to make a usually 'boring' topic much more interesting for learners. However, there are a number of barriers that would need to be surmounted first such as the training and commitment needed from the college IT support staff for supporting students placed in different locations. There may also be interoperability issues depending on whether the college has decided to provide one standard device or to rely on students' personal devices. Lastly one major question arises with this scenario about the ethical issues of (a) using GPS to 'track' people such as the students in this scenario (b) recording possibly privileged information about the workplace's business strategies. While students may not object to their friends knowing where they are through GPS, they may not want tutors to know their location. Whilst employers are happy to train Business Studies students within their organisation they may not want multimedia records leaving the premises. For this scenario to be realised it appears clear that there needs to be agreement in advance between employer and college about all possible processes involved in students' collection and sharing of data for assignments.

FE 2: Recording experiential learning in Leisure and Tourism

A leisure and tourism student moves between several different fashionable venues on a work placement day release scheme. She has been asked to create a portfolio to link conceptual ideas from the course syllabus with her experiential learning in leisure and tourism. The actual technology used would all be web-based. This would mean that excuses such as 'I forgot my laptop' will be obsolete as everything would be based on an online e-portfolio system including VLE / blog / wiki style tools, i.e. with inbuilt, well-integrated social networking tools. This online e-portfolio system can be updated by handheld camera phones and netbooks as well as by laptop and desktop computers and assumes high-speed mobile broadband is permanently available through wi-fi or the cell network. The system would have both private and public spaces so that, as the student goes around recording her work, she can keep that in a private space. She can then develop her records via a laptop or desktop with a larger screen at college or at home and transfer the resulting assignment to the public space when finished to be viewed by her tutor, supervisor, mentor and others as required. She would also have access to online tutorials while out in the field, to provide conceptual principles and pointers for her to link them to her practice.

Outcomes for the student would include: having the e-portfolio assessed for an industry recognised qualification from the HE Institution or FE College; new skills relevant to leisure and tourism and in managing new mobile technologies to support learning. She could keep the e-portfolio as something to build upon in the future.

This scenario was also viewed by other respondents from the network as likely to be in effect before 2015. They considered that this style of assessment is likely to appeal to work placement providers and that leisure and tourism would be a suitable subject. Students in this field can easily capture their experiences which can be less easy or even disallowed in other subjects; for example, engineering placement students are not allowed to bring mobile devices near production lines as manufacturers wish to keep their designs secret. Respondents disagreed over whether this scenario would be cost-effective weighing up the savings of having all assessment completed online against the potential cell phone network costs. Also who would fund the broadband usage? Who would own the technology? There was also some concern over the assumption that all students would have personal access to smartphones or Netbooks, particularly in a student population where many come from disadvantaged backgrounds. Nor have e-portfolios been an overwhelming success to date provoking a number of practical, technical and conceptual issues (Adamson, 2006). However, the scenario would probably appeal to students (though possibly only until they discovered how much work is involved) and, as everything is accessed via a web-browser customised for the device it is running on, will not be hampered by interoperability issues.

WBL 1: Projecting handheld device

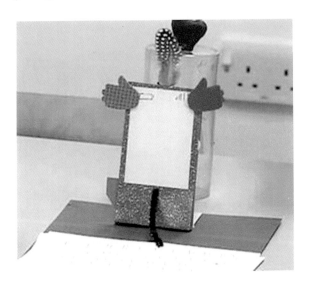

Figure 15.3 Model of 'Projecting handheld device'

This scenario centres on an organic handset made out of as much natural material as possible with a small display on the handset and no keys or buttons. It has a projected virtual keyboard on a second separate screen (at the bottom of the image). When not needed as a keyboard, this can become an interactive touch screen acts as an interactive interface, allowing scrolling and selection by touch. A stylus stored neatly within the body of the device, also acts as a digital pen for note-taking and can transfer recorded information back to the main unit via Bluetooth. In this scenario the handset with a projection display, multiband communication and multimedia is being used to support trainees in workplaces such as pharmaceutical companies and pharmacies.

In the future (but not before 2015) this device will continue to be developed to include a holographic projector display as in science teaching situations 3D models are effective. The image shows a projected 3D model heart behind the handset and the keyboard/ input at the front. The handset includes a removable universal memory card that can be read by most devices, especially computers, that will replace portable hard drives so students can have separate workplace, college or university and home storage media. There is a solar panel on the back and removable rechargeable battery packs to aid use in developing countries. The device is capable of receiving and sending any kind of information from the universal WiFi connection expected in five years' time. The disability-friendly version has an optional speech-to-text input device, with the additional capacity to convert to sign language for deaf students.

Such a device would enable two-way multimedia communication between the university or college tutor and the student on a science-based placement in the pharmaceutical, chemical or medical industries. The university or college tutor can send images, animations and instructions to be projected so that the student and their mentor or groups of students can discuss them. The student(s) can sketch out diagrams and capture images to send back to their tutor.

Whilst aspects of this scenario are fantasy, for instance speech-to-text remains an issue despite decades of research; others such as pico-projection and solar power are appearing in mobile phones being released as announced by Samsung at the GSMA Mobile World Congress in Barcelona in February 2009. The respondents from the network though were very divided as to whether this scenario would come about within five or even ten years. One makes an interesting and relevant point.

> Most of these technologies are around now but a change of priorities would be required for manufacturers to produce these. That is they would have to start from the premise that they would make available what education needs rather than adapting something made for a commercial, less price-sensitive market.

Other barriers include the necessary change in attitude and development of digital literacy skills amongst learners and tutors: not all will be equally well equipped to operate devices such as these.

WBL 2: Connecting student doctors

This scenario focuses on connecting student doctors to external services and expertise and using the information sent back and forth to create learning objects. It involves a consulting room in a hospital, with a student doctor and a critically ill patient. The trainee doctor uses a mobile device that can record and display video, the room has a PC next to the bed and a wall-mounted information screen for displaying patient information, such as X-rays, calendars, case history, and facilities associated with mobile devices, such as SMS. The student can use the PC to search electronic databases, such as patient records or medical bibliographies for information. Using their handheld (which has facilities for speech-to-text conversion), they can record case notes that are automatically added to the patient's records. Or, if necessary, the trainee can use it to contact a more experienced clinician, who may be elsewhere in the hospital or at another location and who can supply advice or information via voice and video. The student uses this technology to record their experiences and data for later reflection. With appropriate permissions it can also be shared with peers for joint reflection and stored as a learning object for future use. The content generated by each device may be repurposed for different stakeholders and devices. All content is held in the same shared data store but different users will have access to different parts of the data or access to it in different ways on different devices. This access to a remote store assists in maintaining security and confidentiality, as each device especially the mobile does not retain data, but merely displays it. In terms of creating this technology, all that is needed to achieve this scenario is better, faster versions of what is already available.

Respondents from the network were agreed that this scenario would be very likely to come about within the next five years. Yet, whilst clinicians are proving receptive to new technologies and all that is needed is faster, always-on versions of what is already available, working cultures in hospitals may well still prove to be a tough barrier to cross. One issue would be making informal advice permanent; medical staff might need to say things off the record and the ephemeral nature of conversation between tutors and students can be important to aspects of the teaching process such as maintaining student self-esteem. One final concern about this scenario was that the network felt that the voice-to-text input method for entering case notes will not be reliable enough to be trusted with medical information without cross-checking by a human.

WBL: 3 My Life Store

This scenario involves the collection of life experiences, work experiences and associated prompts to learning and reflection. It is much bigger than an e-portfolio and incorporates all of the things that a person generates throughout their life. These could include work experience, academia, qualifications, competencies, case studies of things that people have actually done, things that they may or may not wish to share with others.

These could be separated out into work versus home/lifestyle experiences. In the life space there are stores of different types of information, split into separate areas, such as:

- work;
- qualifications, both academic and professional;
- work-based learning assignments; and
- a personal area.

However, these areas are not completely separate. Parts of life experiences or part of a person's academic experiences could both contribute towards work experience, so these are shared types of information. The store also contains files, be they documents, audio or video, which can reside in/cross link to any of these spaces. As mobile devices become better able to handle data transfer, they will become the medium to handle and transfer items to and from the 'life store' silo. The mobile device is particularly suitable to help people remember that they are learning all the time: at work, in an educational institution, touring or at home and to prompt them to record that learning. The emphasis would be on the device's prompting, making people become more proactive about recording, reflecting and capturing this information. The process will be multi-input through voice and tablet or stylus. The device will help individual learning as it responds to the way that people organise their work. With appropriate viewing permissions set a university or college tutor or employer could come along to a student or trainee's 'life store' and look at what they have done, how they have worked on certain tasks, how they have handled situations, their case studies. They could then view the trainee as a person, to get a rounded picture and see how suitable they might be for a particular role. This scenario could be augmented by adding connectivity between individual's 'life store' that supported a learning community as well as individual learning.

Members of the network held strong, divergent views about this scenario split between those who believed that, as a mega-personal multimedia wiki in Facebook style with updates easily supported by current phone technology, it was very likely to happen to those who believed it was extremely unlikely to happen. The latter pointed to cultural barriers between personal and work lives, concern about security of storage, privacy and fears that information could be passed on by the system. For example the current UK government is working on plans to record every email sent and received in the country.[2] These concerns are fuelled by the publicity surrounding systemic failures of recorded assessments of learning such as

<hr/>

2   Angus Crawford, 'UK e-mail law "attack on rights"'. *BBC News*. Available online at <http://news.bbc.co.uk/1/hi/uk/7819230.stm> (accessed 16/08/10).

the English Standard Assessment Tests (SATs) marking collapse in 2008. Other technical barriers pointed out were the reliance of the scenario on semantic web technologies and intelligent agents that have been predicted for some time but have been slow in arriving and on connectivity. Currently connectivity and bandwidth are a real concern for university and college IT network teams who are reluctant to allow access to many services especially file sharing, peer-to-peer networks and even some sites e.g. social networking sites such as You Tube. Whilst mobile broadband may mean students will no longer have to deal with such institutional mistrust, the cost of mobile data services may make them reluctant to use too much of their own 'airtime' on any systems or tools other than the ones they have chosen to use.

WBL 4: Just-in-time training and information networks

Figure 15.4 Model of 'Just-in-time training and information networks' scenario

This scenario focuses on using mobile devices to connect networks of workers and experts in a multi-location setting. The three 'islands' shown in the image of the model represent three residential schools for children with a disability such as Asperger's Syndrome. In this kind of work setting there is a large team of care workers surrounding the children who get little training. The nature of the work is that they have to learn as they go along because each child is really individual. This is a problem for the management of that care. Also a considerable number of outside experts and sometimes others who are tangentially connected with the children are involved. These might include speech therapists, social workers, relatives and/or someone who knows the child's drug plan. Handheld mobile devices will be used for tapping into this local expertise, remote expertise and any available peer expertise through video connections between phones. Users could consult their phone to see who is available among fellow workers, send text messages to all those who are available and then initiate a video call to whoever responds. The phones can also capture stories, through video and voice recording, which could be edited into a suitable snippet. This edited story could then be uploaded to a private, video-sharing community YouTube-style site for access by appropriate colleagues. Another possibly contentious idea would require that the children were assigned tags of 'need' and local experts were given tags of 'expertise'. Then, if a difficult situation with a child arose where it was becoming impossible to communicate with the child a carer could look up their tags of need which would lead to finding others who had worked with that child and appropriate experts on that need. However, it was recognised that there are concerns associated with such tags. If you are carrying around information in the form of a tag that you are not in control of releasing, you need to know who else may get access to that data. Sharing information through channels such as Bluetooth carries risks of interception by others.

This is another scenario where respondents were divided as to the likelihood of its coming into play before 2015 with cultural barriers playing a greater role in their thinking than technical ones. While technically most aspects of the scenario are perfectly feasible, it is questionable whether manufacturers would have the will to make or to support such devices. Currently the rate at which manufacturers change the designs of their smartphones aimed at the business and entertainment markets is a problem for those attempting to embed their use in education. Also members of the network again raised concerns over data storage and security. One catastrophic failure of care or loss of patient confidentiality caused by a communications failure at a critical moment would destroy all public trust in such an approach. Whilst those young people today who update their My Space, Bebo or Facebook status several times a day clearly share fewer concerns about privacy than members of this network, we have yet to hear much about how those with special educational needs feel. Though results from projects such as those run by the Rix Centre at the The Big Tree (<http://www.thebigtree.org>) on behalf of the University of East London imply many would like to become more involved with Web 2.0 technologies.

Discussion of emerging issues for work-based mobile learning

A range of learning opportunities can be seen to reoccur within many of the scenarios; it appears that these will underpin developments that will impact upon the imminent future for workplace-based mobile learning associated with HE and FE programmes. These include:

Issue 1: The device that enables 'just-in-time' and 'as-and-when-necessary' training

Scenarios such as *FE1: Working together in Business Studies, WBL2: Connecting student doctors* and *WBL4: Just-in-time training networks* foreground the opportunity for learners to seek information relevant to their current context via a mobile device. This information would be both location- and activity-specific and appropriate to the learner's current stage in their progress over time. This source of this information could be a person, peer or expert, the world wide web or a bespoke subject-specific video or animation. The Hairdressing Training programme (Smith, 2008) which allows trainee hairdressers to review videos of cutting techniques on their mobile phone before trying them for real is an example how 'just-in-time' training can work.

Issue 2: An approach to teaching and learning that is more collaborative and learner-centred than didactic or teacher-centred

In the scenarios listed above and also in *WBL1: Projecting handheld device* the workshop participants also draw attention to the opportunities for two-way communication in different modes between tutor and student (and, where relevant, workplace mentor). They view the college or university tutor as taking a more collaborative role than is seen currently and using the mobile device to support a teaching approach that facilitates context-specific learning opportunities.

Issue 3: Always-on affordable connectivity and power

All of the envisaged scenarios rely on permanently available, affordable connections to the world wide web and the mobile phone network. In scenarios *WBL2: Connecting student doctors* and *WBL4: Just-in-time training and information networks* having a charged phone in credit could be crucial to patient care. Network participants debated the respective merits of university- or college- or employer-supplied devices versus setting up the institutions' ICT systems to operate seamlessly with a range of student-owned devices. Other members of the network opined that, come what may, students would continue to bring a variety of mobile devices with them. This has implications for the amount of support and training tutors and ICT support staff will need and for network security. Whilst interoperability is currently an issue it was felt that the increasing number of phones with mobile web browsers, such as the Apple iPhone, phones running the Google Android operating system, and phones by LG and Nokia, would be likely to resolve this.

Issue 4: An online repository accessible by different browsers according to device at hand

The importance of the role of the web-browser is clearly an emerging issue for mobile learning. It looks like online access is the lowest common denominator between devices and will lead to the design of applications for education and other courseware for the different browsers such as IE, Firefox, Safari, Opera, Chrome and their mobile versions. All the scenarios generated by the workshop participants involve, more or less obviously, some kind of large online data store to support the information gathered by the students' mobile devices. It would seem sensible to make access to this central repository via the simplest web interface common to as many browsers as possible. Indeed, it looks as if Google has also had this thought with Google Apps Education Edition (<http://www.google.com/a/help/intl/en/edu/>) now being used in dozens of universities and colleges across the world. However, such central repository brings with it huge concerns over managing a huge, ever increasing file store and ensuring its security.

Issue 5: The merging of personal and vocational information and practice

Several scenarios pointed to security issues within the online repository described above. In *WBL 3: My life store* this was linked to the combination online of records of learning in informal and formal contexts to provide a more 'rounded' assessment of an individual's learning progress leading to a loss of privacy. Members of the network pointed out that public confidence in the security of large ICT systems is low, for example, this has held up the development of national electronic patient records in the English National Health Service. However, the way social networking sites such as Facebook and Flickr continue to flourish and the variety of information uploaded suggest that such concerns are not held by everyone. In addition, scenarios such as *WBL 2: Connecting student doctors* and *WBL 4: Just-in-time training and information networks* rely on using personal devices for communication between students and their tutors or supervisors. Requests for such communication could well occur in personal as well as work time. Cook,

Pachler and Bradley (2008) have already found that loaning postgraduate students mobile devices to use with web-based media boards led to a blurring of the boundaries between study, work, and personal time.

Issue 6: Subject-specific opportunities

It is interesting to note that, in the workshop focusing on developing scenarios for work-based learning, though the participating group was multidisciplinary, use of mobile devices within science, particularly bioscience and medical sciences, underpinned three of the four scenarios envisioned. Other experiential learning scenarios generated in the FE-focused workshop included science and engineering, business studies and leisure and tourism. An emerging issue for mobile learning is identifying which subjects will most naturally accommodate learning opportunities for students with devices such as camera or web-enabled mobile phones. Early indications from this workshop series point to subjects and professions with experiential learning and work placements and those, such as science and medicine, where the technology can help bridge contexts and show students the applications of the concepts being taught.

Issue 7: Peer-to-peer networking and collaboration

In scenario *FE1: Learning and working together in Business Studies* the opportunities offered by mobile devices for student-to-student communication and collaboration are foregrounded. Members of the network considered this to be a likely outcome of more students owning more sophisticated mobile devices. Concerns were raised over managing the variety of devices and opportunities they offered, about the training and support faculty needed and, common to all collaborative work, issues of assessment.

Issue 8: Integral projection

Other suggestions made during the workshop, such as mobiles with integral projectors, are novel and their potential has yet to be evaluated seriously by the community. This is not so futuristic as once thought, pico-projection phones are already available in Korea. The potential disruption caused by projecting images as well as audio into a classroom or lecture theatre is clearly an emerging issue to be addressed sooner rather than later.

Whether the learning opportunities described in this report are realised is dependent on whether sufficient numbers of employers, students and tutors engage with the new technologies in a responsible fashion with an eye to their potential to support learning. In several scenarios including *WBL 2: Connecting student doctors* and *FE1: Working and learning together on placement* members of the network highlighted concerns over socio-cultural barriers that they believe are more likely to impact negatively on these scenarios than technical barriers. Examples include people's concerns over privacy, potential loss of data, disruption and being 'always available' that may well prevent these opportunities being taken up. Clearly an emerging issue for mobile learning is developing an appropriate cultural climate within the institution(s) involved and that will need ground rules accepted by all parties. It is known that mobile devices used irresponsibly are disruptive, some states in the US and India and even a country, Brunei, have entirely banned their use by students in schools. As Wishart et al. (2007) found, such bans impact negatively on staff trialling new technologies to support learning even if their own use is not formally restricted.

Thus further emerging issues for workplace-based mobile learning in HE and FE include both ethical and practical implications. Examples of those highlighted in the discussion workshops include resistance to change, especially potentially disruptive change amongst faculty, concerns about new learning practices impacting upon employers' and tutors' personal time, data security and privacy issues. There are particular concerns about how images are used, the ease of their capture and uploading to an online store and their usefulness in supporting learning and revision visually has meant that learner-captured multimedia is part and parcel of nearly all the scenarios envisioned. Yet not all establishments who host students on placement, especially those manufacturers who carefully guard their designs, are likely to be as free as suggested in *FE2: Recording experiential learning in Leisure and Tourism* about allowing students on placement to take images and use them outside the building, even if only for assignments. Wishart (2009) also includes ownership in her discussion of the range of ethical considerations relevant to the use of mobile devices for work-based learning. Both ownership of the device, if the institution has a loan scheme in place, and of the data and images collected on it by a student on placement.

Finally, it is interesting to note how the different futures prediction tools used were related to the scenarios that were generated. Whilst in all workshops participants were reminded that they were considering only five years hence the *Futures Technology Workshop* led to a greater range of scenarios for which the technology is not yet in place than did the other techniques. Using the *Cognitive Foresight Toolkit* meant that the drivers chosen for axes on which to pin the scenarios led and, in some cases constrained, participants' thinking. The 3D modelling component of the *Futures Technology Workshop* was more liberating in relation to participants' ideas than the images in the *Building Visions for Learning Spaces* scenario cards where the participants tended to make their scenarios fit the image rather than use the image to generate free-flowing ideas from which to create a scenario.

Conclusions

It was concluded that there was an extensive and strong match between affordances of mobile devices and learning opportunities in work-based and experiential learning. There are particular learning opportunities in specific subjects, especially those where theory and application are both studied or involve fieldwork and data collection such as in the sciences, geography and vocational subjects.

The future for workplace based mobile learning in Higher (HE) and Further Education (FE) is most likely to include the increasing use of just-in-time and as-and-when-necessary training, an increased amount of peer-to-peer networking and collaboration and an approach to teaching and learning that is more collaborative than didactic. Concerns were raised over the need for always-on affordable connectivity and power and the merging of personal and vocational information and practice. There will be a need for design specifications for a secure online all-purpose data repository accessible by different browsers according to device at hand.

Other emerging issues for workplace-based mobile learning include both ethical and practical implications. These include cultural barriers and resistance to change amongst lecturers, tutors and associated professionals. They include fears for the erosion of tutors' personal time, people's concerns over security related to the increasing amount of information and number of images to be stored and privacy issues related to the ease with which information can be captured in a range of locations. One last issue, one that is in need of urgent attention, is the need for the development by students and staff of agreed practice, establishing how mobile devices are to be used responsibly in institutions and workplaces before inconsiderate use or ignorance of their potential to enhance learning results in banning a valuable learning tool.

References

Adamson, V. (2006) Final report on the University of Nottingham's JISC e-Portfolio Reference Model Project Technology and Evaluation Seminar. Inverness: Glenaffric Ltd. Available online at <http://www.nottingham.ac.uk/epreference-model/keydocuments/Glenaffric Final Report.doc> (accessed 18/02/09)

Brown, J. (2008) *M-learning 4 those who care*, Visited: Feb 2009. Available online at <http://www.molenet.org.uk/projects/2007projlist/colleges/Bournville.aspx> (accessed 18/04/10)

Cook, J, Pachler, N., & Bradley, C (2008), "Bridging the gap? Mobile phones at the interface between informal and formal learning", *Journal of the Research Centre for Educational Technology*, Special issue on Learning While Mobile, Spring. Available online at <http://www.rcetj.org/files/RCETJ_4_1_learningwhilem-obile_cook.pdf> (accessed 18/04/10)

Davidson, H., & Lutman, M. (2007) 'Survey of mobile phone use and their chronic effects on the hearing of a student population.' *International Journal of Audiology 46* (3), pp. 113–118

Dearnley C., Haigh J., &Fairhall, J. (2008) 'Using mobile technologies for assessment and learning in practice settings: A case study.' *Nurse Education in Practice 8* (3), pp. 197–204

Lambourne, B. (2008) *Assessing the impact of m-learning with Work Based Learners undertaking Apprenticeships across Rural Lincolnshire*. Available online at <http://www.molenet.org.uk/projects/2007projlist/colleges/boston.aspx> (accessed 01/02/09)

New Media Consortium (2009) *The 2009 Horizon Report*. Available online at <http://www.nmc.org/pdf/2009-Horizon-Report.pdf> (accessed 01/02/09)

Ofcom (2007)*The consumer experience research report*. Available online at <http://www.ofcom.org.uk/research/tce/ceo8/research.pdf> (accessed 01/02/09)

Office of Science and Technology (OST) (2005) *Strategic futures planning: Suggestions for success*. The Cognitive Foresight Toolkit Version 1. London: Horizon Scanning Centre. Available online at <http://hsctoolkit.tribalctad.co.uk/> (accessed 01/02/09)

Reynolds, P., Harper, J., Dunne, S., Cox, M., & Myint, Y. (2007) 'Portable Digital Assistants (PDAs) in dentistry: Part II – Pilot study of PDA use in the dental clinic.' *British Dental Journal 202*, pp. 477–483

Sharples, M., Arnedillo Sánchez, I., Milrad, M., & Vavoula, G. (2007) *Mobile learning: Small devices, big issues*. Available online at <http://telearn.noe-kaleidoscope.org/warehouse/KAL_Legacy_Mobile_Learning_(001143v1).pdf> (accessed 01/02/09)

Smith, S. (2008) 'Delivering mobile services'. Paper presented at *IADIS International Conference on Mobile Learning*, Carvoeiro, Portugal, 11–13 April

Vavoula, G., & Sharples, M. (2007) 'Future technology workshop: a collaborative method for the design of new learning technologies and activities.' *International Journal of Computer-Supported Collaborative Learning 2*(4), pp. 393–419. Available online at <http://www.ftw.org.uk/Portals/4/Publications/FTW_Preprint.pdf> (accessed 01/02/09)

Warren, S. (2008) *My podcast: Developing innovative approaches to personalised learning*. Available online at <http://www.molenet.org.uk/projects/2007projlist/colleges/newCollegeSwindon.aspx> (accessed 01/02/09)

Winters, N. (2006) 'What is mobile learning?' In Sharples, M. (ed.), *Big issues in mobile learning: Report of a workshop by the Kaleidoscope Network of Excellence Mobile Learning Initiative.* Available online at <http://telearn.noe-kaleidoscope.org/warehouse/Sharples-2006.pdf> (accessed 01/02/09)

Wishart, J. (2009) 'Ethical considerations in implementing mobile learning in the workplace.' *International Journal of Mobile and Blended Learning 1*(2), pp. 76–92

Wishart, J., Ramsden, A. and McFarlane, A. (2007) 'PDAs and Handhelds: ICT at your side and not in your face.' *Technology, Pedagogy and Education 16*(1), pp. 95–110

Notes on Contributors

PETER AUBUSSON is Associate Professor and Head of Teacher Education at the University of Technology, Sydney where he is a member of the *Mobagogy* group. He was a school teacher for over ten years, during which time he researched his own practice. He has since researched mainly in the fields of teacher professional learning and science education. His current research includes investigations of mobile learning, action learning in professional community formation and analogical representations. His publications include five books, two edited books and more than forty refereed articles. Recent book publications include P. Aubusson, R. Ewing and G. Hoban *Action Learning in Schools* (Milton Park: Routledge, 2009); P. Aubusson & S. Schuck (eds) (2006) *Teacher Learning and Development: The Mirror Maze* (Dordrecht: Springer, 2006); and P. Aubusson, A. Harrison and S. Ritchie (eds) *Metaphor and Analogy in Science Education* (Dordrecht: Springer, 2006).

MICHAEL E. AUER is Professor of Electrical Engineering at the Systems Engineering Department of the Carinthia University of Applied Sciences Villach, Austria since 1995 and also has a teaching position at the University of Klagenfurt. Furthermore, he works as a visiting professor at the Universities of Amman (Jordan), Brasov (Romania) and Patras (Greece). He is a senior member of the Institute of Electrical and Electronics Engineers (IEEE) and member of Verband der Elektrotechnik Elektronik Informationstechnik (VDE) and the International Society for Engineering Education (IGIP), author or co-author of more than 170 publications and leading member of numerous national and international organizations in the field of online technologies. He is founder and chair of the annual international Interactive Computer Aided Learning (ICL) and Remote Engineering and Virtual Instrumentation (REV) conferences and chair or member of the Program Committees of several international conferences and workshops.

He is editor-in-chief of the *International Journals of Online Engineering* (iJOE, <http://www.i-joe.org>), *Emerging Technologies in Learning* (iJET, <http://www.i-jet.org>) and *Interactive Mobile Technolgies* (iJIM, <http://www.i-jim.org>). Furthermore, he acts as an associated editor for *Middle and Eastern Europe* of the *European Journal of Open and Distance Learning* (EURODL, <http://www.eurodl.org>). In June 2006 Michael Auer was elected as President and CEO of the International Association of Online Engineering (IAOE), a non-governmental organization that promotes the vision of new engineering working environments worldwide.

STUART BOOMER is presently a clinical Lecturer at the Leeds Dental Institute, University of Leeds, where he is actively involved in training members of the dental team through his roles as the Assistant Programme Manager for Graduate Diploma in Dental Hygiene and Dental Therapy and Acting Programme Manager for the Diploma in Dental Technology. As well as having a keen interest in development of clinical teaching practice, areas of research interest include antimicrobial peptide synthesis, drug induced gingival overgrowth and neuropeptide markers within the periodontal tissues. He qualified from the Queen's University of Belfast with BDS in 1993, having also received an intercalated BSC (Hons) in Biochemistry during his dental studies. Following qualification he worked within both general dental practice and the hospital dental services in Northern Ireland and was awarded the FFD in dental surgery from the Royal College of Surgeons in Ireland in 1998. He commenced monospecialty training in Periodontics at Belfast in 1999, being awarded an MPhil from Queen's University Belfast in 2002, before completion of specialist training in 2003. He was awarded the MRD from the Royal College of Surgeons of Edinburgh in Periodontology in 2003 and was subsequently entered onto the General Dental Council (UK) specialist list in Periodontics in 2004. Until taking up his present post at the Leeds Dental Institute in 2005 Stuart worked as a Specialist in Periodontics within both private practice and at the Royal Group of Hospitals Trust in Belfast. He has also been awarded the Postgraduate Certificated for Learning and Teaching in Higher Education from the University of Leeds.

KEVIN BURDEN is a lecturer and researcher in the Centre for Educational Studies at the University of Hull, where he has worked since 1995. Before that he was a school teacher for fourteen years teaching history. He is responsible for continuing professional development within the Centre for Educational Studies and directs the Postgraduate Professional Development programme for teachers across the region. His research interests focus on the social and cultural impacts of new and emerging technologies, with particular reference to professional learning for educators. He has undertaken research and evaluation work into the affordances of mobile technologies and the impact of digital media resources. He has led a number of nationally funded technology projects including commissions for the British Educational Communications and Technology Agency, JISC, Nesta, the BBC and several local authorities. He is currently working with European partners to develop a multi-lingual video library for schools (EduTubePlus) and to investigate the impact of mobile learning devices for learners, including students and teachers.

SELENA CHAN has been teaching at Christchurch Polytechnic Institute of Technology (CPIT) since 1980. She is a baker by trade and completed her trade training in Singapore. She emigrated to New Zealand (NZ) in the late 1970s, where she worked in Wellington before accepting a teaching position at CPIT. She has a BEd (1998), a MEd (Hons) (2002) from Massey University and a graduate certificate in applied e-learning (2005). She is currently working towards the completion of a PhD with Griffith University (Brisbane). Her continual learning has led to a life of teaching, scholarship and research. Currently, her roles at CPIT include teaching in the adult education programme and providing staff development support on various e-learning and research projects. She is also project leader of several externally funded research projects focused on vocational education. These various branches of research are disseminated via bakery journals, writing of book chapters on baking and mobile learning, recipe books, conference presentations and an ongoing blog (<http://mportfolios.blogspot.com/>). Her sustained interests and dedication to teaching, learning and research have been recognised with various awards. Notably, the Service to the Industry award from the NZ baking industry in 2002, the CPIT excellence in teaching award in 2007 and the NZ Prime Ministers supreme Excellence in Tertiary Teaching award for 2007.

SARAH CORNELIUS is Lecturer in the School of Education, University of Aberdeen. Sarah has research interests in the design, facilitation and evaluation of technology-enhanced learning in the post-compulsory sector, focusing particularly on learners' and tutors' experiences. Sarah has previously worked as an independent consultant in online and distance learning as well as in higher education in the UK and the Netherlands. She has published widely in the fields of Geographical Information Systems and e-learning. Recent publications include articles for the journals ALT-J, Educational Media International, Interactive Learning Environments and Open Learning. Sarah is also co-author of the highly regarded textbook *An Introduction to Geographical Information Systems* (Pearson Education: Harlow).

CERIDWEN COULBY is Educational Staff Development Officer for Leeds Institute of Medical Education and the Assessment and Learning in Practice Settings Centre for Excellence in Teaching and Learning based at the University of Leeds. As well as developing the teaching skills of clinical staff, she also manages a module on the BSc in Medical Education. She is currently working on a PhD examining the quality of work-based learning experiences and is interested in developing the educational experience for all students by encouraging the use of emerging technologies such as mobile learning in education. She has had work published in the mobile- and work-based learning fields and is a reviewer for the British Journal of Education Technology.

NANCY DAVIES is Learning Technologist for the Assessment and Learning in Practice Settings (ALPS) Centre for Excellence in Teaching and Learning (CETL). Her main focus is on the enhancement of learning and teaching through technology with particular focus on the application of mobile technologies. She has contributed to many conferences and papers, including an ALT-C pre-conference workshop, the AMEE guide to e-learning and the Medev Subject Centre newsletter. Other roles include promotion of staff and student engagement in Virtual Learning Environments and e-Portfolios at the University of Leeds and the ALPS partner HEIs.

CLAUDIA DE WITT is Professor of Educational Science and Media Education at the FernUniversität in Hagen, Institute of Educational Science and Media Research. She is chair of the mobile learning group in this department. Her scientific activities are in e-learning and mobile learning; she is also expert in theories of media education and media didactics. She researches internet-based knowledge communication and online communities of inquiry, didactic design of internet-based scenarios of communication and collaboration with synchronous and asynchronous tools, their implementation and evaluation in different contexts. She published several chapters about new media (e-learning) and pragmatism and is co-editor of the online journal MedienPaedagogik.org.

ARTHUR EDWARDS holds a masters degree in curriculum and instruction from the University of Colima. He is currently a senior professor–researcher at the College of Telematics of the University of Colima, Mexico, where he has led and participated in several federally funded research projects sponsored by the Mexican National Research Network and the Ministry of Scientific Research. His areas of research include e-learning, mobile learning, distance learning, computer assisted language learning, virtual reality, multimodal learning and social networking.

KAREN EVANS is Chair in Education and Lifelong Learning at the Institute of Education, University of London. Following her PhD in 1982, she spent a large part of her career at the University of Surrey, where she was Director of the Postgraduate Centre for Professional and Adult Learning and Professor of Post-Compulsory Education. Karen Evans's main fields of research are learning in life and work transitions and learning in and through the workplace. She has directed sixteen major studies of learning and the world of work in Britain and internationally. Books include *Learning, Work and Social Responsibility* (2009); *Improving Workplace Learning* (2006); *Reconnection: Countering Social Exclusion through Situated Learning* (2004); *Working to Learn* (2002); and *Learning and Work in the Risk Society* (2000). She was joint editor of COMPARE, the journal of comparative and international education from 2004 to 2009 and is currently leading a programme of research in the UK Economic and Social Research Council LLAKES Research Centre (Learning and Life Chances in Knowledge Economies and Societies).

SONJA GANGUIN has been scientific staff member at the Institute of Educational Science and Media Research at the FernUniversität in Hagen since 2009. She studied educational science at Bielefeld University and received a PhD in Educational Science with the focus on computer games in professional training (serious games). Since 2007 she is member of the joint board of the GMK (Gesellschaft für Medienpädagogik und Kommunikationskultur) and member of the German Price of Computer Games. Her research fields are mobile learning, media literacy, computer games and empirical social research.

DANILO GARBI ZUTIN has graduated in electrical engineering at the State University of Sao Paulo (UNESP), Bauru, Sao Paulo, Brazil, and obtained his master's degree in Systems Design (specialization in Remote Systems) at the Carinthia University of Applied Sciences in Villach, Austria. His research interests are in the fields of remote engineering, online labs, remote control of devices and software development for online labs. He is currently a senior researcher and team member of the Center of Competence in Online Laboratories and Open Learning (CCOL) at the Carinthia University of Applied Sciences (CUAS), Villach, Austria, where he has been engaged in projects for the development of online laboratories. In January 2010 he was appointed Secretary General of the International Association of Online Engineering. He is author or co-author of more than twenty scientific papers published in international journals, magazines and conferences. Most of these papers are in the field of online laboratories and issues associated with their dissemination and usage.

MARTIN GOOD is currently a freelance expert on learning and technology. He was the founding chairman of Cambridge Training and Development Ltd (CTAD), sold to Tribal Group plc in 2001. At CTAD and Tribal he led much of the work on open learning which has gradually migrated into e-learning and mobile learning over the last 15 years. He wrote 15 books on learning to learn. His favourites are *The Effective Learner* (a bestseller for the late lamented Open College) and 'On the way to online learning', a chapter in *Teaching and Learning Online*, edited by Professor John Stephenson (Kogan Page 2001). He remains fascinated with the learning process, especially its relationship with technology, and believes that, intelligently used, technology can and will contribute more and more value to education and training. His blog is found at <http://martingood.blogspot.com> and he often works as a consultant <http://www.m-learning.org>.

DAVID GREEN is a Research Associate with the Graduate School of Education at the University of Bristol. He works as a combined technologist and researcher creating and evaluating internet and other Web 2.0 projects for education. With a background in psychology and arts as well as technology, David is able to cover a wide range of skills for online projects. He has built and managed large-scale complex websites such as the successful BioEthics Education Project website (BEEP, funded by the Wellcome Trust) and its companion site PEEP (Physics & Ethics Education Project), funded by the Institute of Physics. Between them these cover some 1,400 pages of information and data, including online video, discussion and other interactive features. He was responsible for carrying out the formal evaluation projects for both sites. He has also managed the data collection for further projects funded by Becta and JISC.

URS GRÖHBIEL is Researcher and Lecturer for e-Learning at the School of Business, University of Applied Sciences Northwestern Switzerland. He is the executive director of edunovum consulting and the Swiss Network for Educational Innovation. In research he focuses on questions of innovation in education and e-learning management such as Web 2.0 in the financial sector, innovation management in corporate training, controlling and quality development of training. Urs Gröhbiel has been supporting and supervising funding schemes for innovation and projects for different institutions of higher education since 1999. He is consulting government agencies, enterprises and non-profit organizations such as the Swiss Federal Institute of Technology, the Federal Office for Professional Education and Technology, UBS and development organizations.

MACIEJ KUSZPA studied business and social sciences at the University of Dortmund and the University of Memphis. As a long-time Mobile 2.0 Entrepreneur and Scientist he has two areas of expertise: on the one hand, the field of mobile social networks, based on his work in the mobile industry since 2000 as founder and CEO of Peperoni Mobile & Internet Software GmbH, which develops software solutions around user-generated content and social media; and on the other hand, the field of mobile learning. In 2000, he started as a research associate at the FernUniversität in Hagen, Department of Business Administration and Economics and there in 2002 he founded the Mobile Education Center of Excellence, which is an international research project on Mobile Learning. In 2008, he also joined the mobile learning research group at the Institute of Educational Science and Media Research, FernUniversität in Hagen.

JULIE LAXTON is the Centres for Excellence in Teaching & Learning; Assessment & Learning in Practice Settings (CETL ALPS) Teaching Fellow for the Faculty of Medicine & Health, University of Leeds. A dietitian by background, she has considerable experience in the field of education, learning and teaching particularly from a practice (NHS) perspective. In her role as Teaching Fellow, she has implemented the roll-out of the ALPS programme for undergraduate students within the Faculty and enabled the research, evidence base and effective learning programme for students and tutors involved. Recent publications include J. Holt et al. (2010) 'Identifying common competences in Health and Social Care: an example of multi-institutional and inter-professional working', *Nurse Education Today* 30 (3), pp. 264–270. She is a reviewer for *European Journals of Dental Education* and a QAA reviewer for healthcare commissioned programme in Higher Education.

PHIL MARSTON is a Learning Technologist and Research Student in the School of Education, University of Aberdeen. He has research interests in the role of contexts and context setting in mobile learning, virtual worlds, simulations and game-based learning, particularly in higher education. He has previously worked in the fields of management training, community ICT training and more recently as part of a team of learning technologists supporting a variety of disciplines in higher education.

SIMONE MARTINETZ is a senior researcher and project manager at Fraunhofer IAO. Simone Martinetz has been working in projects co-funded by the German Ministry for Education and Research since 2002. The project's focus is on the early recognition of new qualification needs (<http://www.frequenz.net>). Simone Martinetz was leader of the AdeBar research project (Permanent close-to-the-job observation of the qualification development aimed at early recognition of changes in employment). Furthermore, she has been involved in topics related to the development of skills, such as analysing training options for IT-supported work forms that are not specifically drafted as learning environments. Her current research activities relate to projects in the fields of innovation-friendly business design and business performance, knowledge-sharing in organisations, organisational change, e-learning and the eColleagues project.

SANDRO MENGEL studied media education and human resource development at the University of Dortmund. He is an expert in media didactics and practical application of e-learning scenarios and tools in educational institutions. Since 2005 he is scientific staff member at the Institute of Educational Science and Media Research at the FernUniversität in Hagen. His activities contain didactical conceptions, consulting and research for innovative e-learning and mobile learning applications as well as the management of such projects. Further activities are the e-moderation of online-based trainings and live online collaboration courses in virtual classrooms. Since 2008 he is member of the mobile learning research group at the Institute of Educational Science and Media Research, FernUniversität in Hagen. His field of activities in this group includes the consulting and the development of didactical conceptions for mobile learning scenarios in the context of learning on the job and their evaluation.

NORBERT PACHLER is Professor of Education and Pro-Director: Professional Learning at the Institute of Education, University of London. In addition to the application of new technologies in teaching and learning, his research interests include teacher education and development and all aspects of foreign language teaching and learning. He has published widely and supervises in these fields. Since 2007 he has been the convenor of the London Mobile Learning Group (<http://www.londonmobilelearning.

net>), which brings together an international, interdisciplinary group of researchers from the fields of cultural and media studies, sociology, (social) semiotics, pedagogy, educational technology, work-based learning and learning design. In the book *Mobile Learning: Structures, Agency, Practices* (Springer: New York, 2010), the group developed a theoretical and conceptual framework for mobile learning around the notion of a socio-cultural ecology. Norbert has (co)organised a number of research symposia in the field of mobile learning and has (co)edited *Mobile Learning: Towards a Research Agenda* (WLE Centre: London) and *Researching Mobile Learning: Frameworks, Tools and Research Designs* (Peter Lang: Oxford).

CHRISTOPH PIMMER is a research fellow at the learning.lab/Competence Center E-Learning at the Institute for Information Systems at the University of Applied Sciences Northwestern Switzerland. He studied at the Johannes Kepler University Linz, Austria and at the Università Roma Tre, Italy. Focusing on learning and information systems he graduated with a degree in social and economic sciences. He worked as a research associate at the Ars Electronica Center Linz in the field of e-government and as an assistant for e-learning at the Department of Social and Economic Psychology at the J. Kepler University, Linz. Completing his alternative civilian service abroad, he engaged in educational and vocational projects with vulnerable children and young people at a non-profit organisation in rural Costa Rica. In Switzerland he has coordinated and worked on several projects in the field of technology-enhanced learning and information management. For example, he acted as a project manager in the study mLeap: mobile learning and performance that was conducted in co-operation with several Swiss universities and enterprises. He has published in the fields of technology-enhanced learning, mobile learning and information systems. His current research interest is in the field of work-based mobile learning with a focus on the clinical sector and on organisational learning. He was teaching in programmes at the J. Kepler University Linz, University of Basel, University of Applied Sciences Northwestern Switzerland and at the Boston College. He currently is member of the Swiss Network of Educational Innovation and associate member of the London Mobile Learning Group.

ALEXANDER SCHLETZ studied sociology, economics and law at the Technische Hochschule Darmstadt. He is the senior researcher and project manager at Fraunhofer IAO's competence management team. Since 2000 his main research interests have been organisational anchoring of learning processes, compilation of qualification needs and early recognition of changes in qualification. In addition, he is concerned with organisational and technical issues related to IT-supported training and cooperation processes. His current activities include different projects on foresight topics. He is a project leader in various research, consulting and industrial projects.

SANDY SCHUCK is Associate Professor in Education in the Faculty of Arts and Social Sciences at the University of Technology, Sydney. She is the Education Coordinator of Higher Degrees by Research. She is on the management group of a University Research Strength, the Centre for Research in Learning and Change, and heads the research program in Teaching, Learning and Schooling. Her research interests include teacher development and learning, the use of new media by teachers and students and mentoring and induction. She has led a number of funded projects in these areas, including projects on student-created digital video, use of interactive whiteboards in schools and retention of early career teachers. Sandy has published extensively in the field of teacher and student use of new media, including papers on mobile learning. She supervises higher degrees in the fields of teacher learning and new media.

JUDITH SEIPOLD is a professional in media education, and a member of the London Mobile Learning Group (LMLG). After graduating from the University of Kassel with a Master of Arts degree in Educational Sciences, Politics and Psychology, she worked as Academic and Project Manager at the University of Kassel and as European Affairs Adviser for the Directors' Conference of the State Media Authorities (DLM) in Germany. She is involved in a number of projects within the field of socio-culturally informed Media Education, focussing on media literacy, media formation (Medienbildung) and media use in everyday life and educational contexts. Her current research is on mobile learning as agentive and meaningful activity in school and everyday life, with a focus on the transformation of informal contexts and their structures into formal learning contexts. Further research interests relate to use of children's television, protected PC use in elementary school and media literacy in everyday life.

GEOFF STEAD is the Director of Tribal's Digital Learning Studio and one of Tribal's thought leaders on how to use new and emerging technologies for better learning, communication and collaboration. He leads on a range of work, from micro-sized mobile phone learning apps to enterprise-level, online learning communities. He has been championing Tribal's use of innovative ideas to solve learning challenges for over 15 years, as well as using the power of Web 2.0, social media and open source solutions to help to make learning work better for all. His team focuses particularly on hard-to-reach, excluded or disadvantaged learners and does two jobs at once: one is research and development, using cutting-edge technologies and refining them to empower all stakeholders. The second is to take those learning visions and weave them into mainstream service and product offerings. Websites: <http://www.tribalgroup.com/dls>, <http://www.m-learning.org>, <http://moblearn.blogspot.com>.

LUCY STONE has worked at Leicester College since 1993. Originally trained as a chef and a secretary, she started at the College in an administrative role. She started teaching computing in 1994 and began her own lifelong learning journey by achieving a Cert HE in Computer Science, City and Guilds teaching qualifications and finally a PGCE some seven years later as a distance learning student. In 2000 she left teaching in the Curriculum Area of Computing and moved into Information Learning Technology where her practice focused on the use of technology in teaching and learning. She has been an Advanced Practitioner, supporting staff across the organisation with their teaching practice. In 2007 Lucy moved into Project Management for Leicester College's first JISC funded project – WoLF. Lucy is currently managing and carrying out the research for the JISC funded HELLO Project and managing the JISC funded HE Net project. She continues on her lifelong learning journey and is currently using her project work towards a Masters Award in Education with the particular focus being on the use of technology in teaching and learning and the impact of technology on learners.

RUTH WALLACE is the Director of the Social Partnerships in Learning Research Consortium at Charles Darwin University, Darwin, NT. Ruth's particular interests are related to engaging in research that improves outcomes for stakeholders in workforce development and education across regional and remote Australia. Ruth's research focus is in vocational education and training practice and workforce development in regional and remote contexts. Ruth has undertaken research into flexible learning, engaged learning and developing effective pedagogy, materials and assessment for marginalized students. In particular, this work explores approaches that focus on recognising marginalised learners' diverse knowledge systems. Her research examines the links between identity and adult's involvement in post-compulsory schooling and development of effective pathways through flexible learning and recognition of diverse knowledge systems.

JOCELYN WISHART is Senior Lecturer with the Graduate School of Education at the University of Bristol. She is Senior Academic Advisor to ESCalate, the Higher Education Academy Subject Centre for Education and convenor of the Institute of Advanced Studies' workshop series 'Adding a Mobile Dimension to Teaching and Learning'. She became involved in mobile learning through her interest in using handheld devices to support teacher trainees on placement in schools. Her interests lie primarily in the psychology of mobile learning and in the corresponding pedagogy of using handheld devices for teaching. She follows a paradigm drawn from cognitive psychology, finding explanations based on cognitive constructs such as challenge, control and constructivism to be the most helpful in describing learning through mobile technologies. She is also moderator of the Teaching with Handhelds discussion group at <http://www.handheldlearning.co.uk>.

LIZA WOHLFART is a senior researcher and project manager at the University of Stuttgart's Institute for Human Factors and Technology Management (IAT). She has been involved in various research and consulting projects, both national and international, on innovation/R&D management, corporate strategy development and knowledge management (including Communities of Practice). Her past activities include the EU co-funded projects 'RUSMECO' (Establishing a Community of Practice on innovation in between Russian SME clusters) and 'KnowledgeBoard 2.0' (Supporting a global online community on knowledge management, <http://www.knowledgeboard.com>). The German 'eColleagues' project, aimed at providing on-demand support to service technicians in machine-building and plant construction industries, is one of her current activities. Liza Wohlfart is the author of various publications and the co-editor of two books including *The Secrets of the Six Principles: A Guide to Robust Organisational Development* (2004) and *Hands-on Knowledge Co-creation and Sharing: Practical Methods and Techniques* (2007).

Index